ART FOR WALES

THE LEGACY OF DEREK WILLIAMS

DAVID MOORE

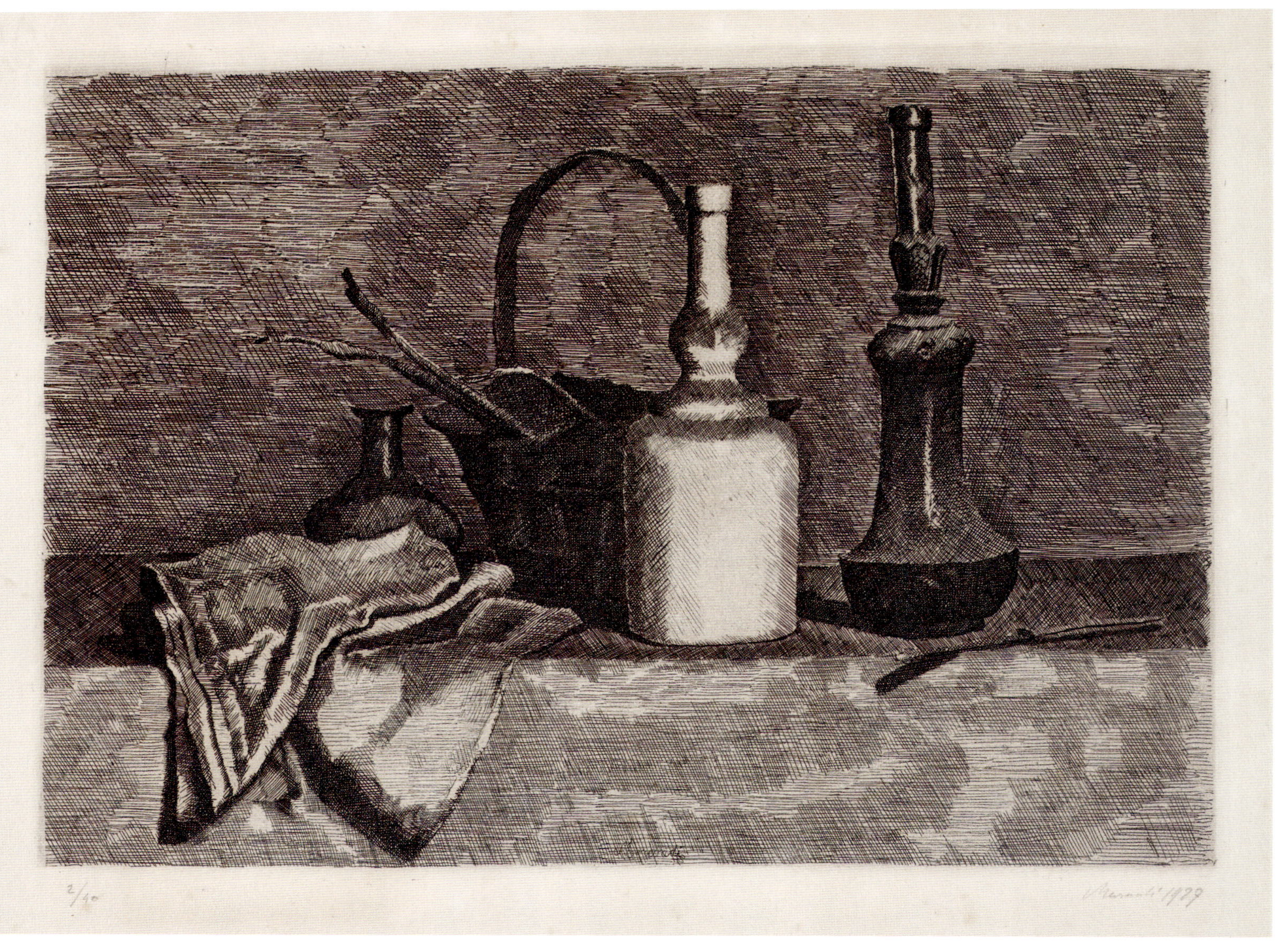

Art for Wales: The Legacy of Derek Williams. Published in Great Britain in 2020 by Graffeg Limited.

Written by David Moore copyright © 2020. Designed and produced by Graffeg Limited copyright © 2020.

Graffeg Limited, 24 Stradey Park Business Centre, Mwrwg Road, Llangennech, Llanelli, Carmarthenshire, SA14 8YP, Wales, UK. www.graffeg.com.

David Moore is hereby identified as the author of this work in accordance with section 77 of the Copyrights, Designs and Patents Act 1988.

A CIP Catalogue record for this book is available from the British Library.

The publisher gratefully acknowledges the financial support of this book by the Books Council of Wales. www.gwales.com

ISBN 9781913134730

1. Georgio Morandi, *Natura morta con il panneggio a sinistra*, etching on zinc, 1927, sheet size 35 x 50 cm. Trust purchase, 2017.

Cover image: **Ceri Richards, *The Dragon Pot,*** ink and watercolour, 1950, 39 x 56 cm. Bought by Derek Williams from Howard Roberts Gallery, Cardiff.

ART FOR WALES

THE LEGACY OF DEREK WILLIAMS

DAVID MOORE

In gratitude to Ivan Sadka OBE, Howard Evans and Joan Winter,
without whose dedication for over twenty-five years to the memory of
Derek Williams and his wishes this legacy would not have existed.

GRAFFEG

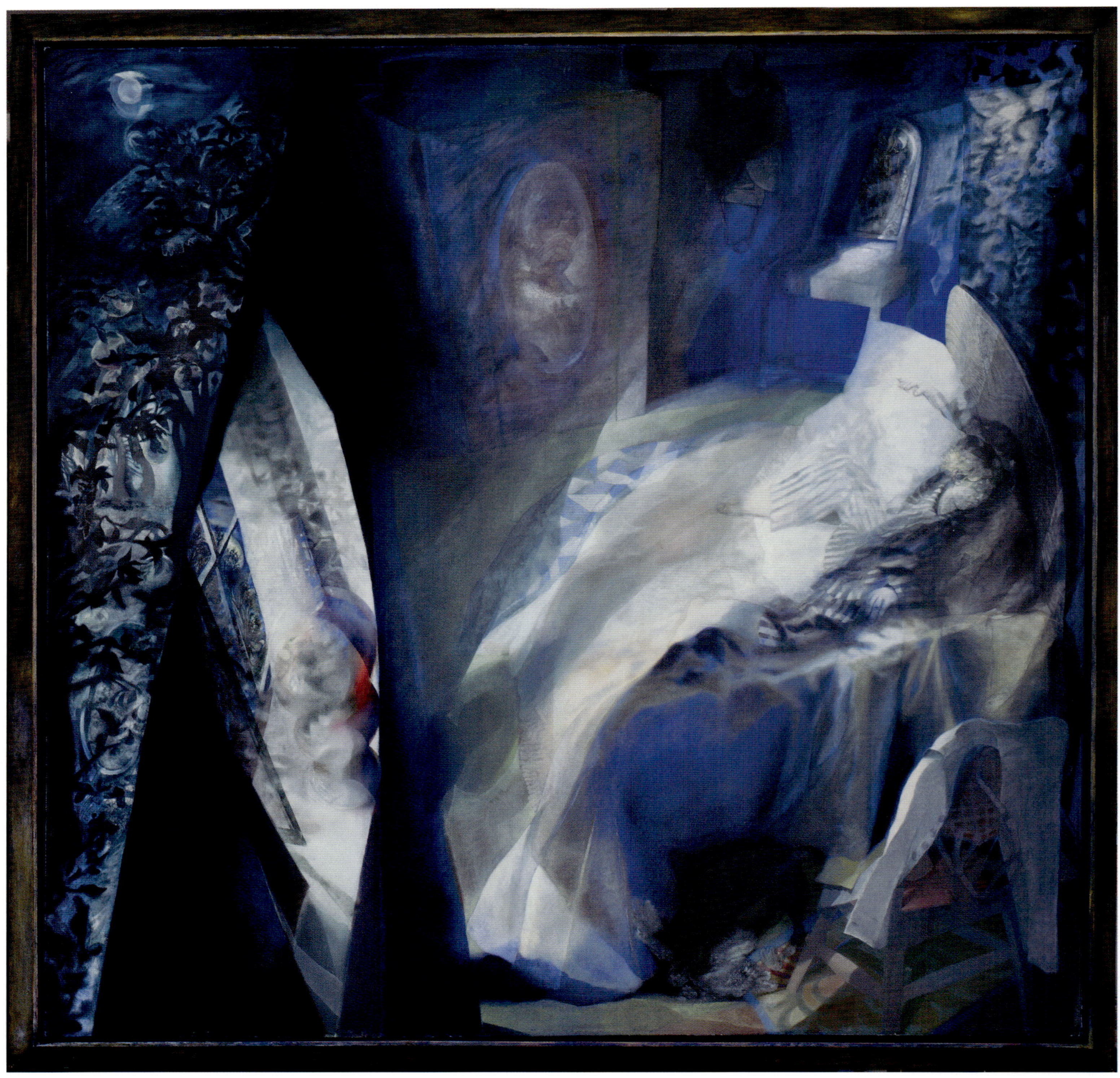

CONTENTS

2. John Selway, *'As I rode to sleep'*, Fern Hill series, oil on canvas, 2002, 183 x 183 cm. Trust purchase, 2011.

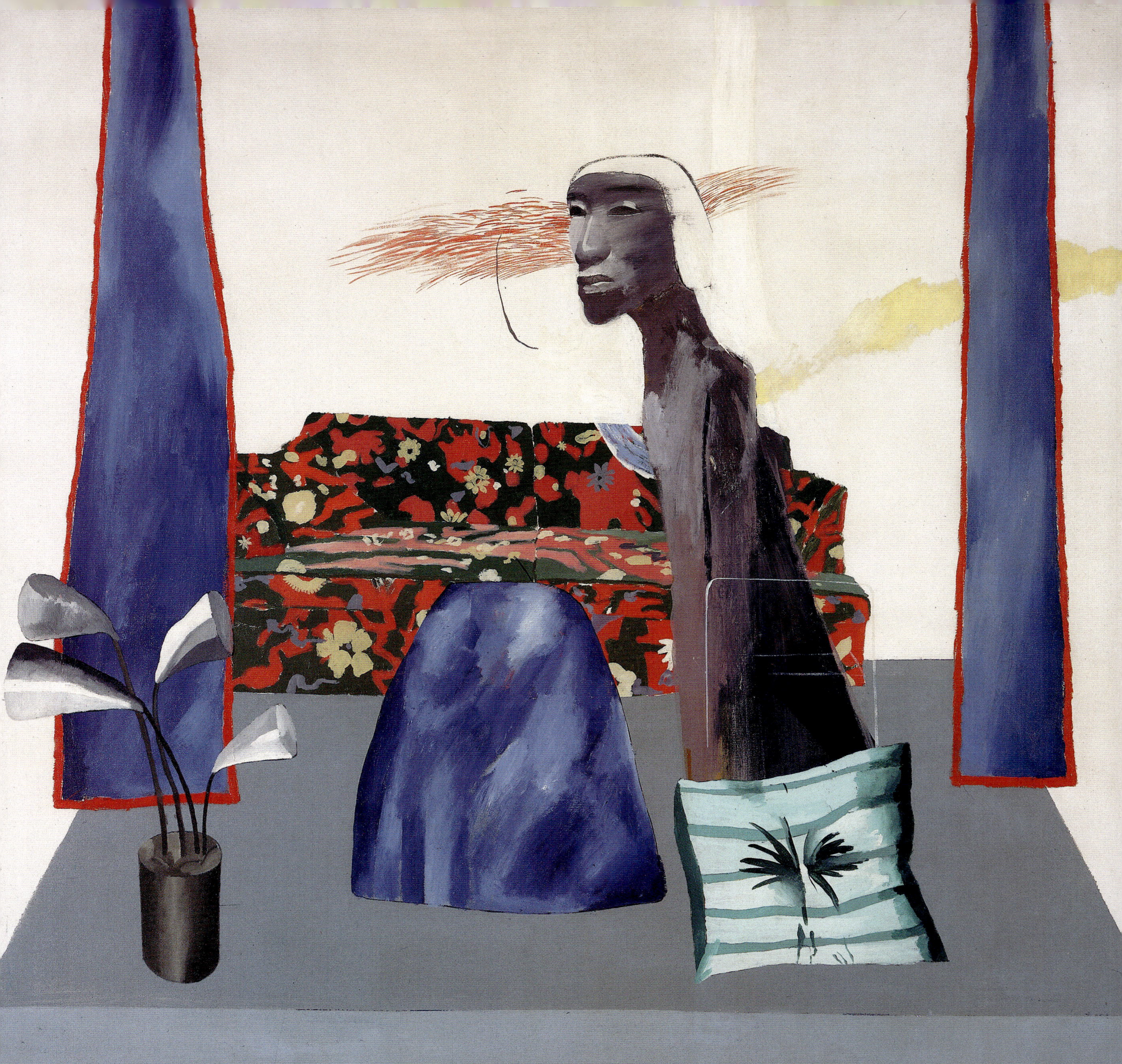

FOREWORD BY DAVID ANDERSON

3. David Hockney, *The Actor*, acrylic on canvas, 1964, 167 x 167 cm. Acquired by Amgueddfa Cymru – National Museum Wales with support from the Derek Williams Trust, 1999.

The decision of the Derek Williams Trust to display Derek Williams's collection at Amgueddfa Cymru – National Museum Wales, and to use the income from his estate to maintain and enlarge the collection, was a landmark in the history of the museum. As the then director, David Dykes, wrote in 1989, this 'resulted in a benefaction to the National Museum of Wales surpassed only by the bequests of French art from Gwendoline and Margaret Davies.'

Even so, neither the museum nor the trust could have imagined just how successful this relationship would prove to be. Their shared belief in the relevance and public benefit of modern and contemporary art has led to the blossoming of these collections into holdings of national prominence, enhancing Wales's reputation in the visual arts and enabling audiences here to enjoy works of the highest quality.

From the perspective of Amgueddfa Cymru, the partnership has consolidated its role as the home of modern and contemporary art – both Welsh and international – in Wales and for Wales. This has enabled the museum's collecting to stay current and relevant at a time when many public institutions have struggled for funding and when its own acquisition funds have diminished significantly.

The Derek Williams Trust's commitment has also been clear in its support for the infrastructure required to house and exhibit its collections in Amgueddfa Cymru and its support of the role of a Derek Williams curator. Since 1993, in recognition of this, the museum has named a gallery in honour of Derek Williams.

The trust made a statement of intent with its first addition to the collection, Michael Andrews's monumental *The Cathedral, The Southern Face / Uluru (Ayers Rock)* (fig. 35), purchased in 1993. It has demonstrated its ambition ever since, growing its collections from the seventy-one works bequeathed by Derek Williams to over two hundred and seventy-five works today.

While many of the Derek Williams Trust's acquisitions – which include works by artists such as John Piper, Ceri Richards and Henry Moore – have paid homage to Derek Williams's own collecting, the trust has recognised the need to collect more broadly. The collection has grown to embrace major Welsh artists such as Ernest Zobole, Ivor Davies, Iwan Bala, David Nash and Lois Williams; leading figures in British art such as Anthony Caro, Howard Hodgkin and Richard Long; and international artists like Giorgio Morandi and Sean Scully. It has embraced sculpture and, in a significant way, studio ceramics.

One of the greatest of the trust's acquisitions has been the bequest of an important collection of modern and contemporary ceramics by Anita Besson, one of the most influential dealers in artist ceramics, who died in 2015. This collection is dominated by the work of her friend Lucie Rie but includes other fine works by Hans Coper, Michael Cardew, Ewen Henderson and international figures from Japan, Russia, France and Spain.

The Derek Williams Trust has had a major impact on Amgueddfa Cymru's own collecting, helping it to bring in key works that are now some of the most popular and significant in the collection. These include: Gwen John, *A Corner of the Artist's Room in Paris* and *The Japanese Doll*; David Jones, *Elephant*; Stanley Spencer, *Souvenir of Switzerland*; Lucian Freud, *Cedric Morris*; David Hockney, *The Actor*; Peter Blake, *Kamikaze*; Bridget Riley, *Kashan*; Richard Deacon, *Empirical Jungle* and *Tall Tree in the Ear*; James Turrell, *Raethro Pink*; and John Akomfrah, *Vertigo Sea*.

A further major achievement has been the creation of the Centenary Fund in 2007 to mark a hundred years of the museum's existence. Using this the museum, with the

A further major achievement has been the creation of the Centenary Fund in 2007 to mark a hundred years of the museum's existence.

support of the trust, acquired a group of highly significant works – Wassily Kandinsky, *Acid Green Crescent*; Pablo Picasso, *Nature Morte au Poron* and four unique ceramics; and Richard Long, *Blaenau Ffestiniog Circle*.

The Derek Williams Trust has often returned to the roots of its collection when considering how to apply its funding. A major example of this is the important acquisition of twenty views of north Wales and Snowdonia by John Piper – one of Derek Williams's favourite artists – acquired by the museum with trust support. This provides a good example of how the funding has, over the years, unlocked very significant funds from other sources such as the National Lottery Heritage Fund and the Art Fund.

Amgueddfa Cymru's partnership with *Artes Mundi* has placed Wales and its National Museum firmly on the stage of international contemporary art, attracting to Cardiff some of the major figures in the field. The Derek Williams Trust, through its *Artes Mundi* Purchase Award, has played its part in guaranteeing the success of the project.

This, in turn, has enabled Amgueddfa Cymru to acquire a collection of growing significance from Welsh and international artists. These purchases include Bedwyr Williams's video *Tyrrau Mawr* (2015), which shows Cadair Idris, an iconic location that has over centuries inspired artists from Richard Wilson to Kyffin Williams, in an imagined near future.

With the support of the Derek Williams Trust, the museum has, in addition, also acquired the film *Snow White* (2001) by mixed-race artist Berni Searle, a work that reflects on the impact of the discriminatory racial classification system of South Africa's apartheid regime on her own sense of identity. Another acquisition is Tania Bruguera's *Destierro (Displacement)*, a 1999 mixed-media work that draws on Congolese animistic religious practice and comments on social promises that were made in Cuba and never kept. Other *Artes Mundi* works obtained with support from the trust include: *The Train* (2003) by Russian Olga Chernysheva; *Throw* by Dias and

Riedweg (Brazil/Switzerland, 2005); Finnish artist Eija-Liisa Ahtila's *The Hour of Prayer* (2005); and Lida Abdul's *Tree* (Afghanistan, 2005). In 2018 the museum acquired its first co-commissioned performance piece, Icelandic artist Ragnar Kjartansson's *The Sky in a Room*.

Art belongs to everyone but, traditionally, only a small number of curators have been empowered to make decisions on what is displayed and how it is interpreted. In 2018 the museum, with the visionary support of the Derek Williams Trust, invited service users of a charity, The Wallich, many of whom had experienced homelessness, to co-curate their own selection of modern and contemporary art and draw on the trust's collections and trust-supported works. The extraordinary and moving exhibition, Who Decides?, was displayed in the whole of the West Wing Galleries of the museum for nearly a year and was widely regarded as a landmark in the development of museums as centres for cultural democracy in Europe.

The Derek Williams Trust's unique contribution to the visual arts will provide a lasting legacy for the people of Wales and will ensure that every child, student and adult can experience modern and contemporary art of the highest quality. It is upon such foundations that open, generous and inclusive nations are built.

David Anderson OBE

Director General, Amgueddfa Cymru – National Museum Wales.

4. Lucian Freud, *Cedric Morris*, oil on canvas, 1940, 31 x 36 cm. Accepted in lieu of inheritance tax by HM Government and purchased by Amgueddfa Cymru – National Museum Wales with support from the Derek Williams Trust, 1998.

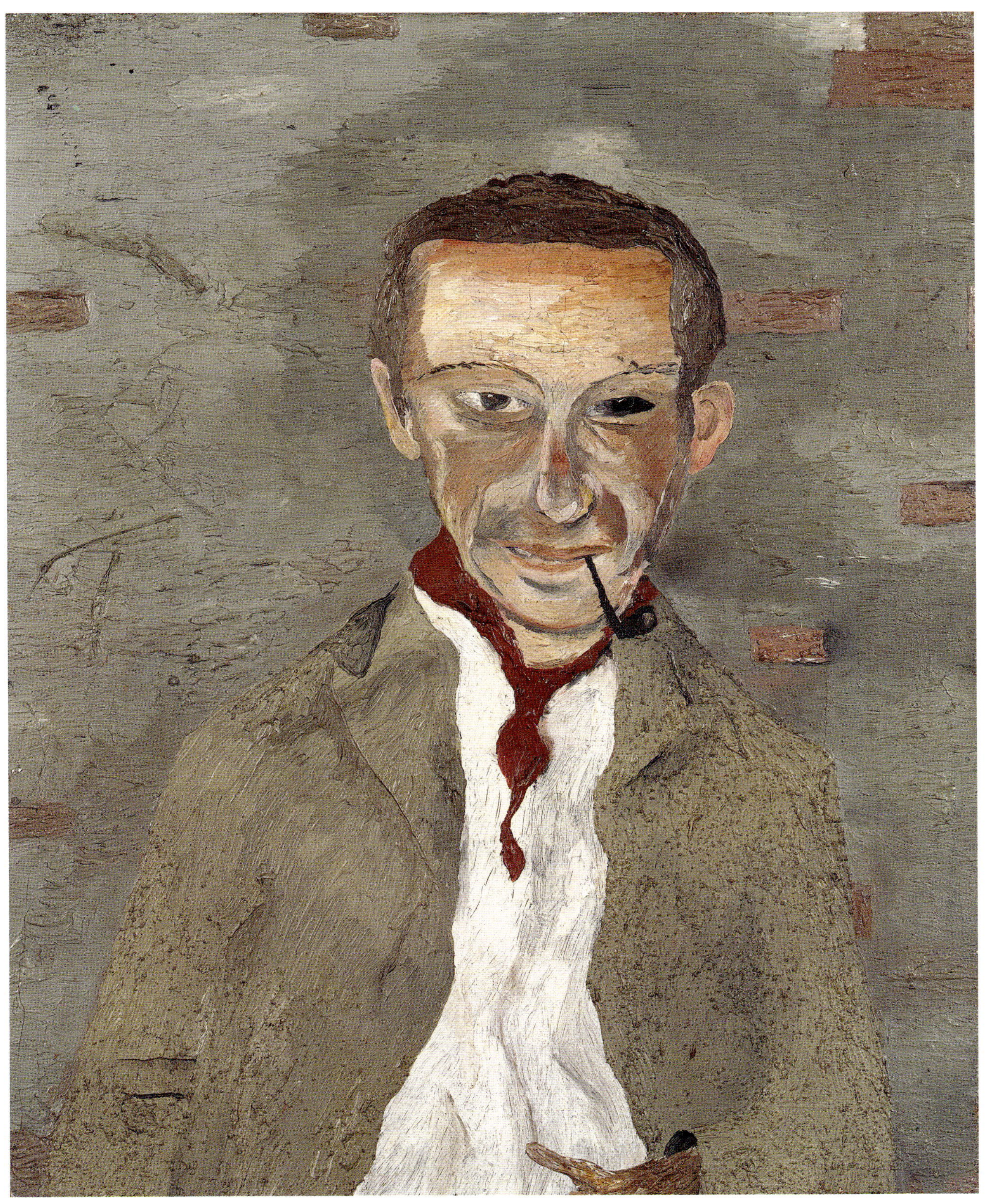

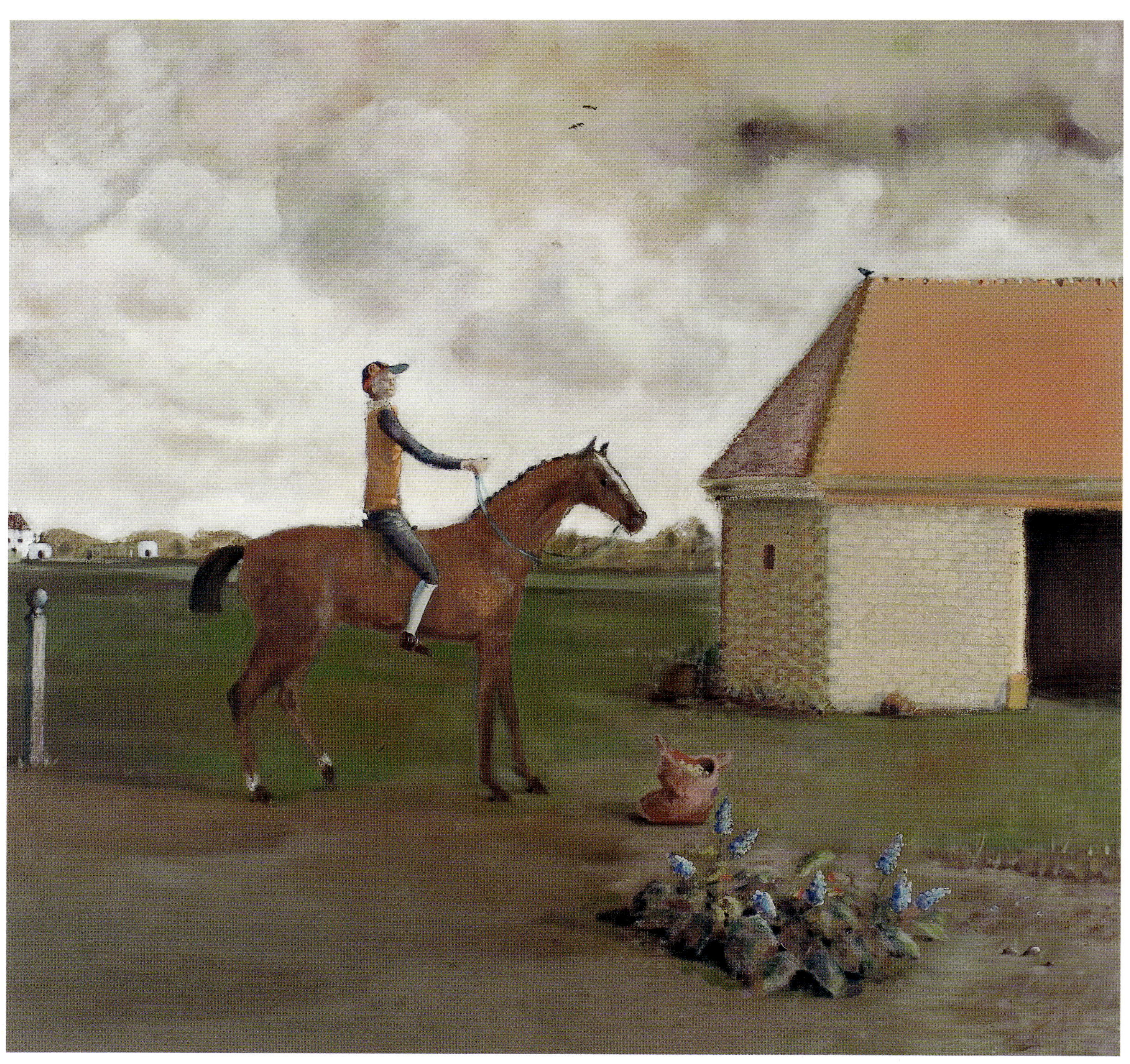

5. Merlin James, *Horse with Jockey Up*,
acrylic on canvas, 2008, 109 x 118 cm.
Trust purchase, 2009.

Derek Williams was a Cardiff born and based chartered surveyor who died in 1984 at the early age of fifty-five. As well as an interest in golf and bird watching, he was a keen collector of modern and contemporary art, and, when he died, his will directed that his estate, together with his collection of paintings and drawings, be managed by his trustees for the benefit of the people of Wales.

The Derek Williams Trust was formally established in 1992 and the original four trustees supplemented their number with an artistic adviser, who later also became a trustee. In order to fulfil Derek Williams's wishes they entered into negotiations with the National Museum Wales and concluded an agreement in 1993 for Derek's original collection to be curated and displayed by the museum and for a joint committee to be established to agree acquisitions that would either be added to the Derek Williams collection or be made by the museum but grant-aided by the trust.

Two significant initiatives commemorated the twenty-fifth anniversary of the Derek Williams Trust in 2017. A major exhibition, Who Decides?, was mounted by the museum based to a large extent on the trust's collection and work grant-aided by it alongside other recent acquisitions by the museum. The other initiative was the commissioning, in collaboration with the *Western Mail*, of a series of monthly articles celebrating the legacy of Derek Williams. This work was commissioned from the distinguished author and curator David Moore and forms the basis for this book.

One of the very distinctive features of the trust is its concentration on strengthening the collections of art accessible to the Welsh public. Though it has, occasionally, made grants for the purposes of display or publication these have been outside its normal parameters. A particular exception was the grant made to the museum to assist in the creation of the West Wing Galleries. If the trust is not unique in what it does

One of the very distinctive features of the trust is its concentration on strengthening the collections of art easily accessible to the Welsh public.

in the United Kingdom, it is very rare and its determination to stick to its principal purpose is a subject of some envy and admiration by other museums. Derek Williams almost entirely collected modern and contemporary work and the trust follows the donor's direction in only supporting the acquisition of post-1900 art. It sees its role as one of helping the museum to fill perceived gaps in its existing collection as well as in expanding its collection of contemporary art. The agreement with the museum emphasises the importance that the donor and the trustees place on the display of works supported by it and in its possession, although the trust is not unaware of the pressure on existing display space. Nonetheless it believes that the development of a new modern and contemporary gallery will take place in the foreseeable future and that the acquisition of high quality works of art therefore remains a matter of great importance for the future of the national collection.

Though Derek himself only collected two-dimensional artwork, the collaboration with the museum has allowed the trust also to acquire and support the acquisition of three-dimensional work. Principally this has been sculpture by Anthony Caro, David Nash and Richard Deacon, among others, as well as ceramics and some contemporary silver.

The ceramics have boosted the museum's existing good collection into one of the most outstanding in the United Kingdom. It particularly benefited from the legacy to the trust of Anita Besson, one of the country's most distinguished modern and contemporary ceramics dealers. The trust had acquired many important works from the gallery and she knew of its devotion to Derek's concern that his collection and that of the trust should have maximum exposure, being on display, rather than in store, as far as possible.

We are grateful to David Moore for undertaking the revisions and expansion of his articles and for editing as well as writing this book. For many years David was the curator of the Brecknock Museum and Art Gallery putting on exhibitions of modern and contemporary work. He is the author of many articles and a book on the history of the 56 Group Wales and, while the trust has an existing website and has previously published catalogues, the decision to produce this book was taken in order to make the trust's work more accessible and to reach out to a wider audience. Copies of the book will be given to the libraries of all universities and colleges of further education as well as secondary schools in Wales.

In a time of straightened public finances the work of the trust has increased in importance and, thanks to the successful management of its financial affairs, it continues to be able to make substantial grants and acquisitions. By 2019 the total income expended for these purposes was just over seven million pounds. In addition to continuing to collect modern and contemporary Welsh painting, sculpture and ceramics, it adds work from British and European artists and, through the Derek Williams Trust Purchase Prize awarded to one of the shortlisted artists in the *Artes Mundi* exhibition, it has enabled the museum to acquire work from South Africa, Ireland, Russia and Cuba among many others.

Williams Wilkins CBE
Trustee and art adviser, the Derek Williams Trust

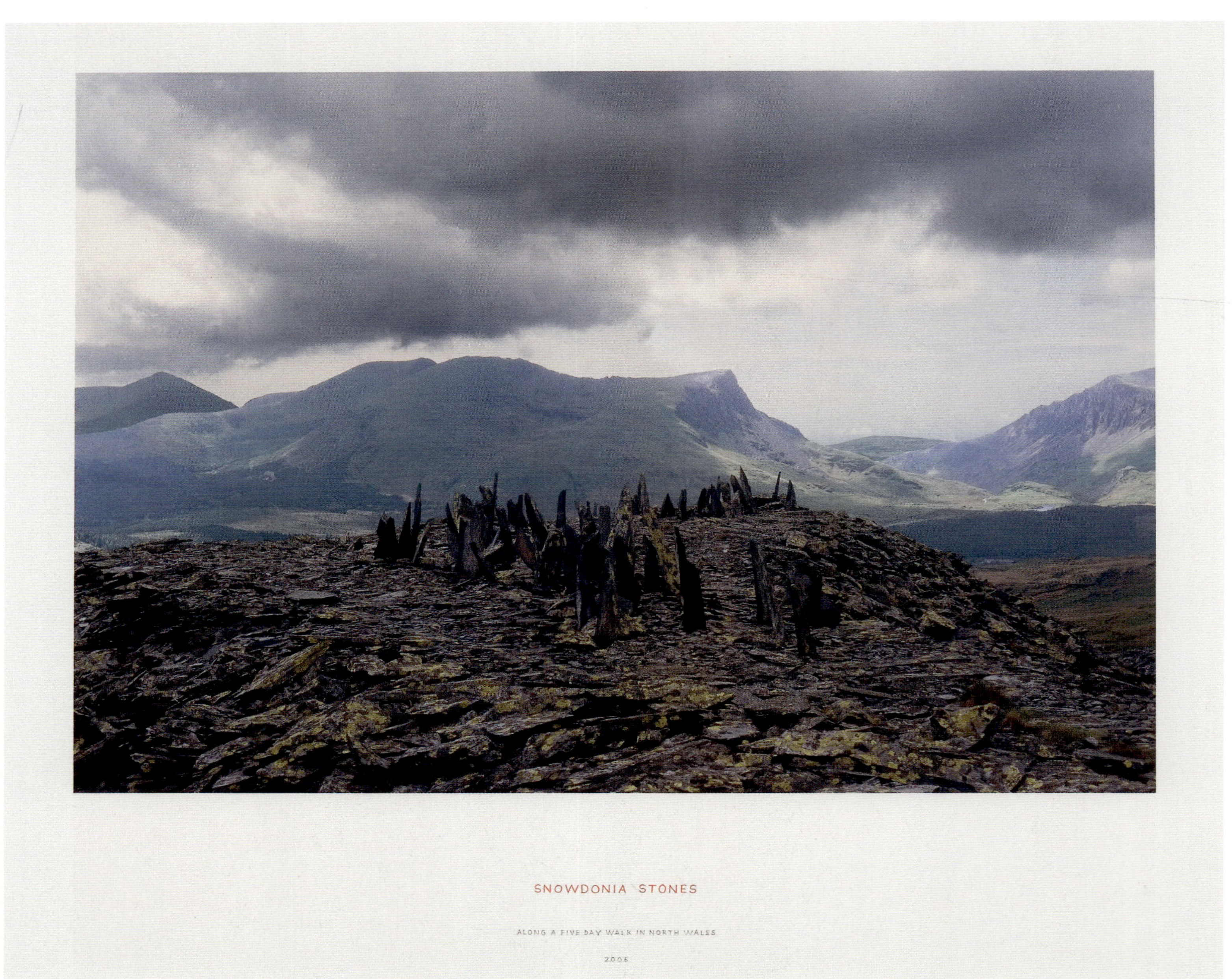

SNOWDONIA STONES

ALONG A FIVE DAY WALK IN NORTH WALES

2006

PREFACE BY DAVID MOORE

6. Sir Richard Long, *Snowdonia Stones (along a five day walk in North Wales)*, inkjet print, 2006, 100 x 113 cm. Trust purchase, 2010

Art for Wales: The Legacy of Derek Williams originated as a series of sixteen newspaper articles exploring, thematically, a selection of artworks either in the collection of the Derek Williams Trust or grant-supported by it. Following a partnership agreement in 1993 the large majority of these are in the care of Amgueddfa Cymru – National Museum Wales.

The trust was established in 1992 from the estate and personal art collection of Derek Williams who died in 1984. Celebrating the trust's twenty-fifth anniversary, the articles appeared in the *Western Mail Weekend* magazine between November 2017 and August 2019. Much of the character of the articles remains although they have been edited and rearranged with an expanded introduction, now chapter one, as well as three additional chapters on drawing, prints and lens-based media.

The themes do not pretend to be a comprehensive account of the artworks or of all relevant art-historical subjects or art media. It is hoped, however, that they will encourage greater awareness of the sizeable legacy to Wales of Derek Williams. Those themes included in the book should, it is hoped, provide a taste of the works collected or supported.

The themes do not pretend to be a comprehensive account of the artworks or of all relevant art-historical subjects or art media. It is hoped, however, that they will encourage greater awareness of the sizeable legacy to Wales of Derek Williams.

Artworks bequeathed by Derek Williams, as well as those directly acquired by the Derek Williams Trust, are listed in appendices I and II. They are also illustrated on the trust's website (www.derekwilliamstrust.org). Appendix III lists the considerable number of significant Derek Williams Trust grant-funded artworks. Most of these are in the collection of Amgueddfa Cymru – National Museum Wales. Appendix IV lists ceramics bequeathed to the trust by London dealer Anita Besson in 2015.

Derek Williams, whose personality and family background are explored in chapter two, was a senior partner in a family practice of south Wales chartered surveyors.

He was a private, kind, gregarious and wealthy man. His private collection of over seventy mid-twentieth century artworks was much influenced by the Howard Roberts Gallery. These works, now in the trust's collection, are discussed in chapter three.

Chapter four reflects upon aspects of an exhibition, Who Decides? Making Connections with Contemporary Art, which was shown at Amgueddfa Genedlaethol Caerdydd – National Museum Cardiff from October 2017 to September 2018. The selection of works was made in collaboration with one of the museum's community partners, The Wallich, a charity supporting people with experience of homelessness in Wales. The exhibition explored the cultural value and diversity of modern and contemporary art acquisitions by both the museum and the Derek Williams Trust over the past decade. Public engagement with the national art collection and debate about the future of modern and contemporary collecting in Wales were encouraged.

Chapters five to nineteen, explore the themes of figuration, abstraction, drawing, landscape, painting, Welsh identity, surrealism, sculpture, Welsh sculpture, prints, lens-base media, support for *Artes Mundi*, international ceramics, Anita Besson's ceramics bequest and Welsh ceramics. These are not, of course, mutually exclusive.

ACKNOWLEDGEMENTS

The Derek Williams Trust, particularly Williams Wilkins, art adviser, for his essential and meticulous support and advice, Howard John Evans, founder trustee and executive, Syon Ivan Sadka, honorary life president, and Joan Winter, founder trustee, for their insights into Derek Williams's personality and art collecting. Also Myles Davies, legal adviser and vice-chair, John Thomas-Ferrand, chair, Brendan Sadka, James Ronald Seaton and Sian Llinos Williams. The late Howard Nicholls and Thomas Arfon Owen were former trustees.

David Anderson, director general of Amgueddfa Cymru – National Museum Wales, for his kind and appreciative foreword. Museum staff have been very helpful, particularly Melissa Munro, senior curator of the Derek Williams collection, Bryony White, Derek Williams senior curator of modern and contemporary art, and Robin Maggs, photographer, and his colleagues. Also, Bronwen Colquhoun, senior curator of photography, Neil Lebeter, senior curator of modern and contemporary art, Melanie Polledri, curator of art collection management and access, Andrew Renton, keeper of art, and Nicholas Thornton, head of fine and contemporary art.

Peter Gill, Graffeg's managing director, and Joana Rodrigues, Graffeg's senior graphic designer, for considerable support, flair and attention to detail. Also Daniel Williams for his care in obtaining copyright permissions.

Catrin Pascoe, *Western Mail* editor, for publishing the original articles and Paul Rowland, editor-in-chief, *Media Wales*, for permission to reproduce edited versions.

Artists or their estates or agents for copyright permissions and, in some cases, for images. The museum has, kindly, made its artwork images available.

Tim Mathias and Professor Richard Griffiths, relatives of Derek Williams, for further insights into his personality, collecting activities and estate.

Last but not least, Sue Hiley Harris, the author's partner, for much support, invaluable proof reading and assistance with images.

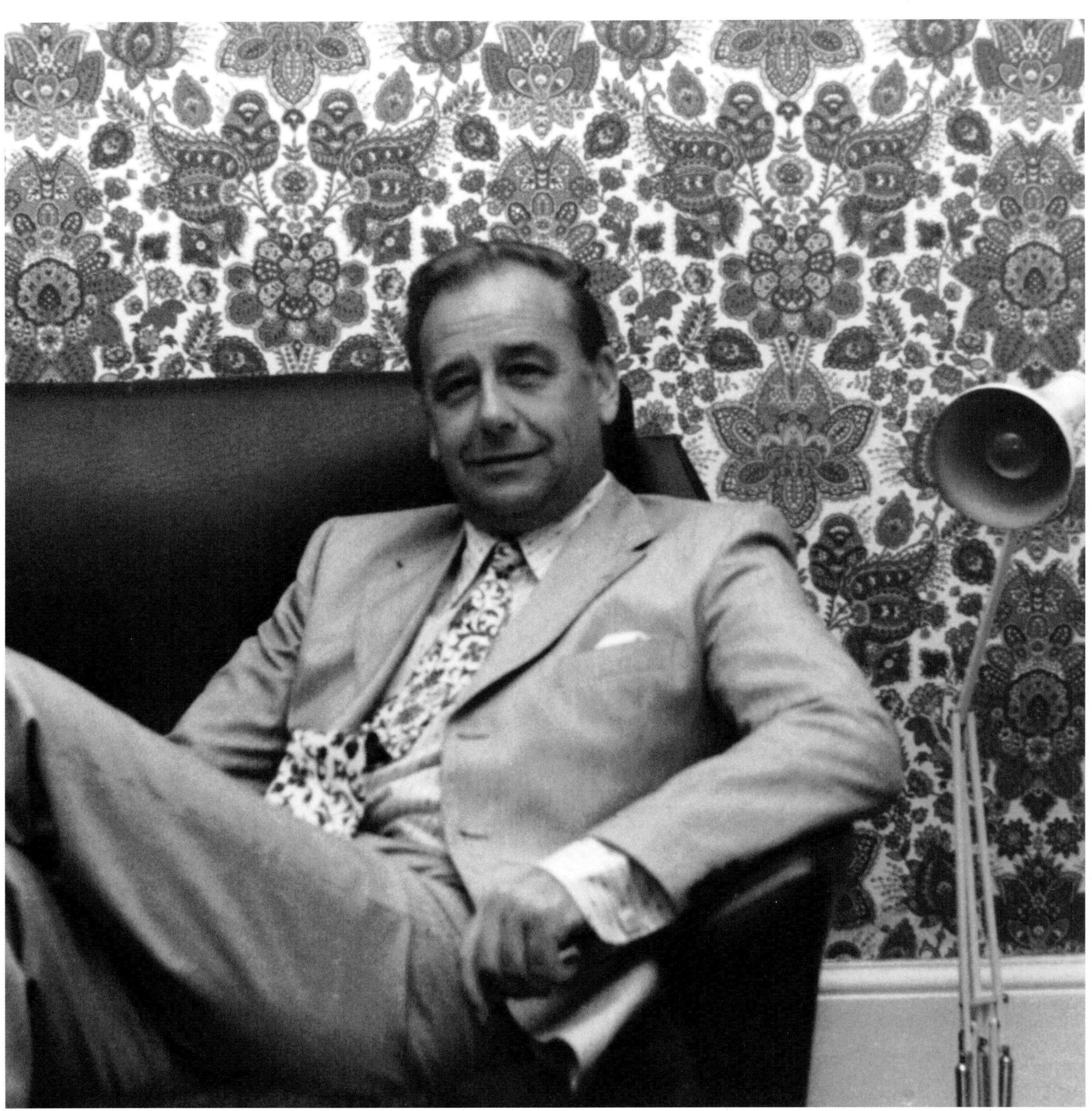

1. DEREK WILLIAMS'S EXCEPTIONAL LEGACY FOR WALES

7. Derek Williams in the 1970s.
Photographer unknown.

This book is intended to demonstrate the significance to Wales of the legacy of Derek Williams (1930-1984), a Cardiff surveyor who died at the age of fifty-five, in bequeathing a significant art collection and his considerable fortune to stimulate an appreciation of visual art.

Today, Derek Williams's former personal art collection, the Derek Williams Trust's own art purchases and its substantial financial support greatly enhance the development of the modern and contemporary art collection, its display and curation at Amgueddfa Cymru – National Museum Wales. It is hoped that an exploration of just a selection of these artworks will provide insights into an exceptional legacy for Wales.

The art collection at Amgueddfa Cymru – National Museum Wales has evolved since the early twentieth century, absorbing works from an earlier museum and carefully buying works, often with grants and other support. Gifts or bequests from generous individuals who wished to share the pleasure they had in an artwork have also been accepted and, sometimes, there have been tax advantages to the donor.

Occasionally, too, exceptional benefactors have come along. The best known must surely be the sisters Gwendoline and Margaret Davies, who died respectively in 1951 and 1963, bequeathing notable artworks to the museum including French impressionist and post-impressionist paintings. The sisters' wealth, inherited from their grandfather, David Davies of Llandinam, derived from the extensive nineteenth-century development of Welsh railways, coal mines and Barry docks.[i]

The legacy of Derek Williams to the appreciation of modern and contemporary art in Wales is just as significant. His personal art collection consisted of over seventy

It is hoped that an exploration of just a selection of these artworks will provide insights into an exceptional legacy for Wales.

---

i   Oliver Fairclough ed., *Things of Beauty: What Two Sisters Did for Wales*, National Museum Wales Books, 2007; Trevor Fishlock, *A Gift of Sunlight: The Fortune and the Quest of the Davies Sisters of Llandinam*, Gomer Press, 2014

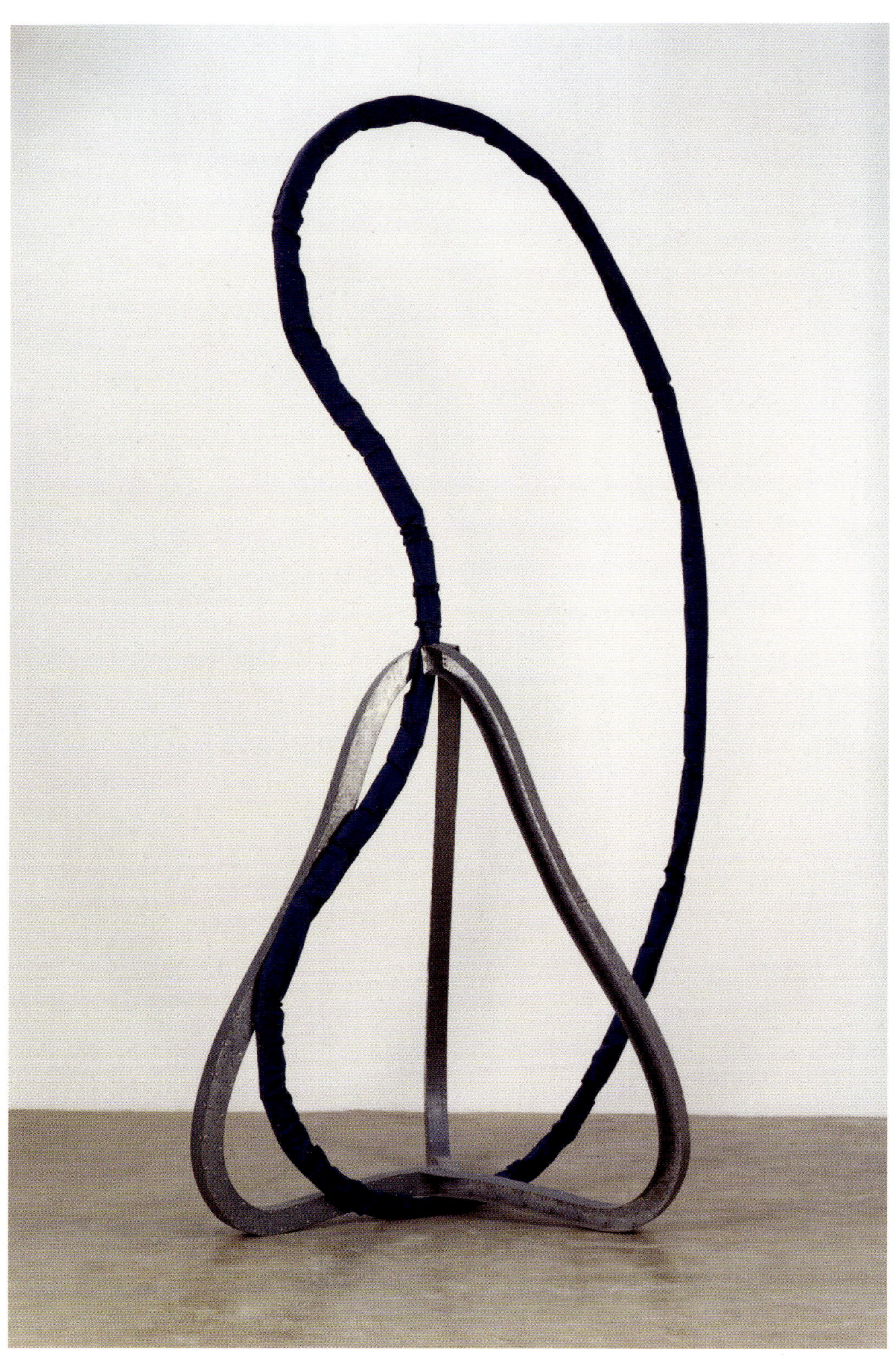

Derek Williams had specified in his will that a trust should exist 'to advance public understanding in and appreciation of the arts by the public display of fine works of art.'

works revealing his strong attraction to the neo-romantics. At least a third of these are associated, biographically or geographically, with Wales. In particular he bought six works by David Jones, twenty-two by John Piper and fourteen by Ceri Richards. Other artists included Graham Sutherland, Josef Herman, Jack Yeats, Kyffin Williams, Stanley Spencer, Victor Pasmore, Ben Nicholson, Henry Moore, L. S. Lowry and Ivon Hitchens. A full list is provided in Appendix I. These works are discussed by Mark Evans in a catalogue published by the National Museum of Wales in 1989.[ii]

The Derek Williams Trust was established in 1992. Derek Williams had specified in his will that a trust should exist 'to advance public understanding in and appreciation of the arts by the public display of fine works of art.' Reflecting his taste for contemporary Welsh and wider British work, the trust's focus has been upon post-1900 fine and applied art. While this has included much Welsh and British art, there has also been increasing interest in acquiring significant work by internationally celebrated artists.

The Derek Williams Trust, while decidedly independent, formed a close and mutually-beneficial partnership with Amgueddfa Cymru – National Museum Wales in 1993. The trust has placed its collections on long-term loan to the museum, has provided considerable grant-funding towards the purchase of modern and contemporary artworks for the museum's collection and has financed gallery improvements and curatorial support. The museum, in turn, has curated, cared for and displayed works from Derek Williams's original art collection and the trust's own acquisitions.[iii] Major decisions between the trust and museum are made at partnership meetings which normally occur twice a year.

ii   Mark L. Evans, *The Derek Williams Collection at the National Museum of Wales*, Amgueddfa Genedlaethol Cymru – National Museum Wales, 1989

iii   Tania Pirsig-Marshall, *A Catalogue of the Derek Williams Trust Collection*, Derek Williams Trust, 2007

The trust's substantial resources, originally in excess of one and a half million pounds, have been carefully managed through the economic down-turn ensuring a continued focus upon the acquisition of high-quality work. This must have partly compensated for a halving of the museum's purchase fund in 2011.

An indication of the scale of meticulously managed funds available to the Derek Williams Trust is that, in its first twenty-five years since 1992, nearly two and a half million pounds were spent on approximately one hundred and twenty-five modern and contemporary fine and applied artworks for its own collection. The first, for £142,500, was Michael Andrews's majestic 1987 acrylic on canvas *The Cathedral, The Southern Faces / Uluru (Ayers Rock)* (fig. 35), which is discussed later and is one of the largest paintings in the museum. Subsequently, the trust has bought remarkable artworks by artists who, to name only a few, include Eileen Agar, Gillian Ayres, Iwan Bala, Sir Anthony Caro, David Nash, Edmund de Waal, Simon Hantaï, Sir Howard Hodgkin, Giorgio Morandi, Shani Rhys James and Clare Woods. The large majority of these artworks are held at the museum although two figurative bronze sculptures by Robert Thomas are on loan to the University of South Wales. These direct trust purchases for its own collection are listed in Appendix II.

The trust's collection has also benefited from a generous bequest, in 2015, of Anita Besson's private collection of ceramics. She ran Galerie Besson off Old Bond Street in London from 1988 until 2011. The collection comprises seventy-four catalogued items by renowned ceramicists including Lucie Rie, Hans Coper, Ian Godfrey and Claudi Casanovas. These are listed in Appendix IV.

The trust has, in addition to direct purchases for its collection, spent over four million pounds on grants in its first twenty-five years up to and including 2017. This has been considerably more than on its own collection and much of it has been in support of around one hundred and eighty art purchases by Amgueddfa Cymru –

9. Clare Woods, *Handsome Devil*, oil on aluminium, 2015, 150 x 100 cm. Trust purchase, 2016.

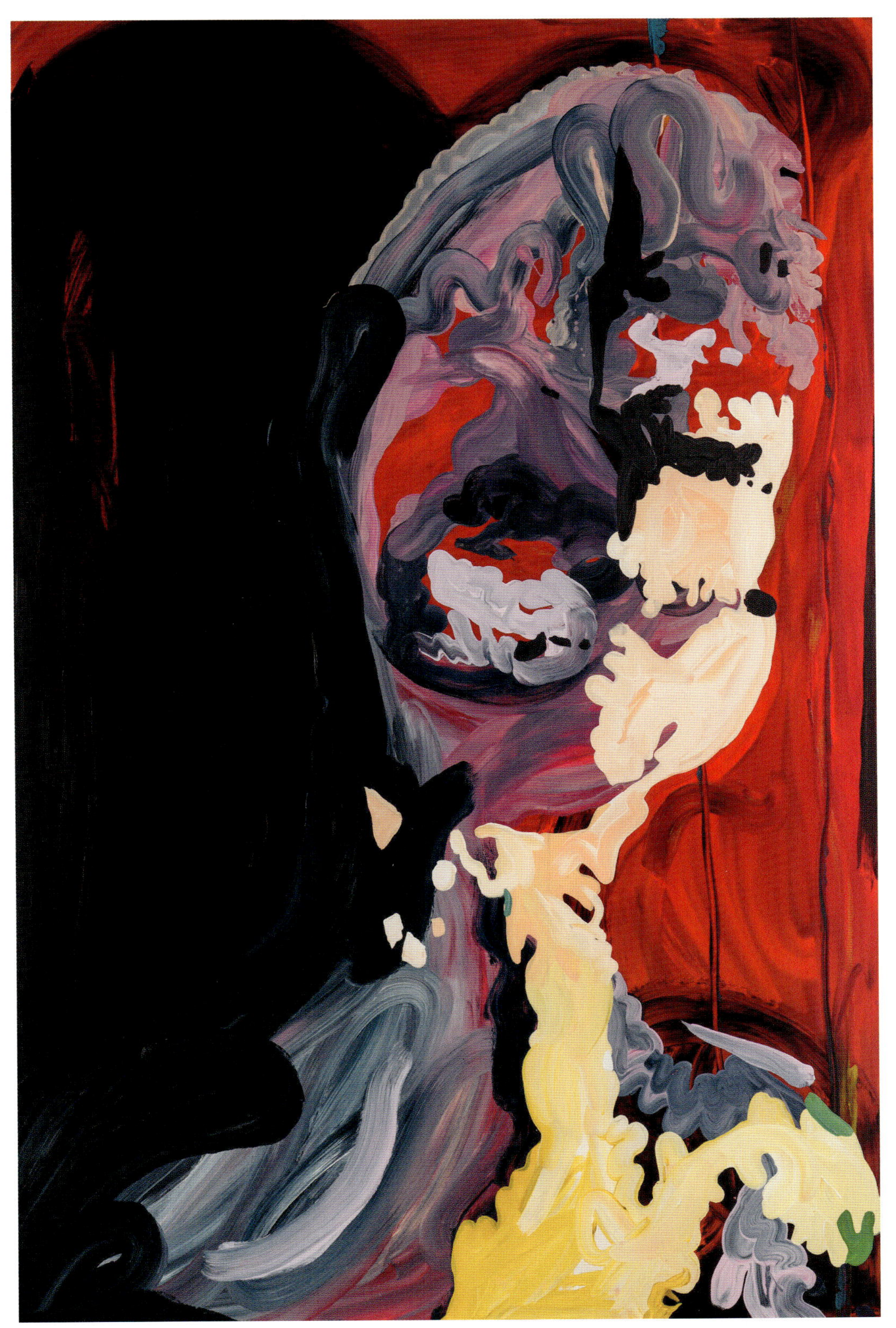

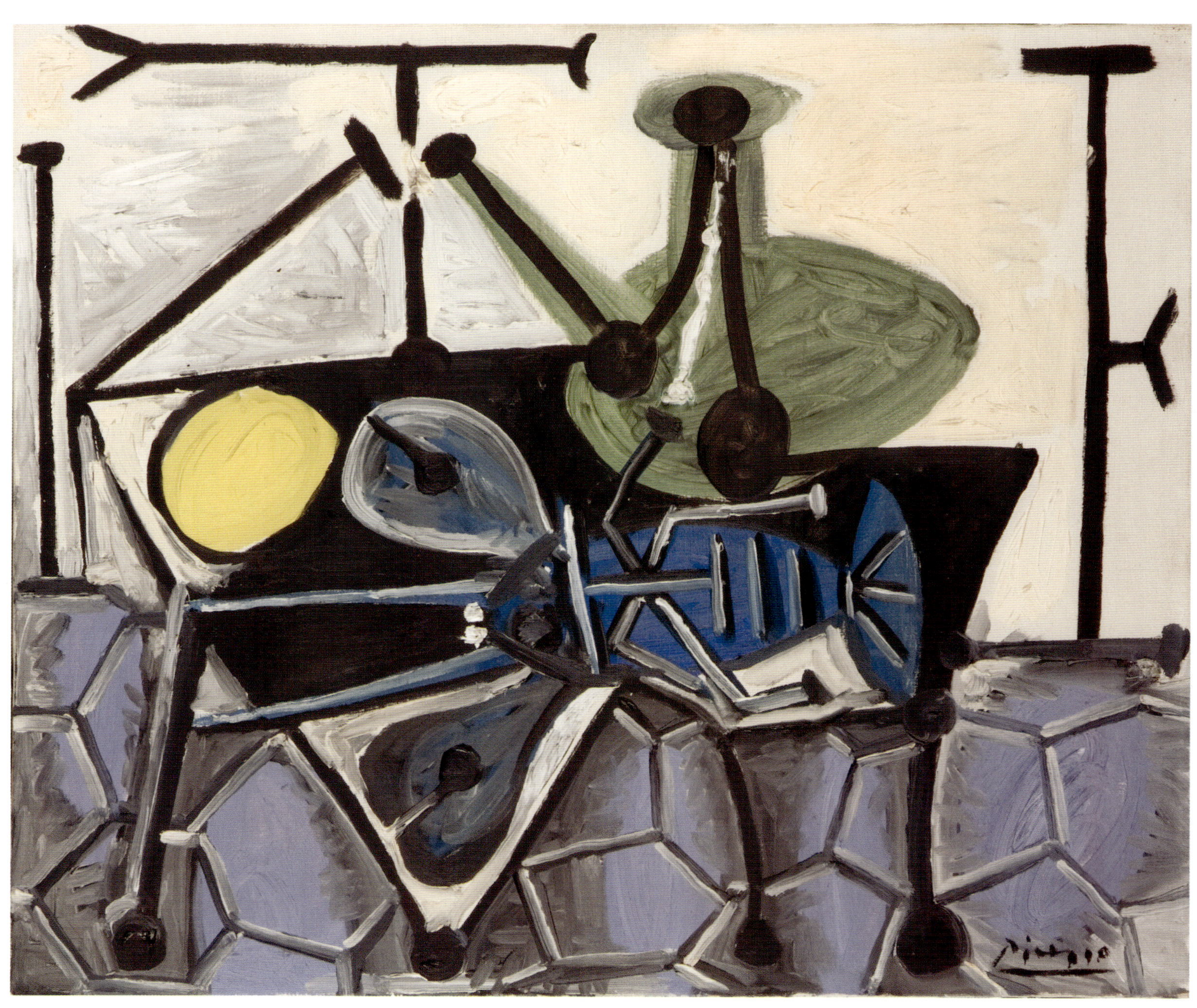

10. Pablo Picasso, _Nature Morte au Poron_,
oil on canvas, 1948, 50 x 61 cm. Acquired
by Amgueddfa Cymru – National Museum
Wales with the support of the Derek
Williams Trust (Centenary Fund) and the
Art Fund, 2009.

National Museum Wales including international _Artes Mundi_ prize-winning works and purchases from the National Eisteddfod of Wales.

A few major trust grants of over £100,000 have greatly helped the museum to attract additional grant funding from other sources towards important acquisitions. While the majority of trust grants have been considerably smaller, major grants indicate the scale of the trust's capacity to support the building of a national art collection. Notable have been: £200,000 in 1997-98 towards Stanley Spencer's 1935 oil on canvas _Souvenir of Switzerland_ (with the Art Fund and the Heritage Lottery Fund); £277,500 in 1999-2000 towards David Hockney's 1964 acrylic on canvas _The Actor_ (with the Art Fund and James Butler Charitable Trust) (fig. 3); £667,500 in 2009, marking the museum's centenary, towards Pablo Picasso's 1948 oil painting _Nature Morte au Poron_ (with the Art Fund) (fig. 10); £350,000 in 2013-14 towards an outstanding collection of John Piper paintings of north Wales and Snowdonia (with the Art Fund and the Heritage Lottery Fund) that had been the subject of an earlier exhibition; and £106,250 in 2015-16 (together with a private donation) to support the purchase of Richard Deacon's 1983-84 sculpture _Tall Tree in the Ear_ (fig. 8). A comprehensive list of artworks at the museum grant-funded by the trust may be found in Appendix III.[iv]

In addition the trust grant-supported with £300,000 the development of the museum's West Wing Galleries between 2009 and 2011.

In addition the trust grant-supported with £300,000 the development of the museum's West Wing Galleries between 2009 and 2011. It had previously funded distinctive gallery seating by David Colwell, in 1992- 93, and had commissioned for the museum's Courtyard Galleries a 1994 ceramic mosaic, _Flowers, Lily Pad, Pictures and Labels_, designed by Patrick Caulfield and made by Jean-Paul Landreau. In 1998 the trust commissioned Nicholas Pryke to make a veneered display cabinet in walnut, sycamore and stainless steel for light-sensitive works on paper (fig. 11). On loan to the museum,

---

iv   Works in the museum's collection grant-supported by the trust up to 2006 are illustrated in Tania Pirsig-Marshall, _ibid._, 126-133. What would later become the Piper acquisition is described in David Fraser Jenkins and Melissa Munro, _John Piper: The Mountains of Wales. Paintings and Drawings from a Private Collection_, Amgueddfa Cymru – National Museum Wales, 2012.

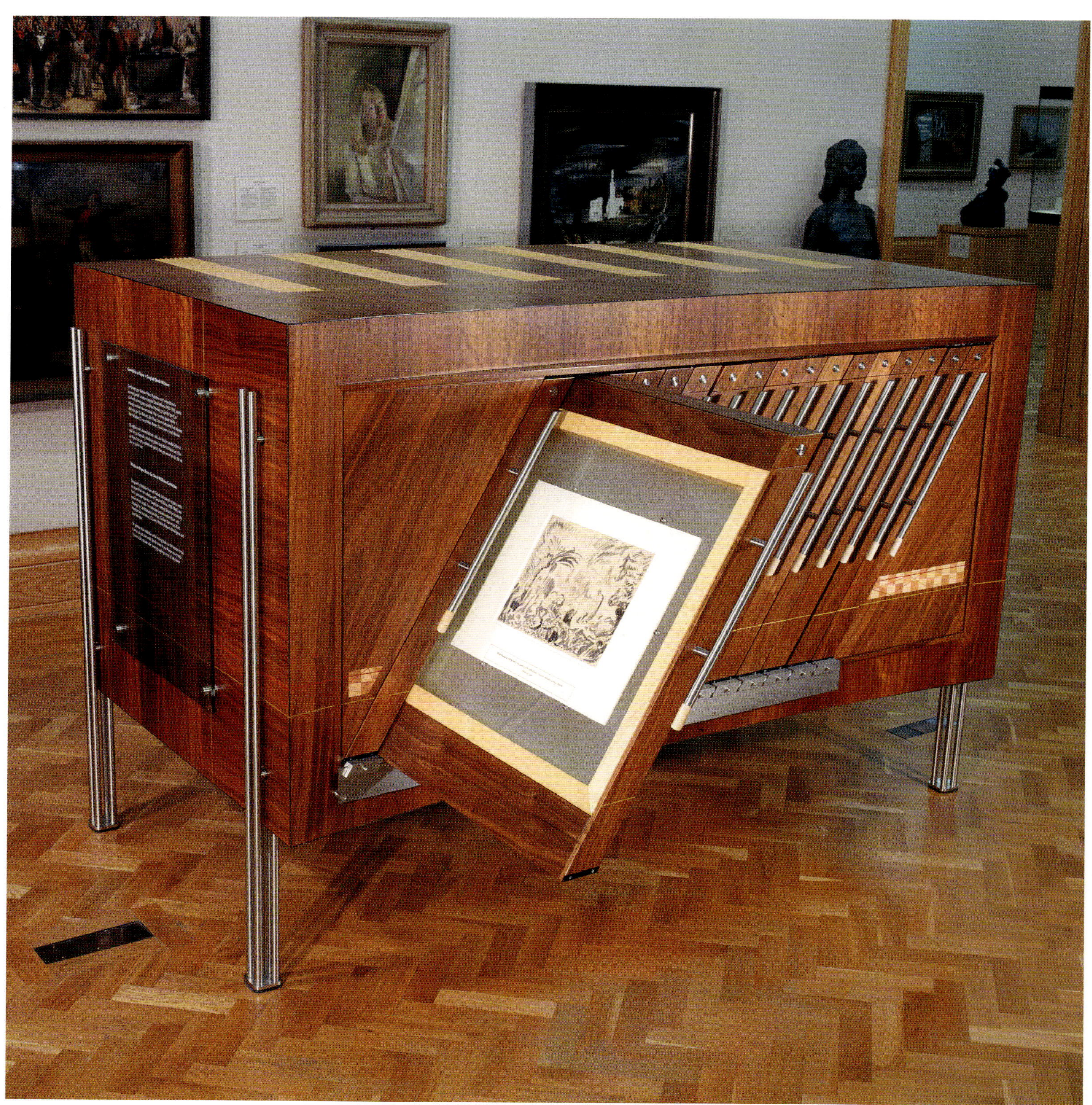

11. Nicholas Pryke, *Display Cabinet for Works on Paper,* walnut and sycamore veneer and stainless steel, 1998-2000, 140 x 217 x 125 cm. Trust commission, 1998.

It is hoped that increased gallery space will eventually be made available to display more of the museum's and trust's artworks.

this shows many works from the trust's collection and Derek Williams's original collection. The trust's ongoing support for curatorial work at the museum has also been of vital importance.

The Derek Williams Trust has, as well as grant-funding art purchases, funded projects outside the museum that include 2000-01 architectural and water features at the National Botanic Garden of Wales by Marion Kalmus and William Pye, an oil painting by Josef Herman for Brecknock Museum and Art Gallery (with Brecknock Museum Art Trust and the V&A Purchase Grant Fund), in 2003, and a panel by Tom Phillips for Cardiff University in 2012-13. Many of these projects are indicated in Appendix III. The trust has also grant-funded art publications.[v]

It is hoped that increased gallery space will eventually be made available to display more of the museum's and trust's artworks. With the Welsh Government having recently commissioned a feasibility study for a 'National Contemporary Art Gallery Wales', the possibility of additional dedicated display space for Welsh contemporary art is, once again, on the agenda. Led by both the museum and the Arts Council of Wales, current advice favours a solution characterised by centralised national support for selected upgraded dispersed galleries, rather than a focus on one location, with a strong agenda for wellbeing and social justice.[vi] The Trust, however, tends to prefer that such a project should be placed centrally.

The museum, in any case, has an ambitious social agenda, set out in a 2015 document *Inspiring People, Changing Lives*. This prioritises enabling as many people as possible to enjoy its collections and to participate in its activities by removing barriers as well

---

v   Examples are: Peter Lord, *The Visual Culture of Wales: Industrial Society*, University of Wales Press, 1998; Mel Gooding, *Ceri Richards*, Cameron & Hollis, 2002; Peter W. Jones and Isabel Hitchman eds., *Post-War to Post-Modern: A Dictionary of Artists in Wales*, Gomer, 2015

vi   Lucie Branczik and Becky Schutt, *National Contemporary Art Galley Wales: Preliminary Feasibility Study and Options Appraisal*, Event Communication, 2018

as supporting the wellbeing of future generations.

The modern and contemporary artworks, whether directly owned or supported by the Derek Williams Trust, are, undoubtedly, a highly significant cultural resource for all the people of Wales, as well as numerous visitors, to appreciate and enjoy. In its first twenty-five years the Derek Williams Trust spent over six and a half million pounds in adding both to its own collection and, substantially, in supporting the national art collection and a small number of visual art projects outside the museum. By 2019 the figure was over seven million pounds. This is a measure of Derek Williams's outstanding – and continuing – legacy for Wales.

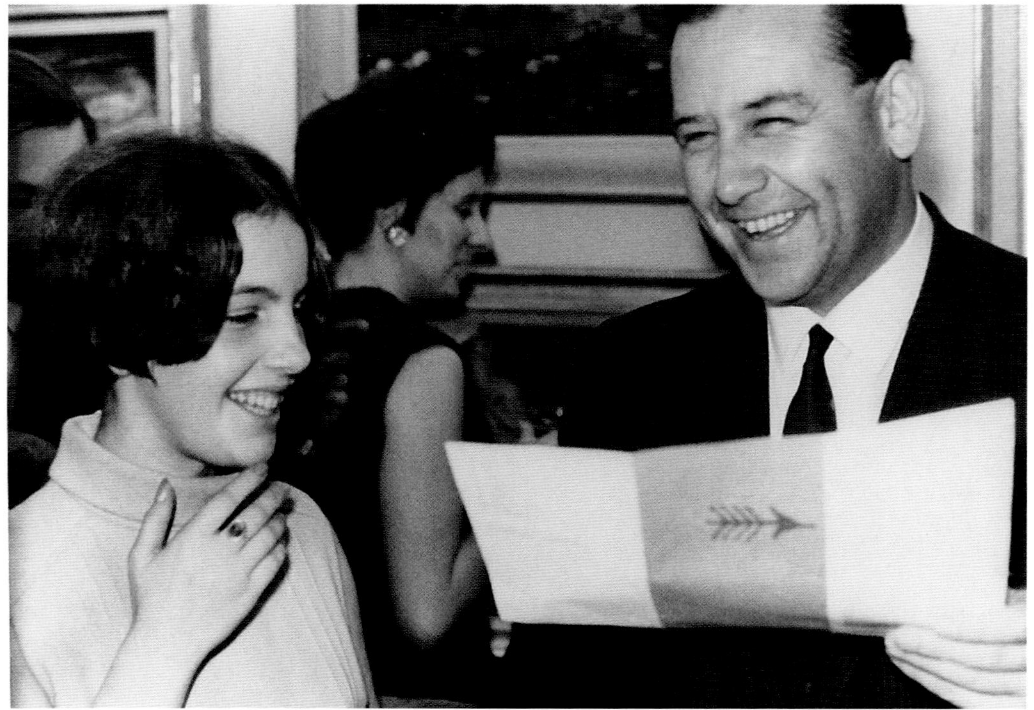

12. Derek Williams at an exhibition launch. Photographer unknown.

The modern and contemporary artworks, whether directly owned or supported by the Derek Williams Trust, are, undoubtedly, a highly significant cultural resource for all the people of Wales, as well as numerous visitors, to appreciate and enjoy.

2. DEREK WILLIAMS: THE PRIVATE MAN BEHIND THE LEGACY

Surprisingly little is known about Derek Williams, a man whose legacy has had as much impact upon the national collection of art as the celebrated Gwendoline and Margaret Davies did earlier in the twentieth century. This chapter focuses upon his character and interests, business and family background.[i]

Derek's great-grandfather was the highly-successful and powerful, if ruthless, Porth and Pontypridd entrepreneur William Henry Mathias (1845-1922). He had built branches and infrastructure for the Taff Vale Railway, developed coal mines and quarries and invested in other properties. Mathias had been a director of companies concerned with everything from coal and electricity to flour milling and insurance. He held influential public offices such as chair of Rhondda Urban District Council and alderman of Glamorgan County Council. At his death, his gross estate was worth over half a million pounds. The Mathias Trust, which he established, would benefit his family for generations. Indeed, a proportion of its income, from a quarry and through Derek's late mother, contributes to the Derek Williams Trust's income today.[ii]

Derek Williams was born in 1929, the only child of Tudor and Dorothy Williams. Derek's mother, as William Mathias's granddaughter, had inherited a share of Mathias money. Tudor was a successful businessman who built up an auction house in Pontypridd and two offices of chartered surveyors, one in Pontypridd and the other in central Cardiff. He and, later, Derek were both very effective at acquiring and developing properties.

---

i   Insights into the personality, activities and family background of Derek Williams have been obtained from conversations with Joan Winter, Ivan Sadka and Howard Evans, founder members of the Derek Williams Trust, as well as Tim Mathias and Professor Richard Griffiths, March 2018

ii   Richard Griffiths, *The Entrepreneurial Society of the Rhondda Valleys, 1840-1920*, University of Wales Press, 2010

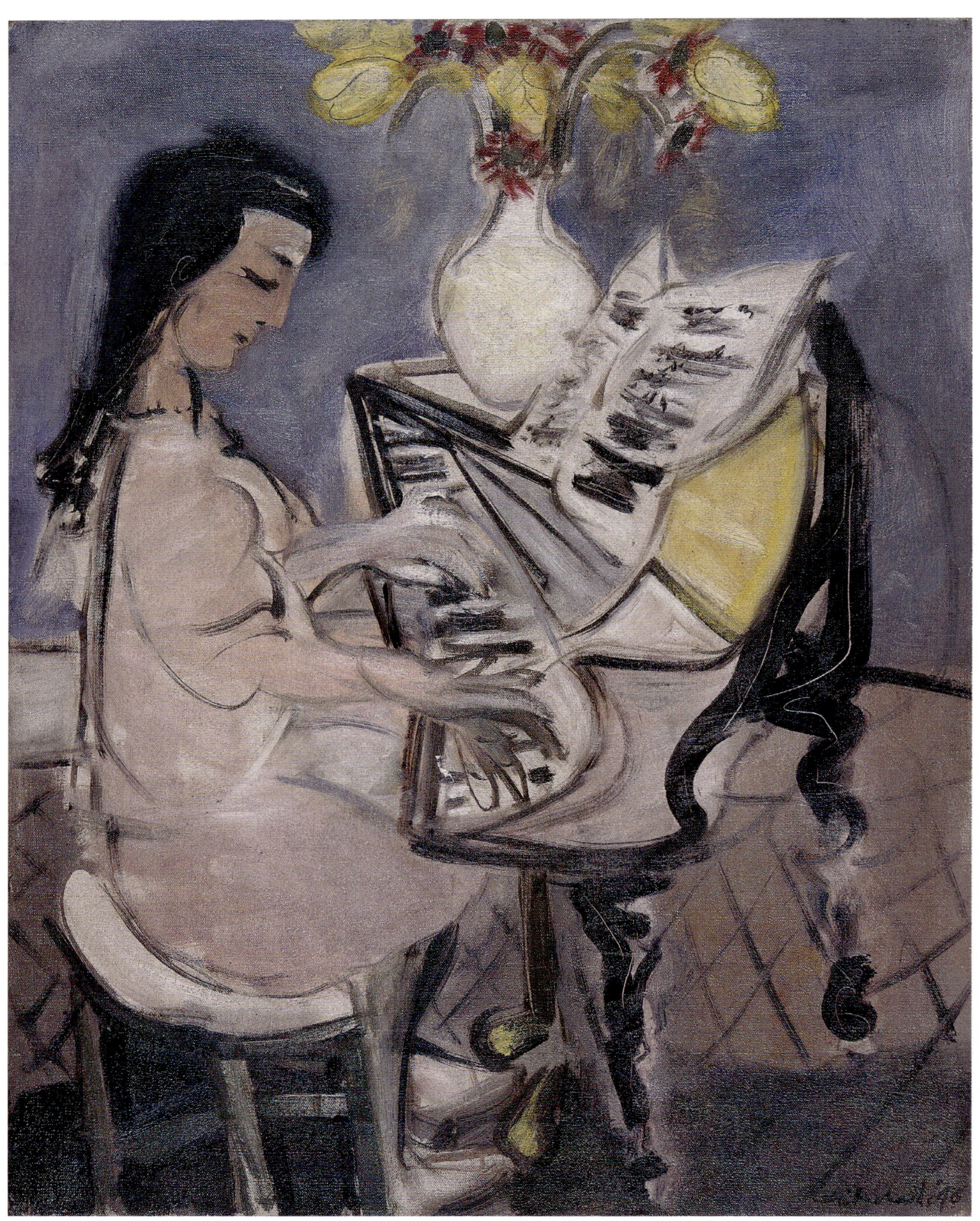

Although Derek had considered a career as a barrister, he became a partner in his father's practice. He learned many business skills from him, inherited useful contacts and, eventually, became a senior partner. A shrewd businessman, he was good at investing money wisely and managing his finances. He became, for a few years, a member of Lloyd's with its exposure to insurance risks.

Derek had been brought up in Llandaff and educated privately at the Cathedral School and at Radley. He became an independent, determined, urbane, polite, smartly dressed and highly personable man. He liked to see fairness and treated people well. A life-long bachelor, he drove a navy-blue Aston Martin with a personalised 'D13' number plate. With a wicked sense of humour he would, sometimes, disconcert people by impersonating voices on the telephone. In many ways, though, he was very private, something of a perfectionist who led a well-ordered life.

An enthusiastic member of Royal Porthcawl Golf Club, he also enjoyed taking photographs and had his own dark room. He regularly attended opera, ballet, theatre and art exhibitions and was a life member of the Cardiff and County Club.

Derek was probably influenced in his art collecting activities by watching auctions at his father's Pontypridd salerooms. Tudor had been enthusiastic about art, although his taste was likely to have been conservative. Derek could be reluctant to reveal his ownership of artworks and, although he displayed some on the walls of his various homes and other properties, many were kept hidden in cupboards. He was, undoubtedly, strongly motivated by the potential investment value of his collection.

Derek was particularly influenced in his art collecting by Howard Roberts who, from 1956 until 1970, ran, in Cardiff, one of the first commercial galleries in Wales. This relationship, crucial to an understanding of Derek's art collection, is explored in chapter three. It was from this gallery that Derek acquired most of his works by

Derek was probably influenced in his art collecting activities by watching auctions at his father's Pontypridd salerooms.

mid-twentieth century British neo-romantics John Piper, Ceri Richards and David Jones and, when the gallery closed, he seems to have felt its loss.

Derek, who had not always enjoyed good health, died at the early age of fifty-five and was outlived by his mother. Never having married or had children and experiencing strained relations with his wider family, he had a keen appreciation of the impact his fortune might have if carefully directed.

He left his residuary estate and art collection to be administered by trustees either in support of the National Museum of Wales or a similar institution to be maintained and enlarged for display to the public. After much consideration, the independent Derek Williams Trust was formed in 1992. A mutually-beneficial long-term partnership with Amgueddfa Cymru – National Museum Wales, with an emphasis upon post-1900 art, was made the following year.

14. John Piper, *Rudbaxton near Haverfordwest,* pencil, watercolour, indian ink and gouache, 1963, 40 x 57 cm. Bought by Derek Williams from Howard Roberts Gallery, Cardiff, c.1964.

Pages 36-37: **15. Ivon Hitchens, *Arched Trees No.12,*** oil on canvas, 1954, 46 x 110 cm. Bought by Derek Williams from Fosse Gallery, Stow-on-the-Wold, 1984.

He left his residuary estate and art collection to be administered by trustees either in support of the National Museum of Wales or a similar institution to be maintained and enlarged for display to the public.

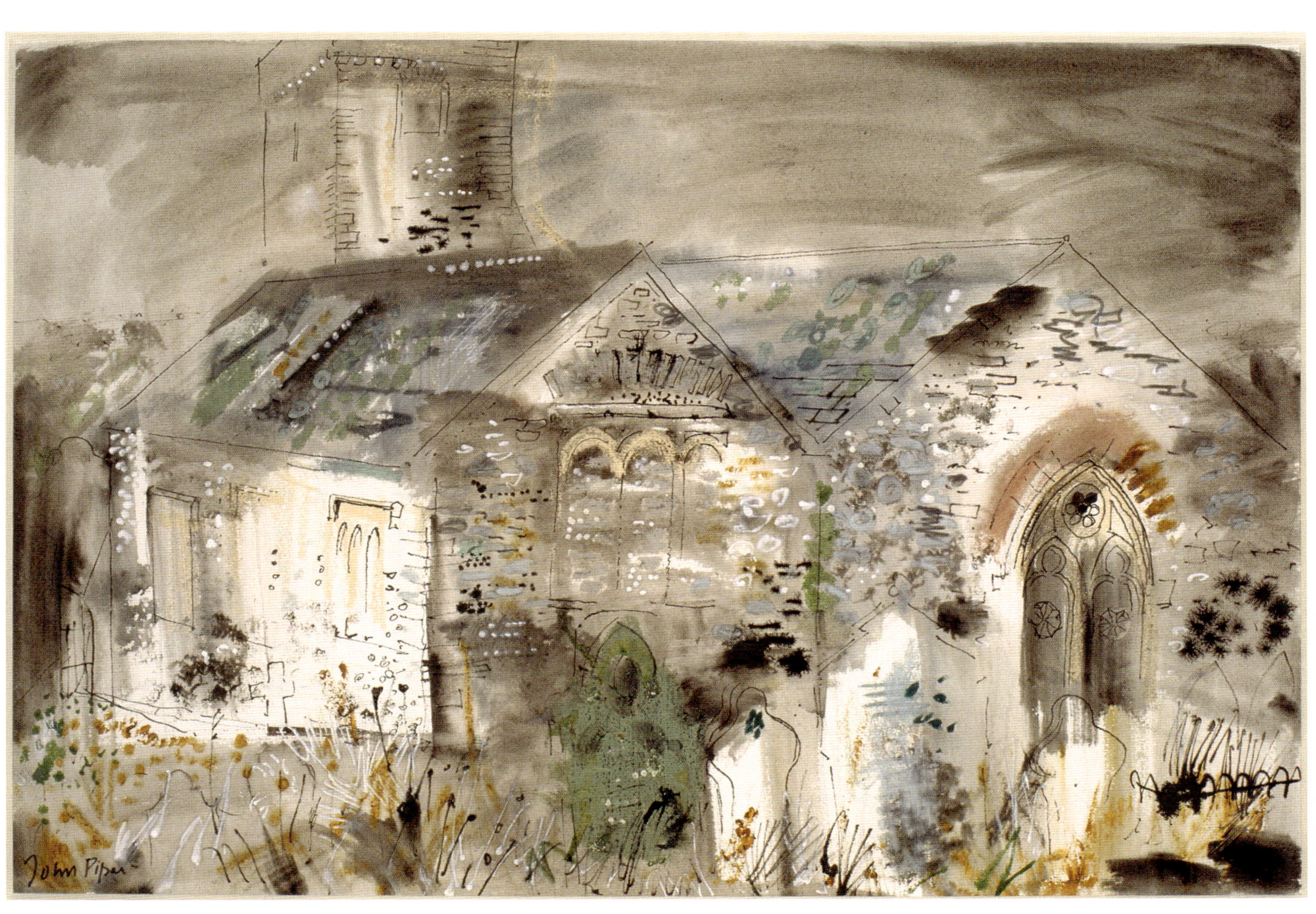

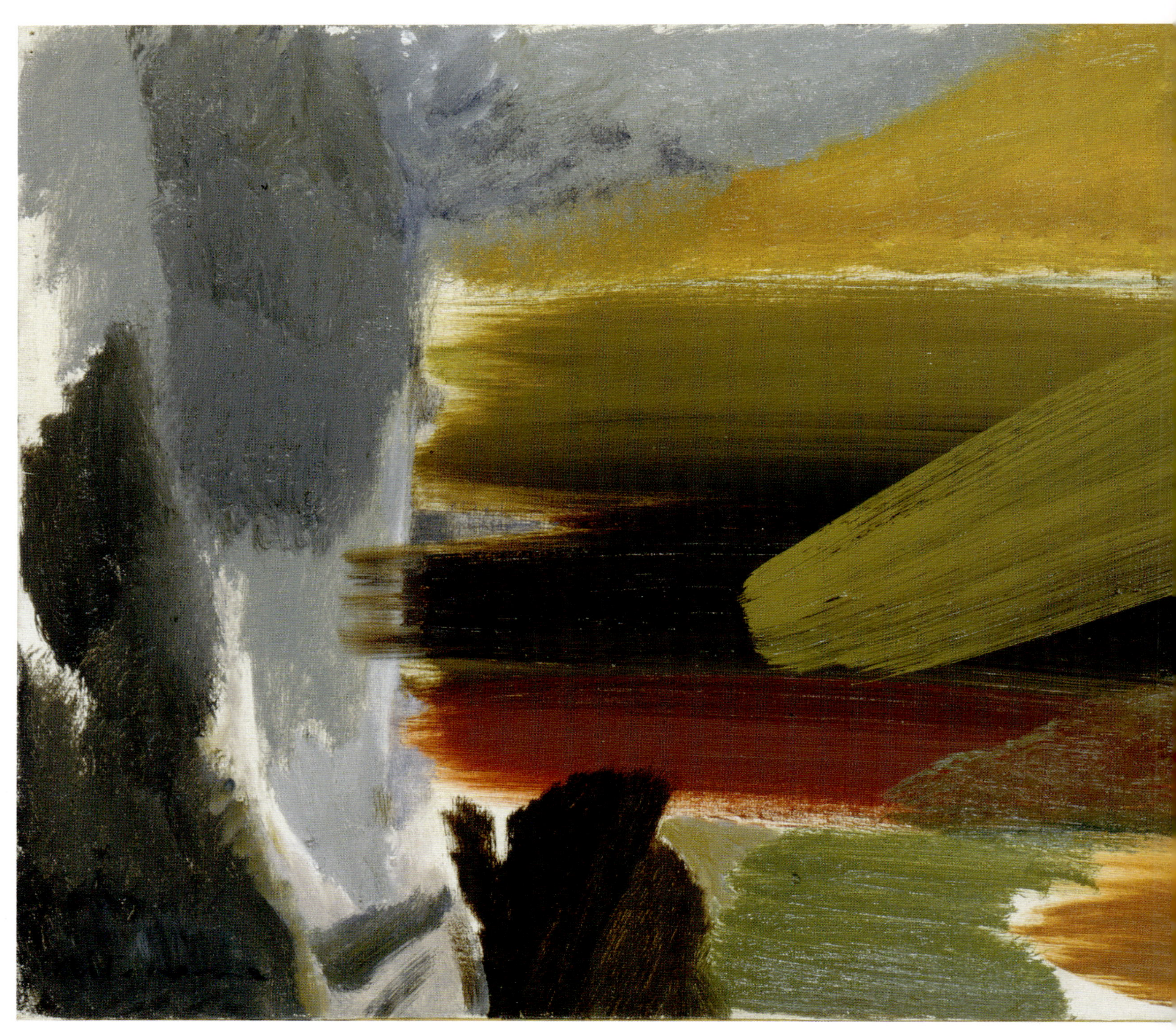

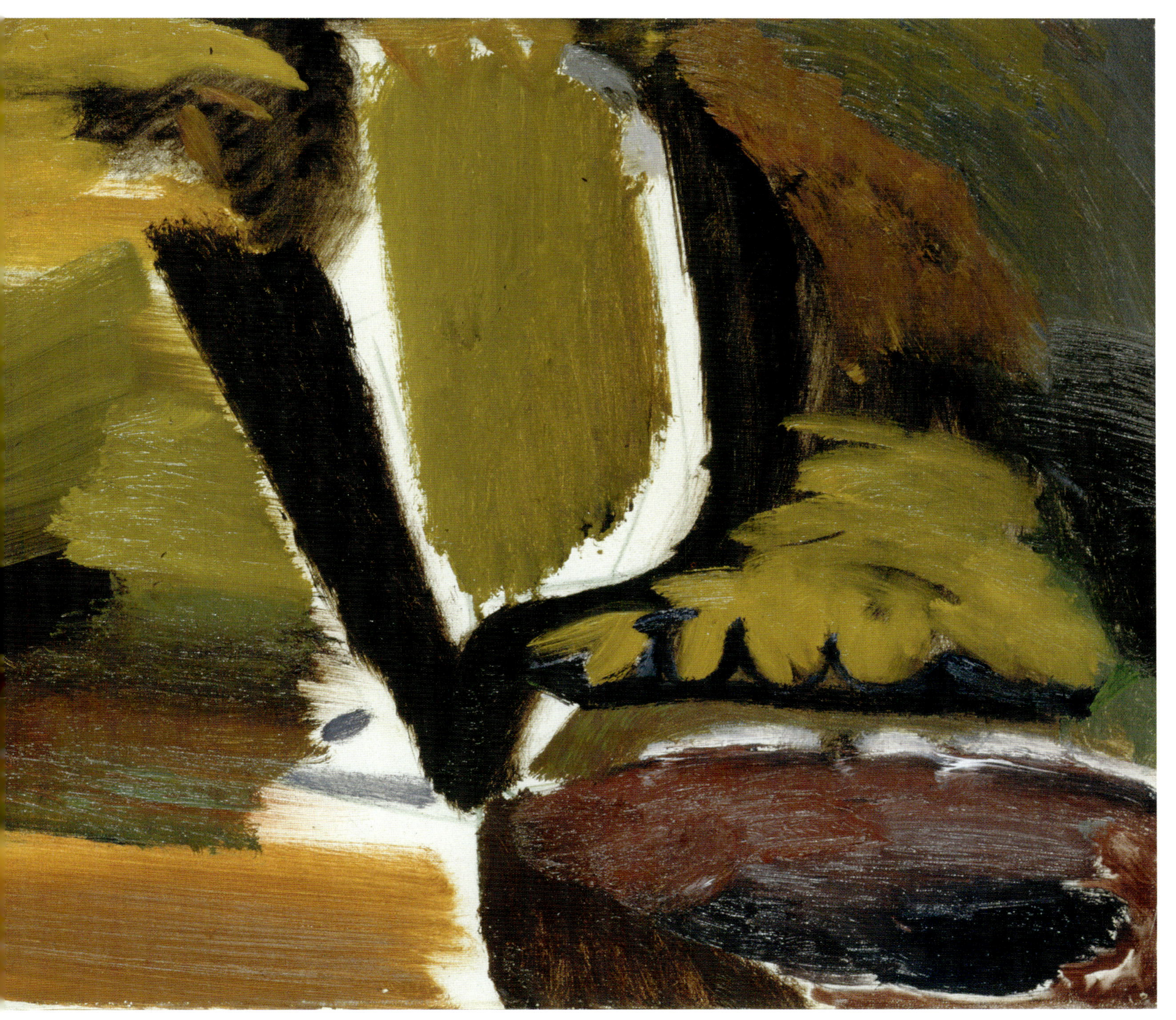

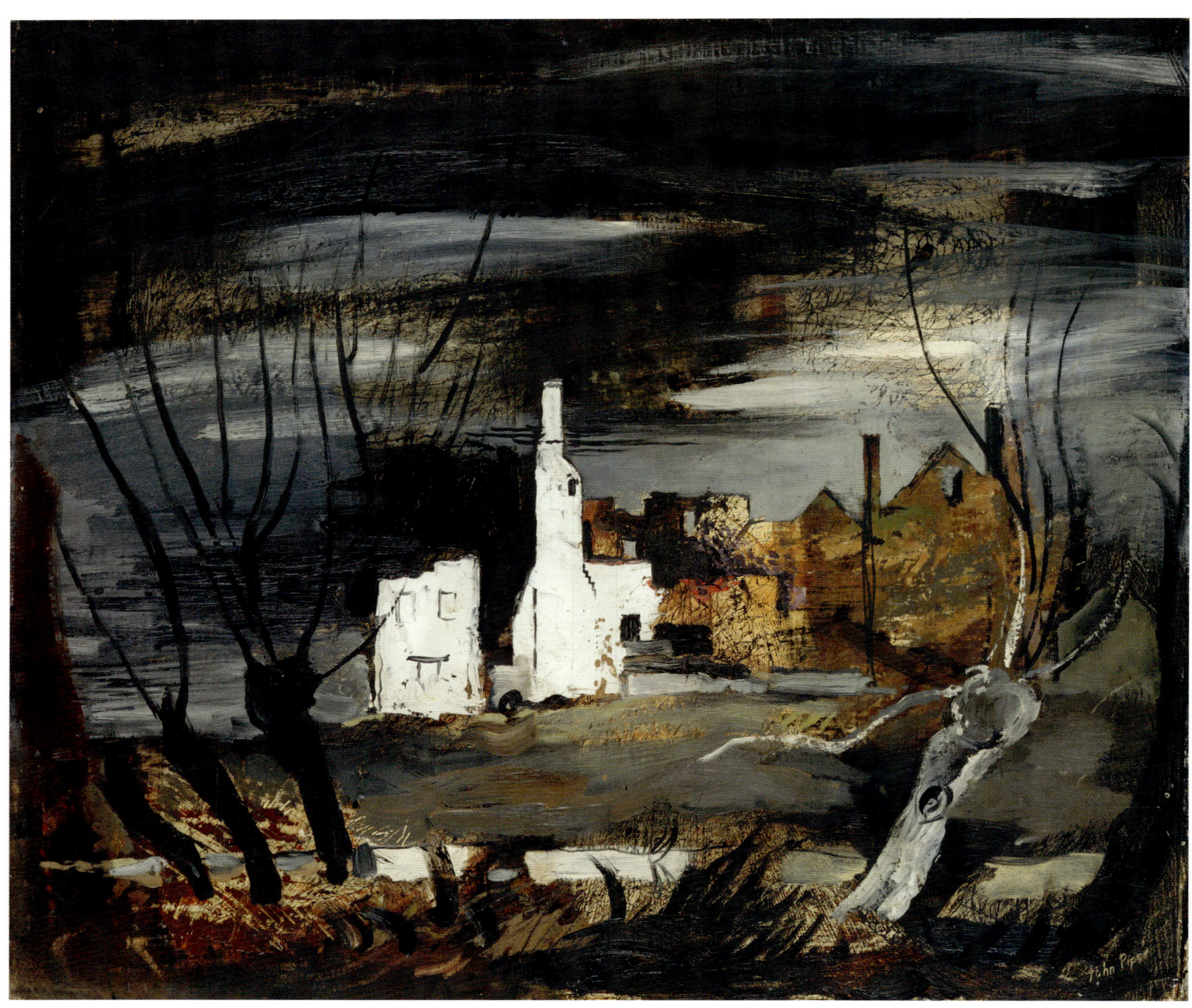

3. A CHAMPION IN WALES OF MODERNISM: THE INFLUENCE OF HOWARD ROBERTS

16. John Piper, *A Ruined House, Hampton Gay, Oxfordshire*, oil and ink on canvas, 1941, 64 x 77 cm. Purchased by Derek Williams from Howard Roberts Gallery, Cardiff.

Derek Williams bought most of his art collection from Cardiff's progressive Howard Roberts Gallery. Howard Roberts was a former art teacher, painter and pupil of Ceri Richards at Cardiff College of Art, where he had also met his wife Joan.

The Robertses together ran one of the earliest, liveliest and most influential post-war commercial art galleries in Wales. Opened in 1956, it was originally located in Howard's studio rooms at the top of Imperial Buildings in St Mary Street, Cardiff. It moved in 1966 to larger, smarter ground-floor premises in Westgate Street. While always focused upon modern Welsh art, it was also a showcase in Wales for modernists such as Barbara Hepworth, Ben Nicholson and Victor Pasmore.[i]

Derek's particular enthusiasm was for neo-romantic work by artists of the mid-twentieth century such as John Piper, Ceri Richards and David Jones. Howard Roberts, who died in 2001, recalled that the first painting which he sold to Derek had been a drawing by Ceri Richards bought, in the late 1950s, as a present. Derek would, eventually, acquire two thirds of his collection through the gallery although, sometimes, works were obtained through a mutually-beneficial commission agreement with Marlborough Fine Art in London's Old Bond Street.[ii]

Derek was particularly attracted to the landscapes of John Piper (1903-92) and would acquire twenty-one of them, mostly from the Howard Roberts Gallery. After a period of abstract work in the 1930s, Piper returned enthusiastically to landscape. His dark, brooding 1941 oil and ink on canvas *A Ruined House, Hampton Gay, Oxfordshire* (fig. 16) is a striking example. Abandoned after a late nineteenth-century fire, the building

Derek's particular enthusiasm was for neo-romantic work by artists of the mid-twentieth century such as John Piper, Ceri Richards and David Jones.

i   Howard Roberts, 'Howard Roberts Gallery', *The Anglo-Welsh Review*, Vol. 18, No. 41, Summer 1969, 169-74; Peter Wakelin, 'Howard Roberts: Proprietor of Wales's first successful commercial gallery', *The Guardian*, 17 April 2001

ii Mark S. Evans, *The Derek Williams Collection at the National Museum of Wales,* National Museum of Wales, 1989

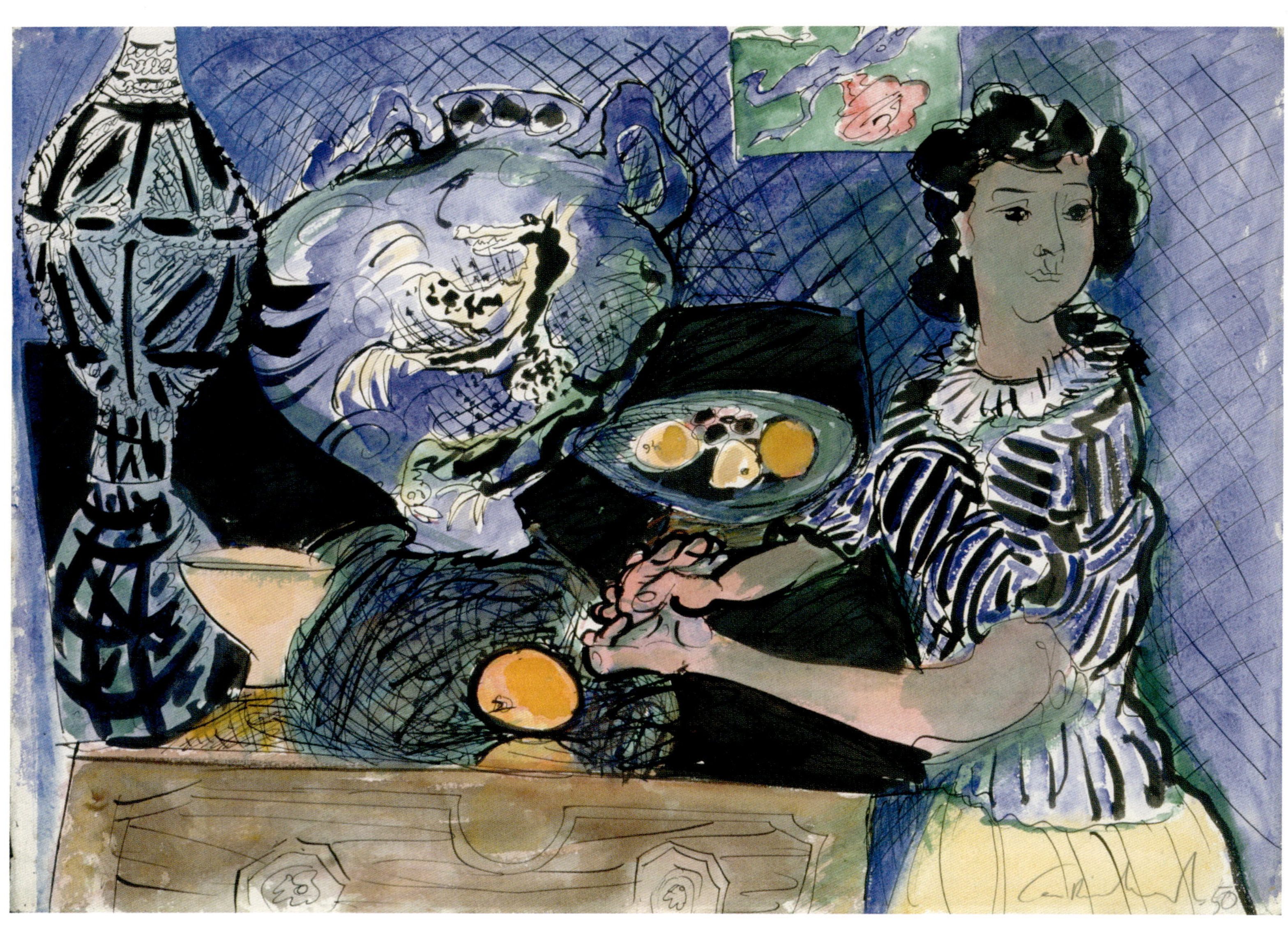

17. Ceri Richards, *The Dragon Pot*, ink and watercolour, 1950, 39 x 56 cm. Purchased by Derek Williams from Howard Roberts Gallery, Cardiff.

appealed to Piper's romantic fascination with derelict buildings and is reminiscent of his contemporary paintings of bomb-damaged buildings. Underlining Derek's interest in Piper, the Derek Williams Trust would, in 2013-14, provide substantial grant support towards the museum's purchase of a significant private collection of Piper's post-war paintings of north Wales and Snowdonia which many regard as among the artist's finest achievements.[iii]

Derek bought from Howard and Joan the majority of his thirteen paintings by Ceri Richards (1903-71). Some of these comprise vigorous responses to the music of Debussy, particularly *La Cathédrale Engloutie*, and to the poetry of Dylan Thomas. They also include comfortable domestic interiors with day-dreaming female figures characteristically absorbed in piano playing. The 1950 ink and watercolour *The Dragon Pot* (fig 17) features, on a table, a giant amphora decorated with a savage-looking beast. While an integral part of the overall design, it is, perhaps, a reminder that the outside world has its dangers.[iv]

Derek also bought from the Gallery six works (two oils and four ink and wash sketches) by the Polish refugee artist Josef Herman (1911-2000). Intriguingly, the c.1966 oil on canvas *Three Welsh Miners* (fig. 18) is the only one of these concerned with coal mining. It is also an example of the artist, having left Ystradgynlais in 1953 after a stay of nine years, returning to a theme which fascinated him for the rest of his life. The dignity and stoicism of working men and women were Herman's chief preoccupation. Depicted in a monumental expressionist style, they embodied, for him, a profound and universal symbol of humanity. He was awarded a gold medal by the National Eisteddfod in 1962 for his contribution to Welsh art.[v]

iii   David Fraser Jenkins, *John Piper: The Forties*, Philip Wilson Publishers / Imperial War Museum, 2000; David Fraser Jenkins and Melissa Munro, *John Piper – The Mountains of Wales: Paintings and Drawings from a Private Collection*, Amgueddfa Cymru – National Museum Wales, 2012

iv   Mel Gooding, *Ceri Richards*, Cameron and Hollis, 2002

v   Monica Bohm-Duchan, *The Art and Life of Josef Herman*, Lund Humphries, 2009

A strikingly abstract and minimalist c.1968 oil on canvas by Kyffin Williams (1918-2006), *Snow on Siabod* (fig. 19), is another of Derek's purchases from the Gallery. A brief moment of sunlight on this snow-capped mountain near Capel Curig is suggested poetically in three contrasting colours by deceptively simple palette-knife strokes. At the time the artist was teaching at Highgate School but, after going part-time, he would resign in 1973 to return to Anglesey to concentrate on painting.[vi]

Other works acquired by Derek from the Howard Roberts Gallery include: six drawings and watercolours by David Jones (three of women, a still life, a landscape and a window seascape), a watercolour and crayon as well as a crucifix figure by Graham Sutherland, an ink and wash drawing by Keith Vaughan, a sketch by Stanley Spencer for *Resurrection Cookham*, an ink and wash study by Augustus John, a bronze maquette by Henry Moore and an oil by L.S. Lowry. The Derek Williams Trust have, subsequently, acquired further work by Herman and Richards and substantially supported an acquisition by Spencer of his major 1934 three-panel oil *Souvenir of Switzerland*.

When Howard and Joan staged a special exhibition in 1969, The Possessors, featuring significant sales to Welsh collections, twenty-six of the exhibits, around a sixth of the total, were, remarkably, lent anonymously by Derek Williams.

The closure of the Howard Roberts Gallery in 1970, partly due to rising costs and competition, greatly affected Derek's art collecting. After some purchases elsewhere, such as a minimalist oil painting by Richard Lin from Marlborough Fine Art and a Piper landscape from Sotheby's, he bought little for a decade. Only towards the end of his life, enticed by the Fosse Gallery near his Cotswolds residence, did he resume buying, acquiring work by Ruskin Spear, William Roberts, Ivon Hitchens and Lucian Freud.

Derek Williams's collection of over seventy works constitutes an important part of

---

vi   Nicholas Sinclair, *Kyffin Williams*, Lund Humphries, 2004

18. Josef Herman, *Three Welsh Miners*, oil on canvas, c.1966, 66 x 51 cm. Purchased by Derek Williams from Howard Roberts Gallery, Cardiff.

The closure of the Howard Roberts Gallery in 1970, partly due to rising costs and competition, greatly affected Derek's art collecting.

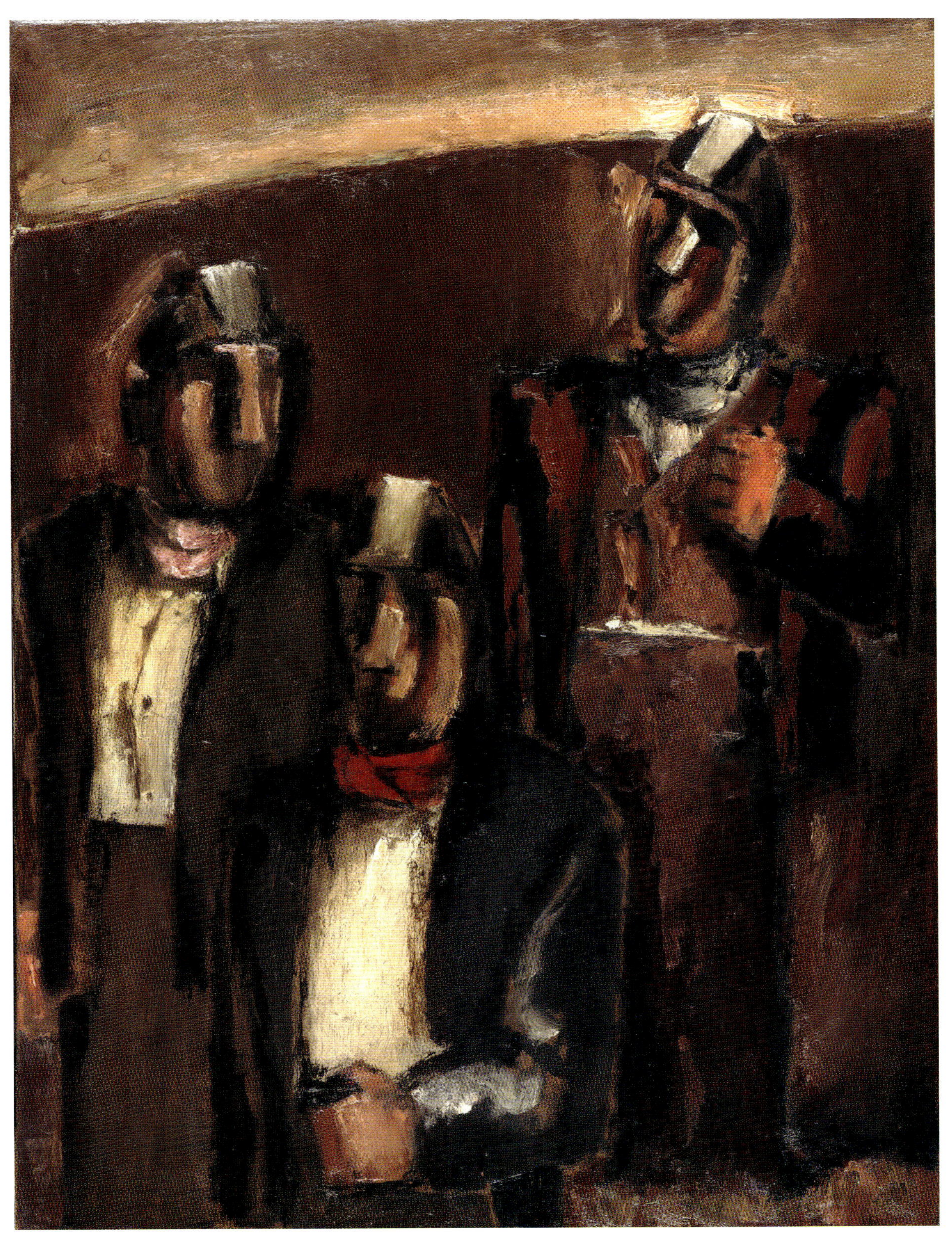

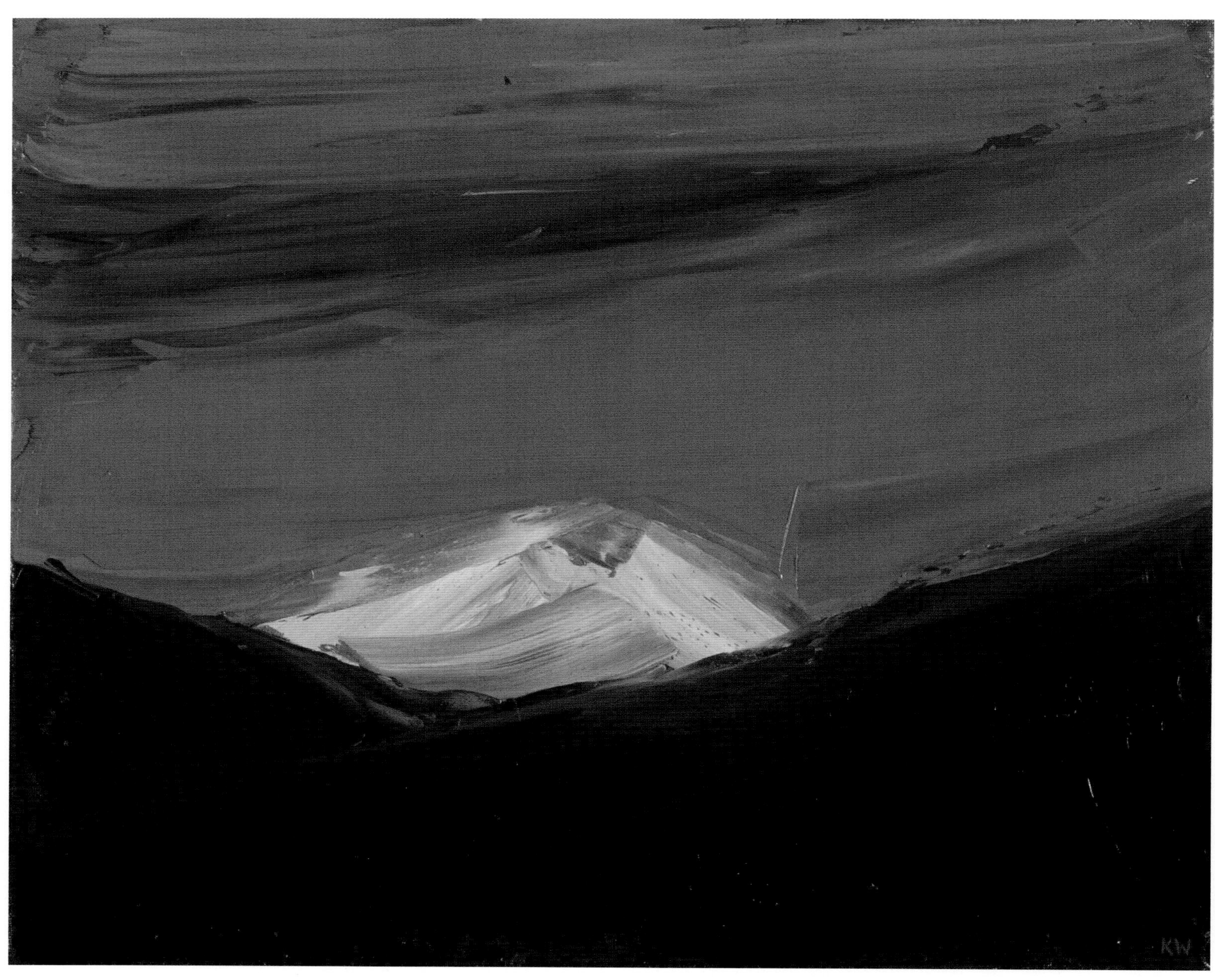

**19. Sir Kyffin Williams, *Snow on Siabod,* oil
on canvas, c.1968, 41 x 51 cm. Purchased
by Derek Williams from Howard Roberts
Gallery, Cardiff.

the mid-twentieth century British art collection held at Amgueddfa Cymru – National Museum Wales. Unsurprisingly, at least a third of his artworks were by artists with close connections to Wales. While reflecting Derek's taste and interests, though, the collection clearly owes much to the guidance of Howard and Joan Roberts. The Robertses moved to Wimbledon where Howard took a teaching post in Battersea. Joan, sadly, died shortly after the move.

Derek Williams's collection of over seventy works constitutes an important part of the mid-twentieth century British art collection held at Amgueddfa Cymru – National Museum Wales.

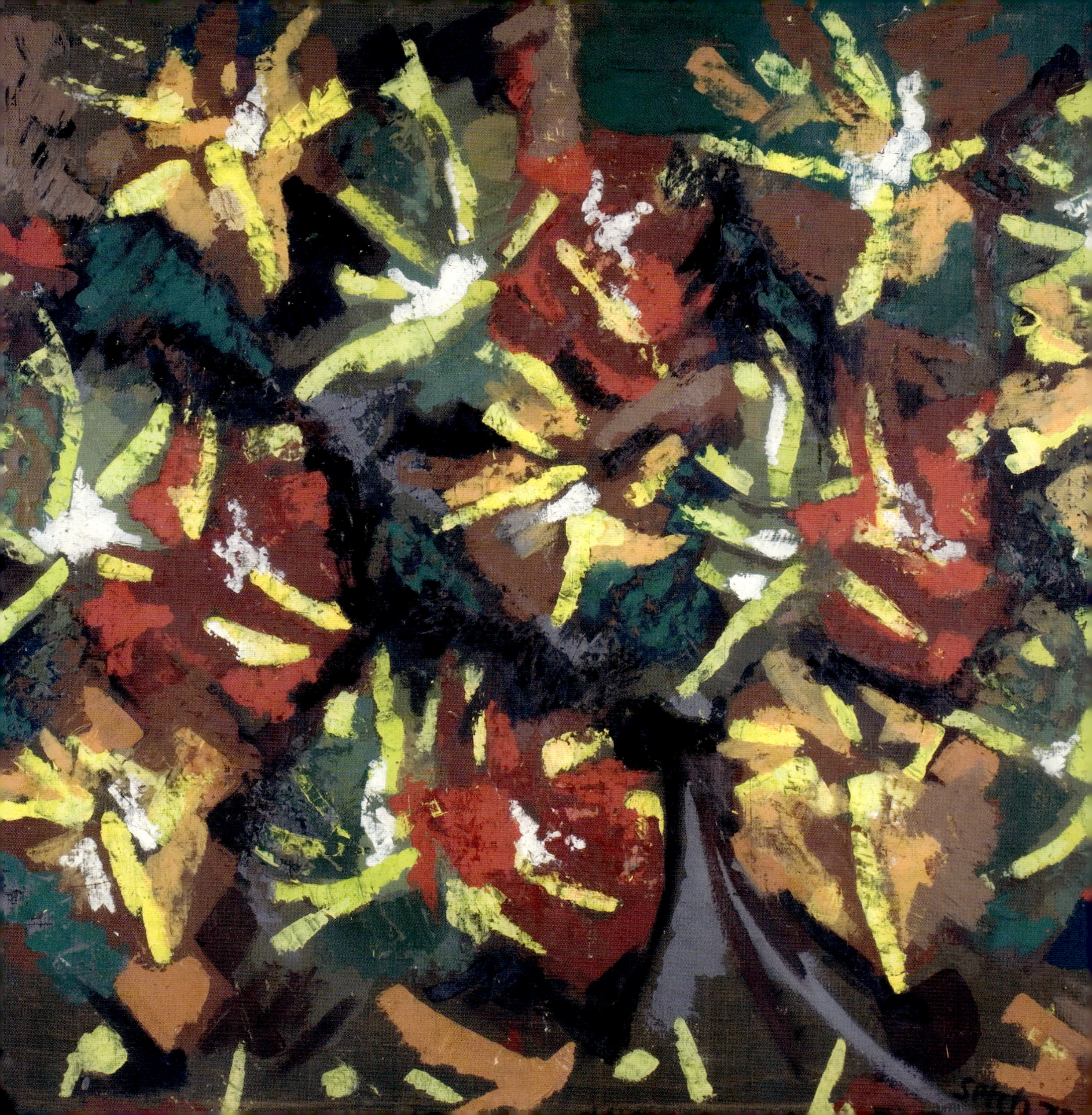

4. ART FOR ALL: WHO DECIDES?

20. **Terry Setch,** *Axminster II,* oil on canvas, 1972, 152 x 151 cm. Trust purchase, 2008.

Art is for everyone. Of course it is. This is what the late Derek Williams wished to see in his generous legacy of art and funding of an art trust in Wales 'to advance public understanding in and appreciation of the arts by the public display of fine works of art.'

This theme and the trust's impact was abundantly apparent in the museum's lively exhibition, Who Decides? Making Connections in Contemporary Art, which ran from October 2017 until September 2018. Celebrating ten years of contemporary art collecting as well as the museum's twenty-five year old partnership with the Derek Williams Trust, the show featured a stimulating selection of recently acquired artworks. It also challenged visitors to reflect upon who art was for.

In the decade prior to this exhibition three hundred and sixty-five paintings, drawings, sculptures, films, prints and installations had been acquired by both the museum and the Derek Williams Trust. A striking and revealing feature of Who Decides? was that the central role in selecting, or curating, what to display from these acquisitions had been played by service users from The Wallich, a charity supporting people who have experienced homelessness in Wales.

This is symbolic of the museum's desire to broaden its appeal to those who, for whatever reason, might be inhibited from entering the building. 'By making our collection more accessible to all,' the introductory panel explained, 'Who Decides? aims to create a more democratic and accountable museum.' To emphasise its point the Universal Declaration of Human Rights was cited: 'Everyone has the right to freely participate in the cultural life of the community, to enjoy the arts.' The Wallich curator team had, indeed, been involved at every stage of this project, not just in the selection of work but also in its arrangement and interpretation.

The result was an exhibition which, from the start, had a refreshing, stimulating and socially relevant quality, embracing issues as diverse as social isolation, religious

'Everyone has the right to freely participate in the cultural life of the community, to enjoy the arts.'

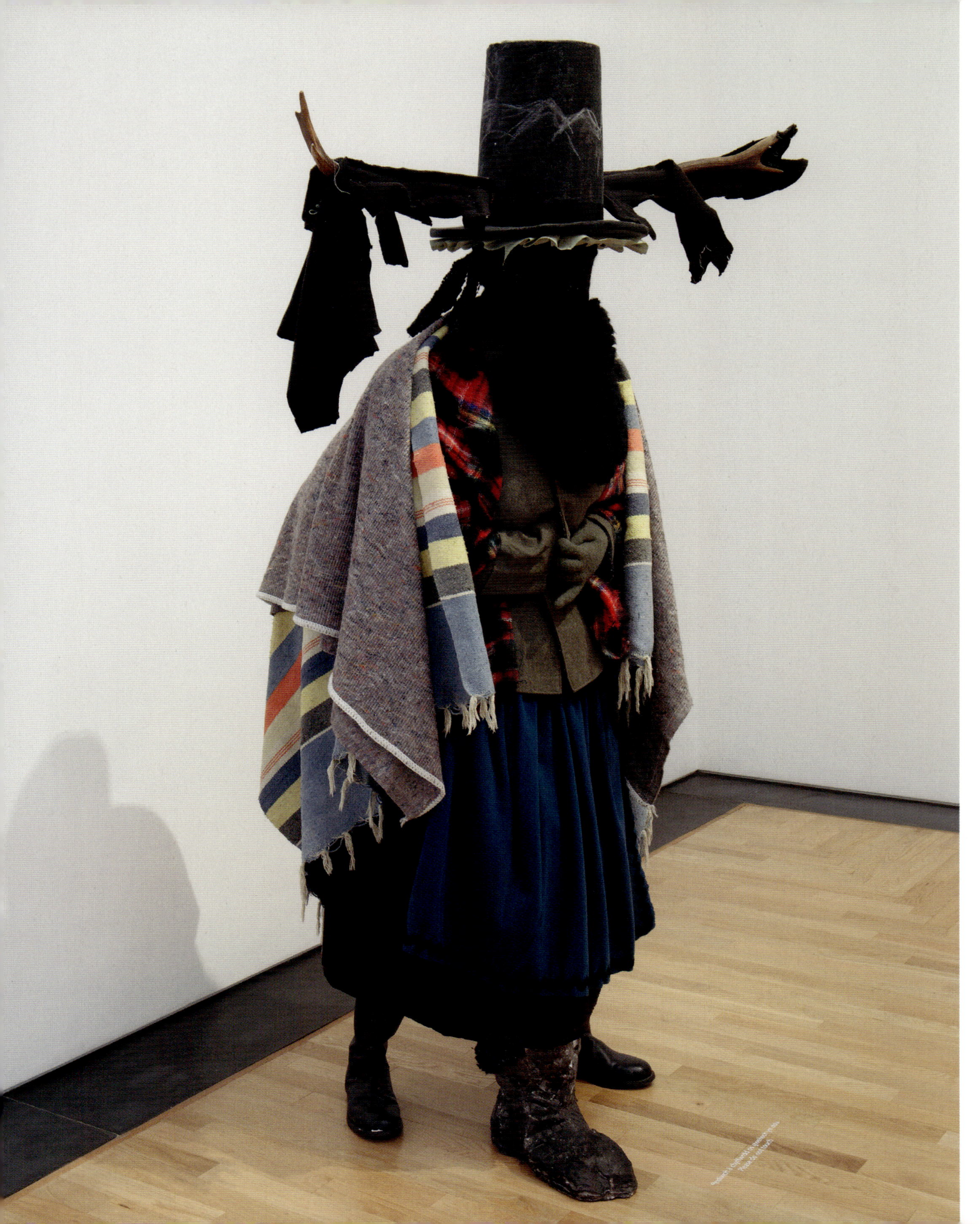

belief, Welsh identity and even, in the powerful etchings and aquatints of Paula Rego, female genital mutilation. It was also visually impressive.

In the first gallery, Terry Setch's abstract 1972 oil on canvas *Axminster II* (Fig. 20) was a work bought by the Derek Williams Trust in 2008 and on loan to the museum. Setch, born in 1936, was, by the early 1970s, a senior lecturer at Cardiff College of Art and a member of 56 Group Wales. He had bought a sample of Axminster carpet in Cardiff and was attracted by its cubist and abstract-expressionist visual qualities. For him, it epitomised absurdities in the relationship between manufacturing and art convention.[i]

Who Decides? curator Dennis King, however, had a very personal take on Setch's painting. 'This piece', he wrote, 'looks like lights in a Christmas tree. Christmas is my favourite time of year when the family get together… It's a sad time now because we haven't got Dad.' Tellingly, he added: 'Before taking part in this exhibition I'd never been into the museum but I'll be coming in more now.'

Laura Ford's 2005 mixed-media sculpture *Glory Glory (Hat and Horns)* (Fig. 21) was bought by the museum with grant-support from the Derek Williams Trust. Included in her Venice Biennale exhibition of the same year, this simultaneously appealing and, yet, disturbingly ambiguous figure plays on a stereotyped yet traditional image of Welsh identity, a woman in national costume. It also raises issues of perceived gender and disability. Ford, born in 1961, encourages us, through unsettling characterisation, to engage with wider social and political issues, to view the world anew and to challenge assumptions.[ii]

Who Decides? curator Helen Griffiths's response to Ford's work was, as the sculptor hoped, of a more emotional kind. For her it was both a reminder of Halloween 'trick or treating' and 'of happier times when all my family got along without many arguments,

---

i   Martin Holman, *Terry Setch*, Lund Humphries, 2009, 46-8
ii   www.lauraford.net

so it wasn't stressful.' Taking part in the museum project had, she reflected, 'opened my eyes to what art is really about and that you don't need to know about art to appreciate it.' Her colleague Steffan Rhys Owen's opinion is eloquent and more complex. He recognises the sculpture, in part, as 'a woman, part-man, moose-headed with a clubbed foot, a malignant spirit from the Welsh hinterland, a shapeshifting figure from our past perhaps, or a more universal apparition...'

John Merion Morris's 1996 bronze sculpture *Cofeb Tryweryn* (fig. 22) was also purchased, in 2008, with grant support from the Derek Williams Trust. Born in 1936, the sculptor has researched Celtic art. He created this maquette for a spiritual memorial, in startled bird-like form, to mark the drowning of Welsh-speaking village Capel Celyn due to the construction of a reservoir to supply Liverpool with water. Hidden in the bird's feathers may be discerned rows of singing or protesting heads.[iii]

Who Decides? curator Ian Harris chose Morris's work 'as it reminds me of my Welsh heritage and it looks almost like a phoenix rising from the flames...' Involvement in the exhibition, he reflected, 'has taught me to appreciate what I'm looking at and I have taken pride in my contribution.'

Visitor participation was further encouraged with a room off the main gallery presented as a museum store with crated and unwrapped paintings and sculpture which visitors were invited to vote to be added, at a later stage, to the exhibition.

The Derek Williams Trust, along with other funders, has acquired and supported the aquisition of a wealth of high-quality artworks at Amgueddfa Cymru – National Museum Wales. People respond to these in different ways according to their background and life experience. Ultimately, however, they help us to understand ourselves better, which is, in essence, what museums are for.

22. John Meirion Morris, *Cofeb Tryweryn,* bronze, 1996, 72 x 60 x 39 cm. Acquired by Amgueddfa Cymru – National Museum Wales with support from the Derek Williams Trust, 2008.

Hidden in the bird's feathers may be discerned rows of singing or protesting heads.

---

iii John Meirion Morris, 'Imagination and the Magic of Tradition', Iwan Bala ed., *Certain Welsh Artists: Custodial Aesthetics in Contemporary Welsh Art*, Seren, 1999, 99-114

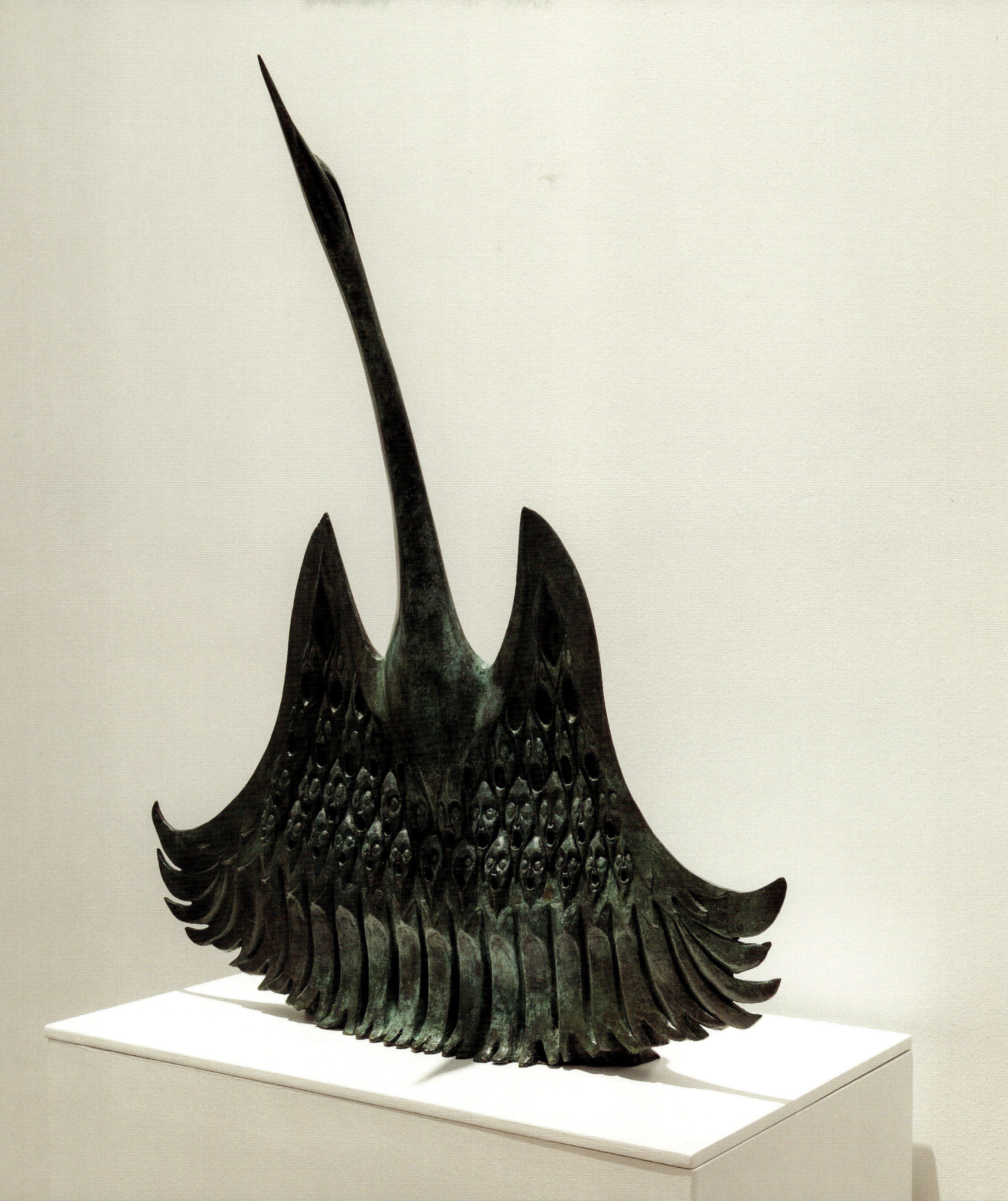

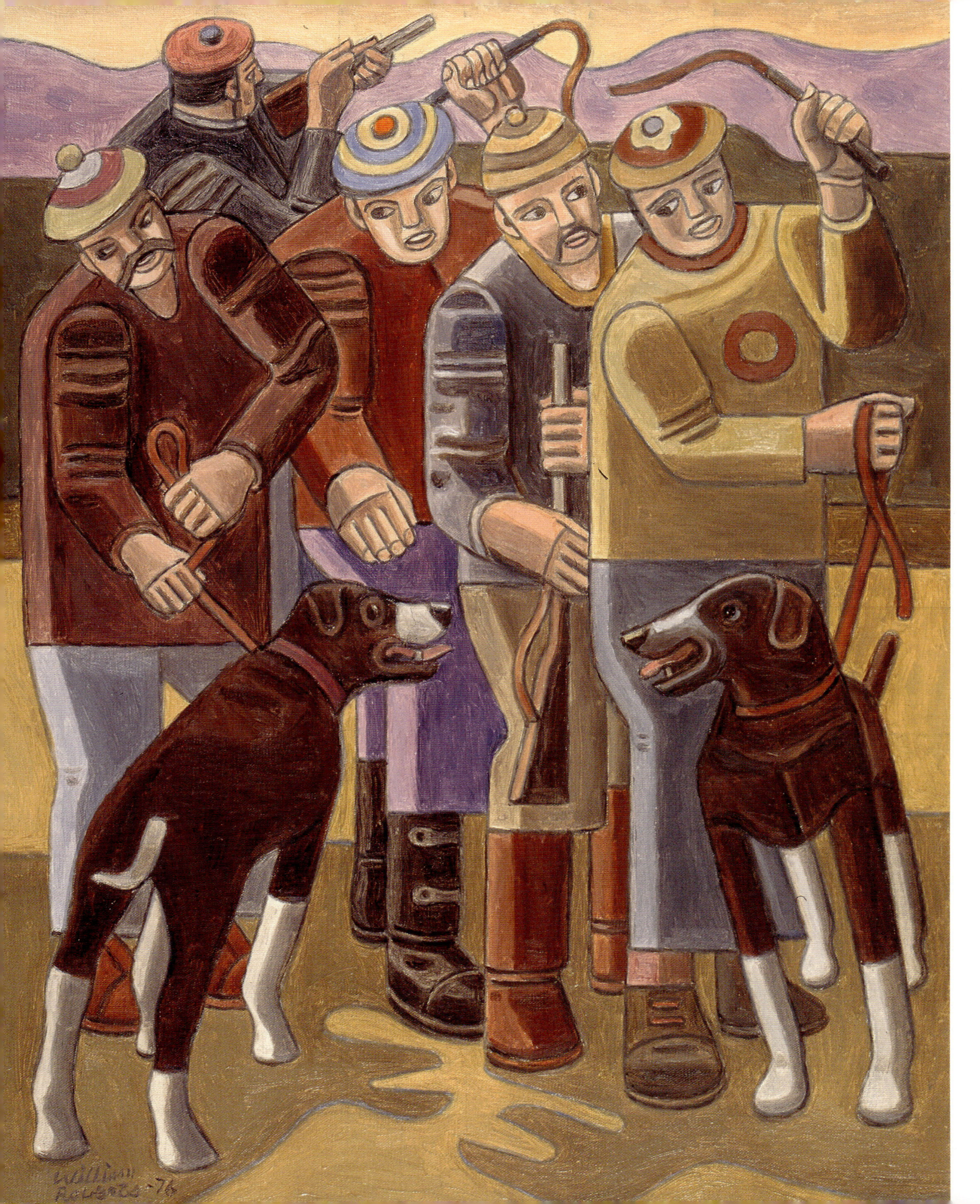

5. FIGURATIVELY SPEAKING

23. William Roberts, *The Shooting Party*, oil on canvas, 1976, 51 x 41 cm. Purchased by Derek Williams from Fosse Gallery, Stow-on-the Wold, 1984.

This chapter explores the diversity of approaches which modern and contemporary artists have taken to figurative or representational art. This is art in which the subjects are recognisable.

William Roberts's 1976 oil on canvas *The Shooting Party* (fig. 23) was one of the last paintings bought by Derek Williams. It exemplifies the artist's stylised, geometrically designed, often satirical and complex compositions of tubular-limbed figures in familiar settings. Roberts (1895-1980), from London, should not be confused with the Welsh Will Roberts, the notable expressive figurative painter who lived in Neath.

William Roberts studied at the Slade School of Fine Art. Having absorbed the principles of cubism, in which, in one work, many viewpoints of a subject were preferred to the tradition of creating a three-dimensional illusion of it, he became a member of the short-lived vorticist movement. Begun around 1914 and influenced by both cubism and futurism, this sought to capture in aggressive angular works the energy, movement and dynamism of modern life and its machinery. Wyndham Lewis, with whom Roberts would later argue in print about their respective roles in the movement, was a leading force.[i]

Roberts, a war artist in both world wars, taught at the Central School, became a Royal Academician and was, eventually, given a retrospective exhibition at the Tate Gallery. Notoriously suspicious of dealers, Roberts, to his financial detriment, had preferred to show his work in Royal Academy summer exhibitions.

William Wilkins's 1994 oil on canvas *Santa Maria Gloriosa dei Frari* (fig. 24), a purchase by the Derek Williams Trust, represents this artist's distinctive pointillist style in which an image is formed in the eye of the viewer by contrasting arrangements of dabs of colour paint which, applied systematically, create an intense effect of light. He has,

Notoriously suspicious of dealers, Roberts, to his financial detriment, had preferred to show his work in Royal Academy summer exhibitions.

---

i   Andrew Heard, *William Roberts, 1895-1980*, Hatton Gallery, University of Newcastle, 2004

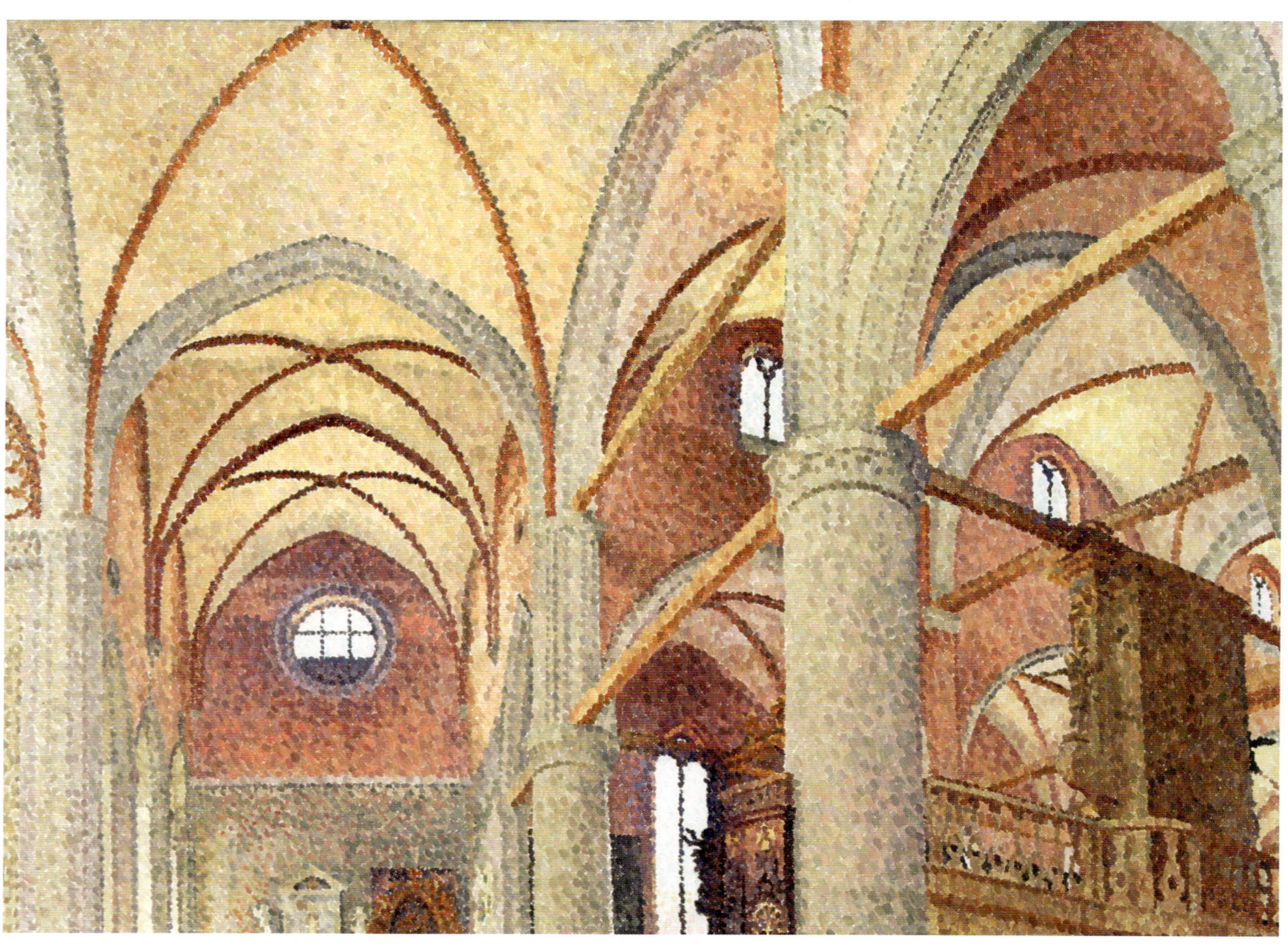

Wilkins's work, often featuring figures, landscape and still lifes with ceramics, is characterised by precision in the use of line, space, restricted colour and tone to form harmonious visual relationships.

since 1987, worked in Venice every year, the location of this Franciscan church. In the 1960s, while in Brittany, he developed a fascination with the way church plans were a key to understanding those buildings' structure, space and light.[ii]

Born in Suffolk in 1938 but brought up in Llandeilo, Wilkins attended Swansea College of Art and the Royal College of Art. After teaching art and working as an architectural journalist he has, since the mid-1970s, concentrated on painting while also being heavily involved in directing historic garden projects in Wales, for which he is, perhaps, more widely known.

Wilkins's work, often featuring figures, landscape and still lifes with ceramics, is characterised by precision in the use of line, space, restricted colour and tone to form harmonious visual relationships. He exhibited regularly in New York from the mid-1970s into the 1990s and was, for many years, an active member of 56 Group Wales. His time-consuming painting technique was first employed in the 1880s by the French painters Georges Seurat and Paul Signac.

Philip Nicol's 2001 oil on canvas *Paw* (Fig. 25), bought by the trust, reveals another approach to figurative art. His work, as here, is often concerned with the psychological effects of inner-cityscapes and, in particular, the sense of isolation their spaces may induce. Figures, curiously, only occasionally occur and, yet, human presence is implied metaphorically through objects such as cars. The paintings may appear to be of actual places but are, often, at least in part, imaginary, drawing upon memory, even novels, and incorporating cinematic techniques such as dramatic lighting and deep shadow. These evoke a poetic and metaphysical quality, a sense of stilled time, of anticipation about a captured narrative. There is also awareness of the uneasy co-existence of nature within the structured urban environment.[iii]

---

ii   David Fraser Jenkins, *William Wilkins*, Graffeg, 2014
iii   Jonathan Clarkson, *Paintings: Philip Nicol*, UWIC Press, 2005

Nicol, born in Caerphilly in 1953, attended Cardiff College of Art and became an art lecturer at various institutions including Leeds College of Art and Design and, latterly, University of Wales Institute, Cardiff. A gold-medal winner at the National Eisteddfod of Wales in 2001, he has also been a member of 56 Group Wales. He initiated and managed the extensive refurbishment of Bute Street Studios, Cardiff, and is today the adjacent Bay Art Gallery's exhibition officer. He is, in addition, fascinated by still-life painting.

These three painters have all shown recognisable scenes, whether peopled or not, and, yet, they are completely different in their vision and technique. There are many other examples in artworks acquired and supported by the Derek Williams Trust.

25. Philip Nicol, *Paw,* oil on canvas, 2001, 144 x 144 x 3 cm. Trust purchase, 2002.

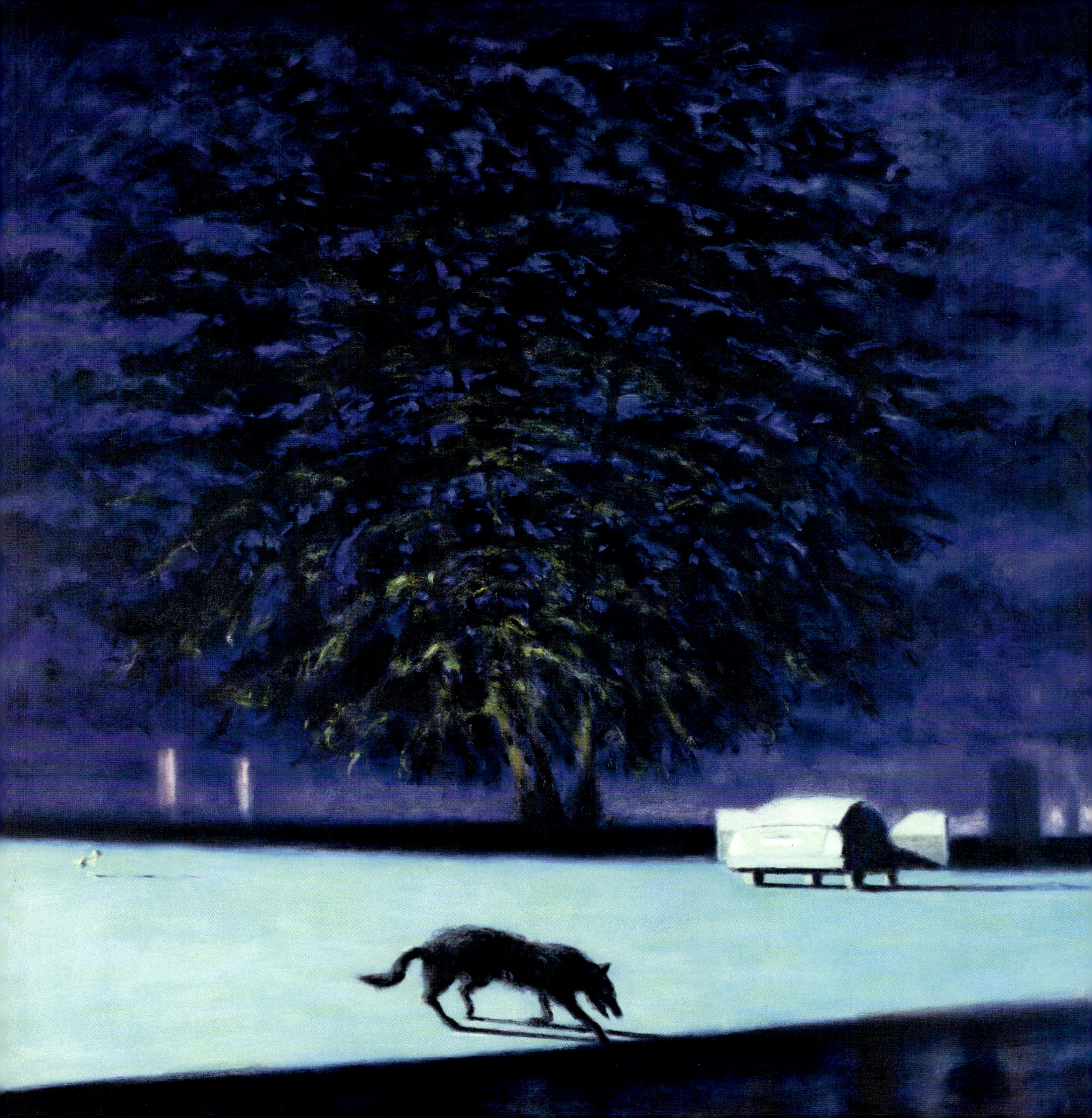

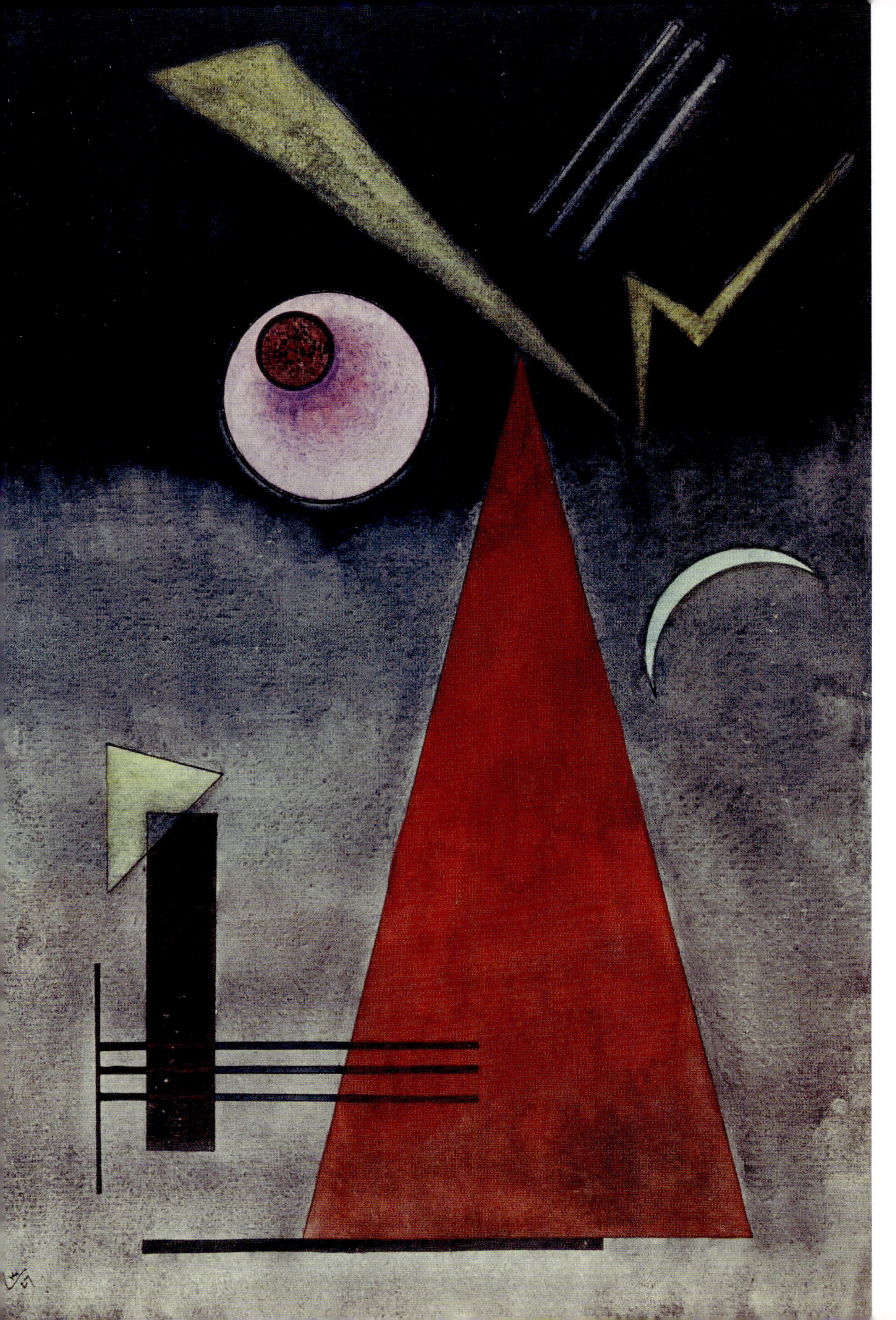

6. CHALLENGES AND PLEASURES OF ABSTRACT ART

26. Wassily Kandinsky, *Acid Green Crescent*, watercolour, ink and bodycolour on paper, 1927, 48 x 32 cm. Acquired by Amgueddfa Cymru – National Museum Wales with support from the Derek Williams Trust (Centenary Fund), 2007.

Abstract art, which does not show recognisable things but consists of colours, forms, marks, lines, patterns, textures and spaces for their own sake, is not always readily appreciated.

It can, for those not open to it, present challenges. Developed independently in several countries during the second decade of the twentieth century, it was a long time before it became more widely accepted. Nevertheless, many members of the 56 Group Wales, in its mid-twentieth century pioneering days, pursued abstraction and endured criticism not only from some incredulous members of the public but, later, from high-profile commentators like Kyffin Williams.[i]

That there is, today, an appetite for abstraction is indicated by the public's choice of a work that was then included in the exhibition Who Decides? Making Connections with Contemporary Art at the museum in 2017-18. This was trust-purchased Maurice Cockrill's *Well You Needn't*, a 2008 mixed-media abstract painting comprising snaking coloured shapes against a bright pink background.

The trust also supported, through its Centenary Fund for the museum, the acquisition in 2007 of a 1927 Wassily Kandinsky watercolour, ink and bodycolour on paper *Acid Green Crescent* (fig. 26). A refined geometric work by a key artist in the development of abstraction, it expresses considerable spirituality and harmony. These were important factors in the early days of abstract art.[ii]

The Derek Williams Trust has recently added a significant abstract painting to its collection, the first in a United Kingdom public collection. This is a large 1973 acrylic on canvas from the distinctive series of *Blancs* by Simon Hantaï (1922-2008). Born in Hungary, Hantaï lived, from 1949, in France. In the early 1950s, supported by André

It can, for those not open to it, present challenges. Developed independently in several countries during the second decade of the twentieth century, it was a long time before it became more widely accepted.

---

i   David Moore, *A Taste of the Avant-Garde: 56 Group Wales, 56 Years*, Crooked Window, 2012, 54-5

ii   Hajo Düchting, *Wassily Kandinsky 1866–1944: A Revolution in Painting*, Taschen, 2000

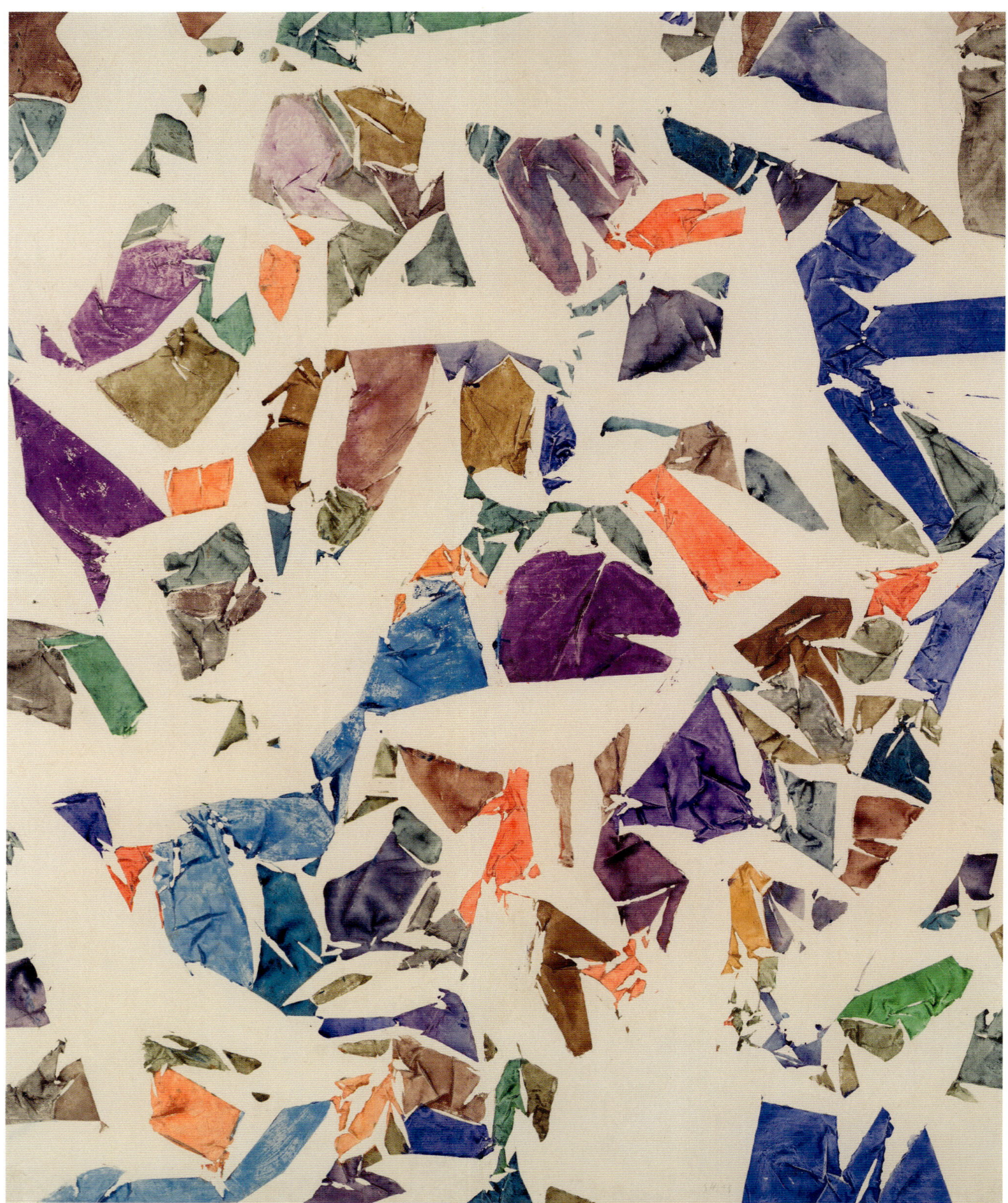

In 1960 Hantaï refocused, in a process-driven series of abstract works, on a new technique called 'pliage', which, literally, means 'folding' and which sought to remove any trace of manual activity.

Breton, he became a surrealist painter before becoming influenced by American abstract expressionist Jackson Pollock.[iii]

Hantaï would find a unique voice, however, with experimentation into untraditional methods of both representation and the application of paint. This included washing, scratching-out and scraping with metal objects. He also copied written texts onto canvases which, thereby, took on a life of their own.

In 1960 Hantaï refocused, in a process-driven series of abstract works, on a new technique called 'pliage', which, literally, means 'folding' and which sought to remove any trace of manual activity. His canvases were rolled up, creased, crumpled, knotted and saturated with paint. When unfolded, the painted and unpainted parts were separated by folds. Some contained one or two bold colours but others, like the series *Blancs* (fig. 27), used a range of bright saturated colours. These were designed so that the fragmented painted parts gave life to a dominant unpainted white structure.

Hantaï held a successful retrospective in 1976 at the Musée National d'Art Moderne in Paris. After representing France at the Venice Biennale in 1982, however, and disenchanted with the art world, he became famously reclusive and largely refused to exhibit. This makes it more remarkable that the trust has acquired one of his major works.

A very different type of abstract painting, employing complementary coloured squares and dating from the same year as the Hantaï, 1973, was acquired by the trust in 2008. This was an oil on canvas, *Four sets of 4 chromatic oppositions in a system of rotation* by Jeffrey Steele (fig. 28). While the title itself is challenging, it does indicate what underlies the work but is not essential for its enjoyment. Influenced by mathematics, the artist has approached, not entirely without intuition, the construction of the

iii   Bénédicte Ajac, *Simon Hantaï: L'Exposition / The Exhibition*, Centre Pompidou, 2013, 44-5

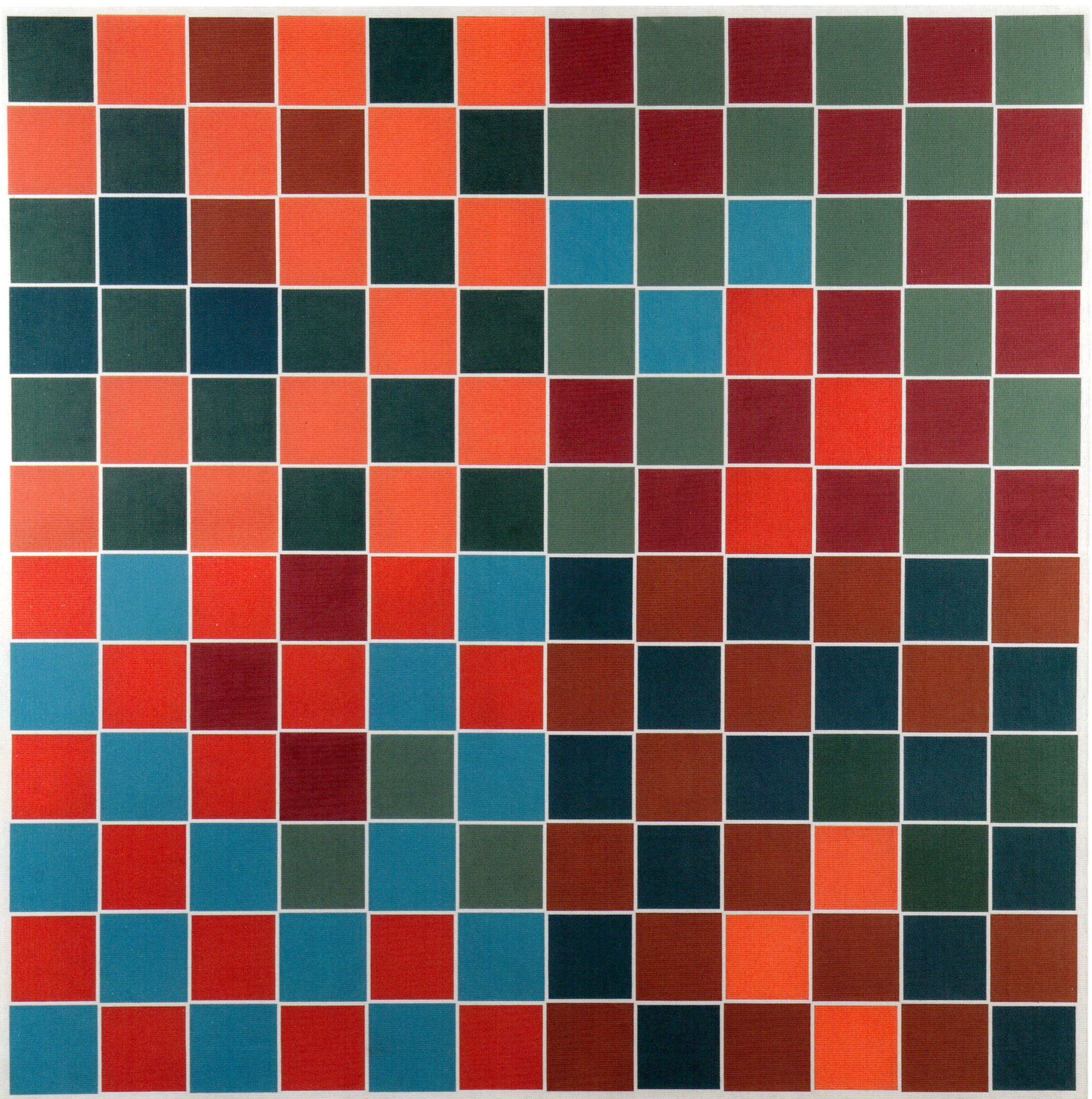

Influenced by mathematics, the artist has approached, not entirely without intuition, the construction of the painting through using a pre-conceived rational system.

painting through using a pre-conceived rational system. Many of his works are black and white with, largely unintended, optical effects.

A celebrated exponent of geometric abstraction, Steele was born in Cardiff in 1931, studied at its art college as well as in Newport and obtained a scholarship to the École des Beaux-Arts in Paris. Returning to lecture at his old colleges and the influential Barry Summer School, he moved on to Portsmouth Polytechnic. An influential 1960s member of 56 Group Wales, he co-founded the Systems Group of artists in 1969. Even by 1965 his work had been included in a landmark international exhibition of optical, systems and kinetic art, The Responsive Eye, at New York's Museum of Modern Art, which also included work by Victor Vasarely, Josef Albers and Bridget Riley.[iv]

Much later, and very different in approach, is Brendan Stuart Burns's 1997 oil on canvas *Swish-Back-West* (fig. 29) which the trust acquired that year. Burns's spiritual paintings from this period, on a knife edge between abstraction and figuration, are an amalgam of multi-sensory responses to close experience of nature at Druidston Haven in Pembrokeshire. His responses to tide, light, colour, wind, spindrift, the feel of sand, rock and seaweed, as well as the sound and smell of the sea, are translated into thick paint with brush and palette knife. Born in Kenya in 1963, Burns studied in Cardiff and at the Slade School of Fine Art. Twice a gold-medal winner at the National Eisteddfod of Wales, in 1993 and 1998, he has also been a member of 56 Group Wales.

These very different examples of modern abstract painting are only three out of many such works which have been carefully selected and acquired by the Derek Williams Trust for the appreciation and enjoyment of museum visitors in Wales. Others discussed and illustrated in this book are by Gillian Ayres (figs. 30 and 59), Adrian Heath (fig. 38), Sir Howard Hodgkin (fig. 60), Sean Scully (fig.33) and Terry Setch (fig.20).

---

iv   Alan Fowler *et al.*, *A Rational Aesthetic: The Systems Group and Associated Artists*, Southampton City Art Gallery, 2008

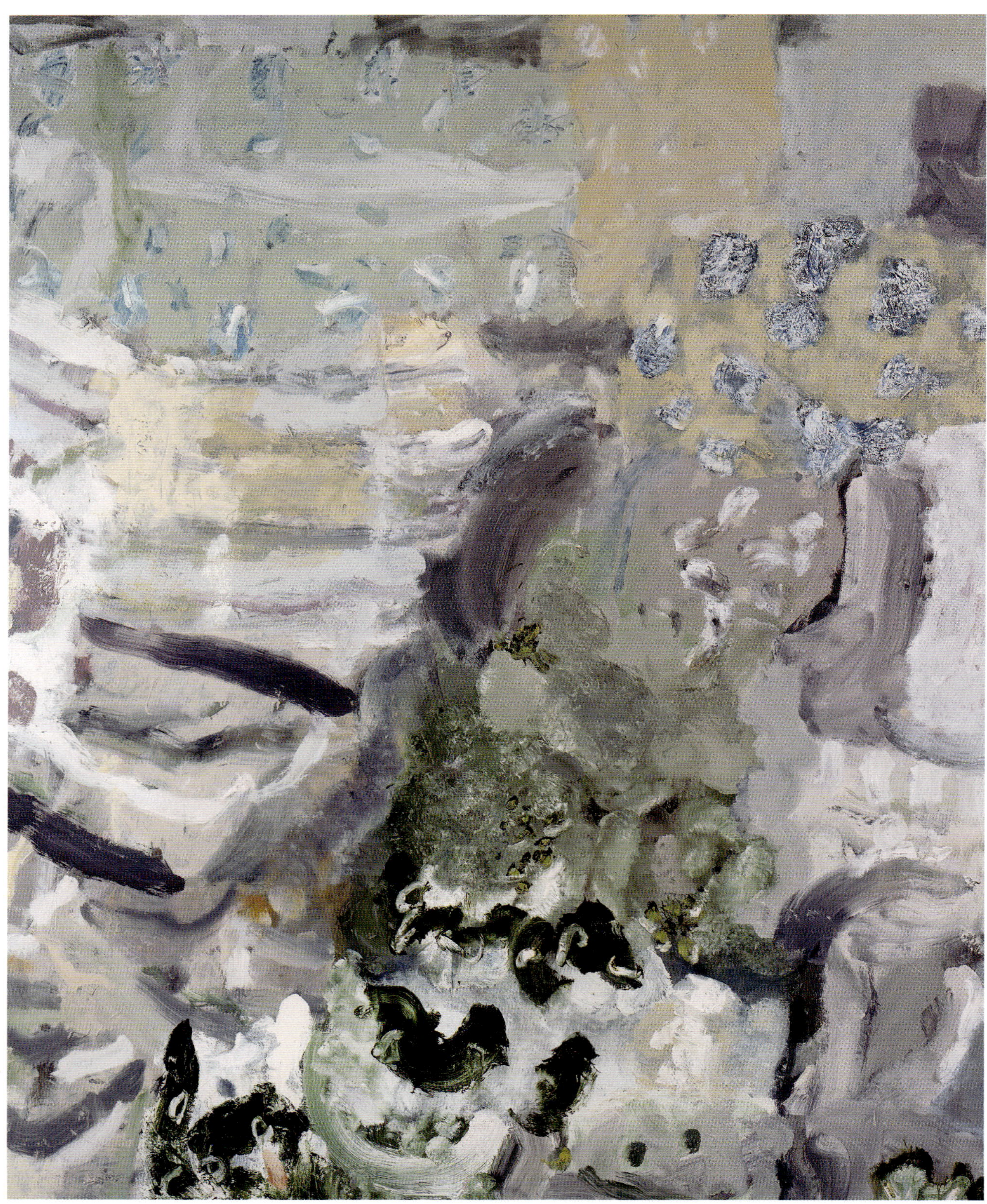

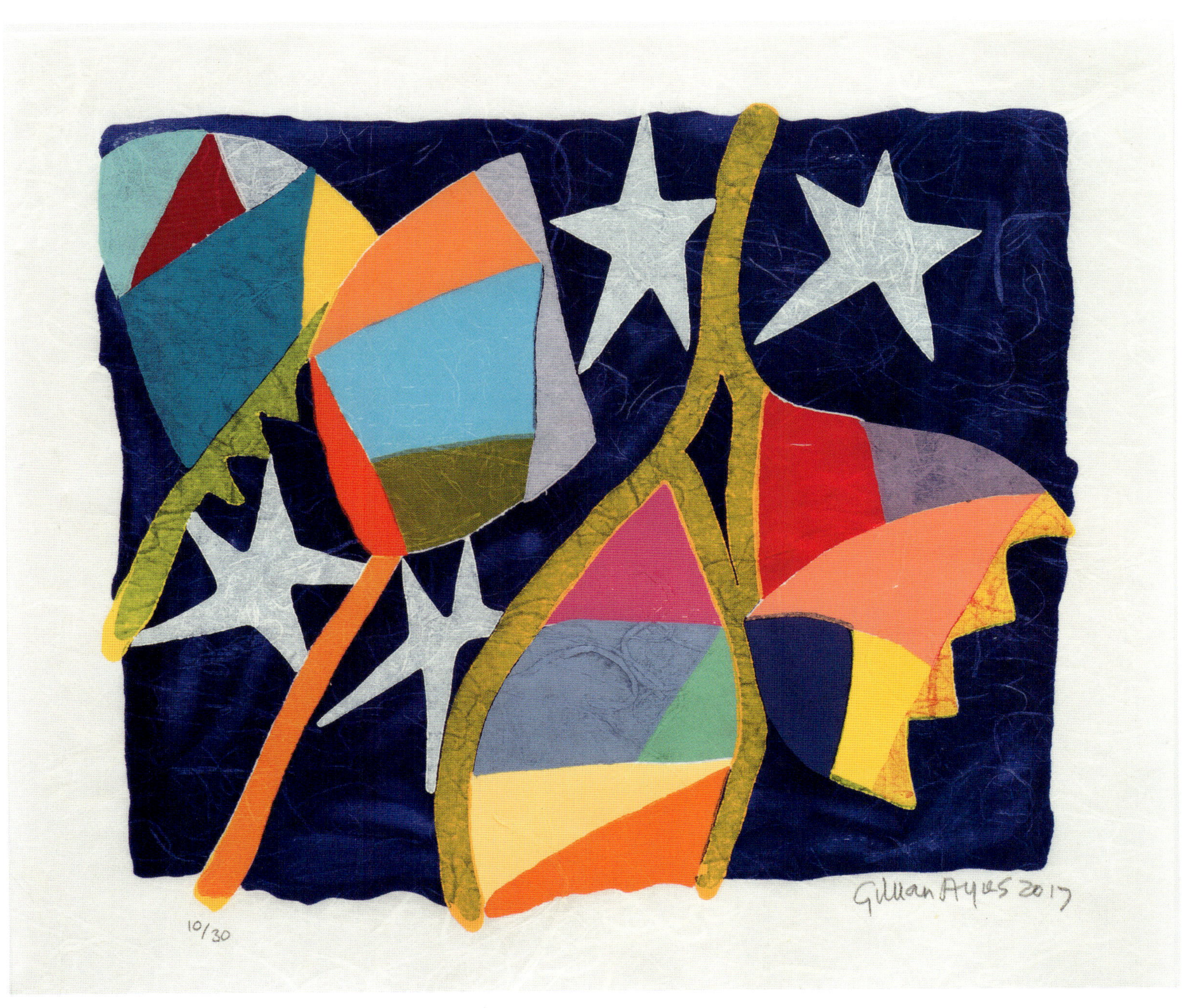

29. Brendan Stuart Burns, *Swish-Back-West,* oil on canvas, 1997, 241 x 201 cm. Trust purchase, 1997.

30. Gillian Ayres, *Thuban,* woodcut on Japanese paper, 2017, sheet size 48 x 58 cm. Trust purchase, 2018.

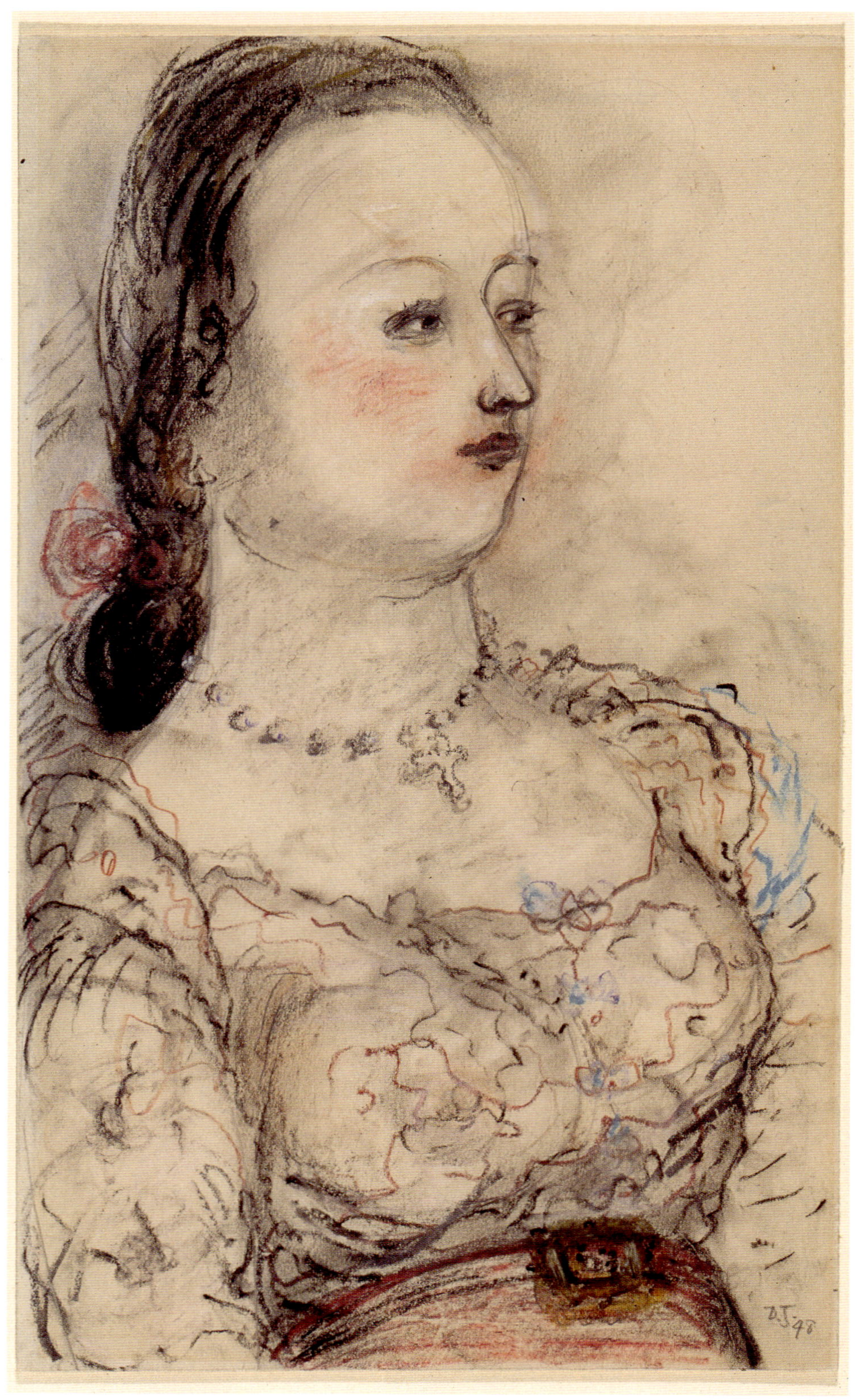

7. THE VITALITY OF DRAWING

31. David Jones, *Half-Length Woman*, pencil, charcoal and coloured chalk, 1948, 33 x 20 cm. Purchased by Derek Williams from Howard Roberts Gallery, Cardiff.

'Drawings are records, observations, discoveries and interventions, sometimes all at once.'

Paul Klee, perhaps recalling earlier explorations of mark-making derived from the imagery of a countryside walk, described in 1925 taking 'An active line on a walk, moving freely without goal.'[i] Intriguingly, an exploration of walking is also an integral part of land artist Richard Long's work (see page 103).

There is more to drawing than might, at first, be imagined. David Maclagan, who has written insightfully on the subject, discerns that it involves marks by human hand deliberately inscribed on a surface and that these may be representational or abstract, a means to an end or end in themselves. 'Drawings are records, observations, discoveries and interventions, sometimes all at once,' he writes. 'Some drawings are consciously directed at an audience, while others seem to be more private; we may draw what we know or what we see outside us, or we may draw "from within"'[ii] Marks may be made in numerous ways using, for example, stone, refined chalk, pencil, ink, paint, crayon, charcoal or pastel.

The Big Draw, a visual literacy charity that promotes the universal language of drawing as a tool for learning, expression and intervention, has, since its foundation in 2000, raised the profile of drawing among the general population, first in the United Kingdom and now worldwide. It has been inspired by Victorian artist, writer and philosopher John Ruskin's belief in the power of drawing to help us to see the world more clearly and as a vital tool for communication and social change.[iii]

Many drawings are represented in Derek Williams's personal collection. Numerous chalk or ink studies by John Piper, often combined with watercolour and gouache, include his 1963 *Rudbaxton near Haverfordwest* (fig. 14). Drawings by another of his

---

i Matthew Gale *et al.*, *Paul Klee: Making Visible*, Tate Publishing, 2013, 18

ii David Maclagan, *Line Let Loose: Scribbling, Doodling and Automatic Drawing*, Reaktion Books, 2014, 17

iii thebigdraw.org

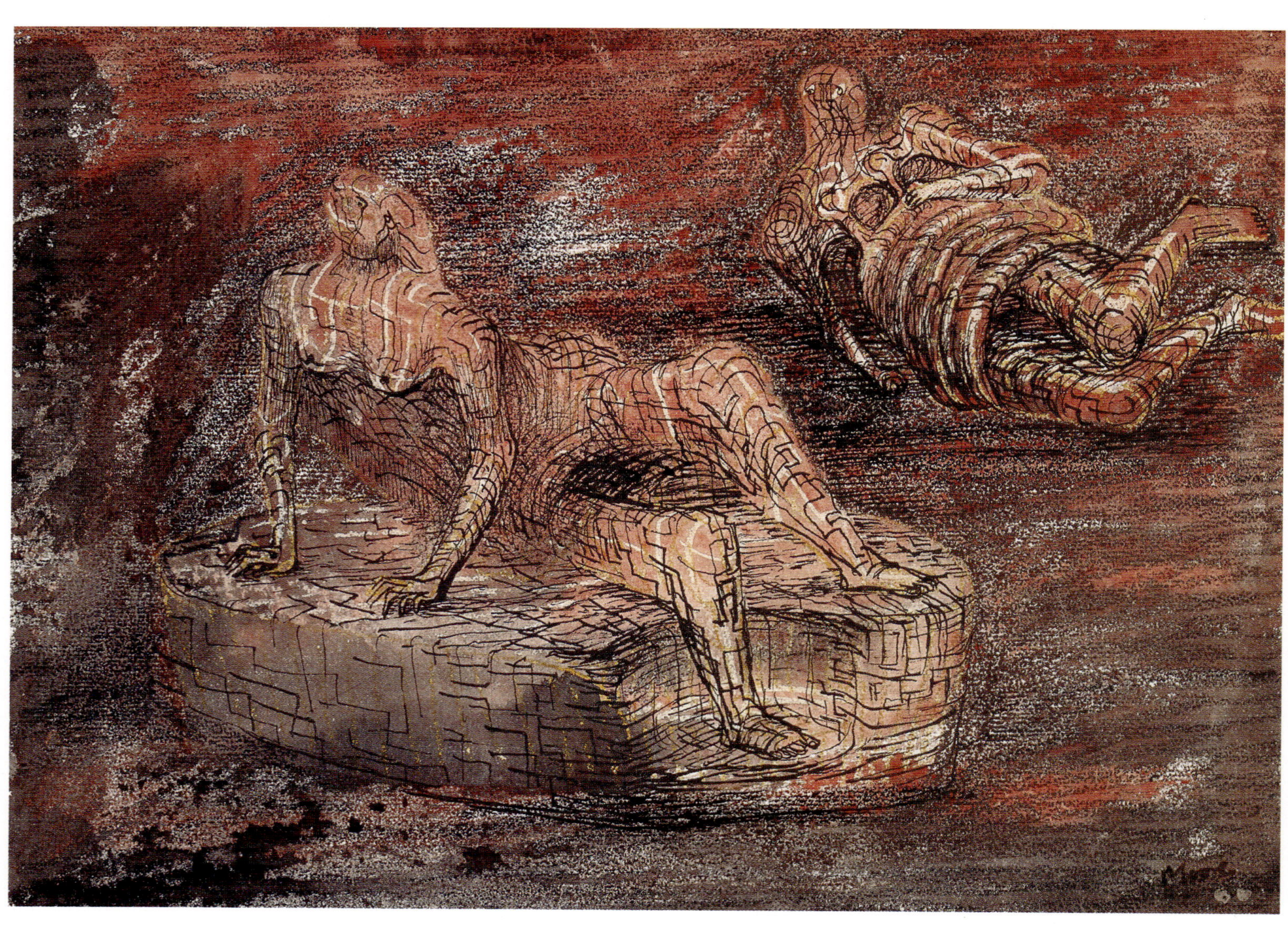

Derek acquired drawings by a wide range of other artists including Augustus John, William Roberts and Keith Vaughan.

favourite artists, Ceri Richards, include a 1950 ink and watercolour, *The Dragon Pot* (fig. 17). Derek was also attracted to ink and wash sketches by Josef Herman.

A drawing by artist-poet David Jones (1895-1974), his 1948 pencil, charcoal and chalk *Half-length Woman* (fig. 31), also from Derek's own collection, is one of many heads of young women at that time observed at Mass and drawn from memory. A suggestion of the spirit of northern Rennaissance devotional painting has been commented upon but, perhaps, there are also parallels with Jones's 1920s profiles of Petra Gill with whom he was, for several years, engaged to be married. Jones, brought up in south London, had converted to Catholicism and frequently stayed with Petra's father, Eric Gill, at Capel-y-ffin in the Black Mountains.[iv] In this delicate drawing there is a contrast between the complexity of her dress, hair and crucifix necklace and the rather idealised face.

Derek acquired drawings by a wide range of other artists including Augustus John, William Roberts and Keith Vaughan. L. S. Lowry's 1919 black chalk full-face *Study of a Head* was one of four of his works that he bought, the others being oils. Lowry constantly made sketches as reminders of what he had seen, the strong outline of early figures contributing to the evolution of his mature style.[v] A 1922 pencil and wash by Stanley Spencer, *Study for the Resurrection, Cookham*, is preparation for the painting, now in the Tate, which established the artist's reputation. There are also doodle-like late 1930s ink sketches attributed to Lucian Freud.

Reflecting Derek's interest in drawings, the trust has bought many examples. These include, in 2000, sculptor David Nash's charcoal, crayon and chalk drawing *Ash Dome* (fig. 36) as well as a charcoal drawing with the same title and related photographs (fig. 54). In the spirit of Derek's collecting, further 1940s neo-romantic drawings by Ceri

---

iv   Ariane Bankes and Paul Hills, *The Art of David Jones: Vision and Memory*, Pallant House Gallery and Lund Humphries, 2015, 115-6; Portraits of Petra Gill in Jonathan Miles and Lottie Hoare, *To Petra with Love: The Petra Tegetmeier collection of works by David Jones*, Wolseley Fine Arts, 2001

v   Mervyn Levy, *The Drawings of L.S.Lowry: Public and Private*, Jupiter Books, 1976

Richards, John Minton and John Piper followed in 2006-07.

Another of these is Henry Moore's 1946 pencil, watercolour, ink and wax crayon *Two Reclining Figures* (fig. 32). Aspects of the artist's wartime underground shelter drawings, also represented in the collection, continued to influence the composition and characteristics of these later drawings as in the suggestion of draped sculpture and the use of a wax-resist technique. Moore (1898-1986) endured a traditional academic art school training but would pursue his own interests by freely drawing a wide range of museum sculpture. Drawing became central to his development as a sculptor. After outlining, perhaps in pencil, he would model with chalk and brush, then use pen and ink to delineate an image more precisely. An inseparable sense of space and form, seen in *Two Reclining Figures*, was becoming a distinctive feature of his sculpture.[vi]

In 2007 the trust bought one of abstract artist Sean Scully's sketchbooks, dating from 2000, which provides insights into his working method. It complements an earlier acquisition, his 2004 oil on canvas *Day Leaving*, comprising his characteristic freely painted blocks of horizontal and vertical layered colour. The works of Scully, who was born in Dublin in 1945, imply rigidity in their structure. Yet, in their lack of precision and looseness of painting, they strongly convey emotion and a sense of spirituality. Expressive sketches are an integral part of the artist's hand-written texts. He has written about how, over many years, the edges of his paint evolved in a unified way with the process of drawing: '...a painting is not a construction. It can't evolve without sensibility. The ambition and the evolution of the painting has to come through time. There's no other way. Because it's an incarnation. It starts out as an idea or a concept, whose destiny is to be converted into material, a subject compressed. That's it, from my own experience, with drawing.'[vii]

---

vi   Ian Dejardin, Ann Garrould and Anita Feldman Bennett, *Henry Moore at Dulwich Picture Gallery*, Scala, 2004

vii Kelly Grovier ed., *Inner: The Collected Writings and Selected Interviews of Sean Scully*, Hatje Cantz, 2016, 178-9

33. Sean Scully, Four drawings from a sketchbook, ink, 2000, sketchbook size 16.8 x 15.6 x 2.5 cm. Trust purchase, 2007.

The works of Scully, who was born in Dublin in 1945, imply rigidity in their structure. Yet, in their lack of precision and looseness of painting, they strongly convey emotion and a sense of spirituality.

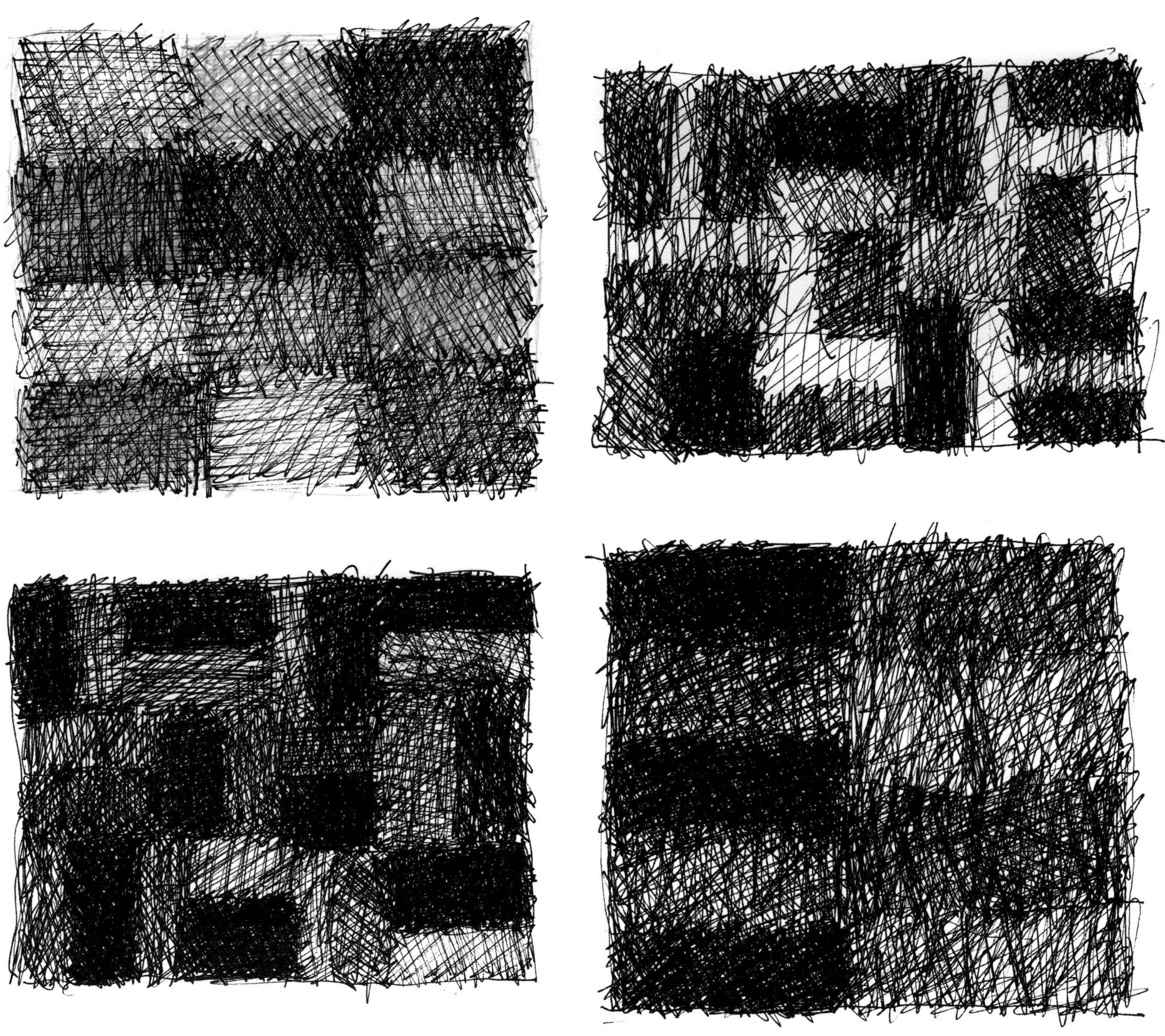

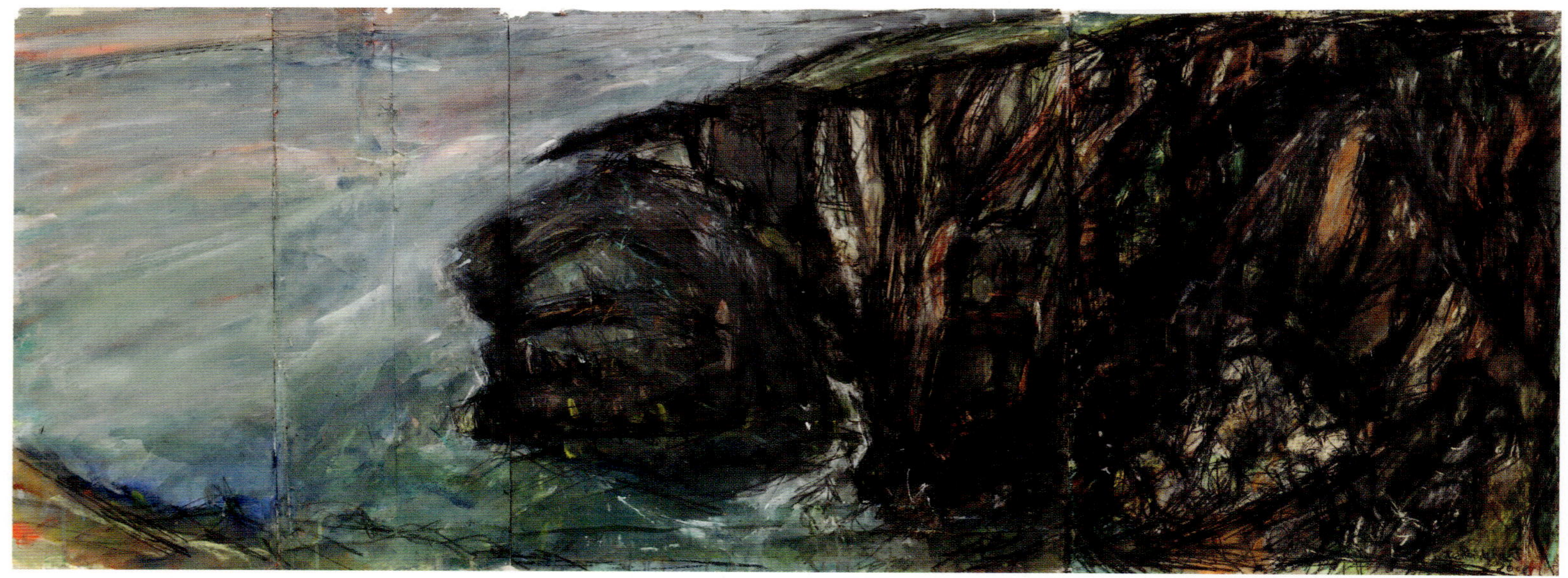

These purchases were followed, in 2008, by two of Peter Prendergast's 2002-03 sketchbooks, his 2004 gouache, chalk, charcoal and pencil *Preliminary Drawing for Tŵr Elin* (fig. 34) and a related, fully-developed, oil on canvas. Prendergast (1946-2007) is particularly associated with deeply felt and understood landscapes around his home in Snowdonia. His process of getting to know the coast between Elin's Tower and South Stack, Holy Island, Anglesey, is reflected in these acquisitions. For him, drawing was a means towards understanding the constantly changing interaction between these dramatic cliffs and the sea that pounds them.[viii]

34. Peter Prendergast, *Preliminary Drawing for Tŵr Elin,* gouache, chalk, charcoal and pencil, 2004, 92 x 276 cm. Trust purchase, 2008.

---

viii David Alston, 'Behold, the sea itself...', in John Russell Taylor et al, *The Painter's Quarry: The Art of Peter Prendergast*, Seren, 2006, 147-62; Richard Cork, *The Art of Peter Prendergast*, Lund Humphries, 2013, 95-103

8. ALL IN THE MIND: LANDSCAPE INTO ART

This chapter discusses three of the diverse ways in which modern and contemporary artists have responded to landscape. The examples are by figurative painter Michael Andrews (1928-1995), environmental sculptor David Nash (born 1945) and silversmith Pamela Rawnsley (1952-2014).

The Derek Williams Trust's collection also includes pertinent works by Sir Richard Long, George Shaw and Clare Woods. In addition, the trust has grant-supported the acquisition of landscape paintings by James Dickson Innes, Cedric Morris, John Piper and Leon Kossoff, drawings by Peter Prendergast (fig.34) and photographs by Richard Billingham, Helen Sear and Paul Seawright.

The very first artwork acquired by the Derek Williams Trust, in 1993, was Michael Andrews's majestic 1987 acrylic on canvas *The Cathedral, The Southern Faces / Uluru (Ayers Rock)* (fig. 35). One of the largest paintings in the museum, it is also part of a series by the artist of acrylics and related watercolours of the iconic Australian landmark dating from 1984-89.

Sacred to Aboriginal Australians and associated with many myths, the intensely coloured rock, rising from a plain, has an extraordinary physical presence with its bare sweeping lines and dramatic gullies. Uluru also has a disquieting quality and is, in this painting, kept at a respectful distance. The artist was intrigued by the impossibility, due to his cultural background, of fully comprehending the Aboriginal spiritual connection with it. This would have involved trying to understand a different form of reality. He did, however, experience a strong sense of the extinction of self which he related to the metaphorical hymn, often sung as a boy, 'Rock of Ages, cleft for me, Let me hide myself in Thee...'[i]

---

i   Catherine Lampert *et al.*, *Michael Andrews: The Delectable Mountain*, Whitechapel Art Gallery, 1991

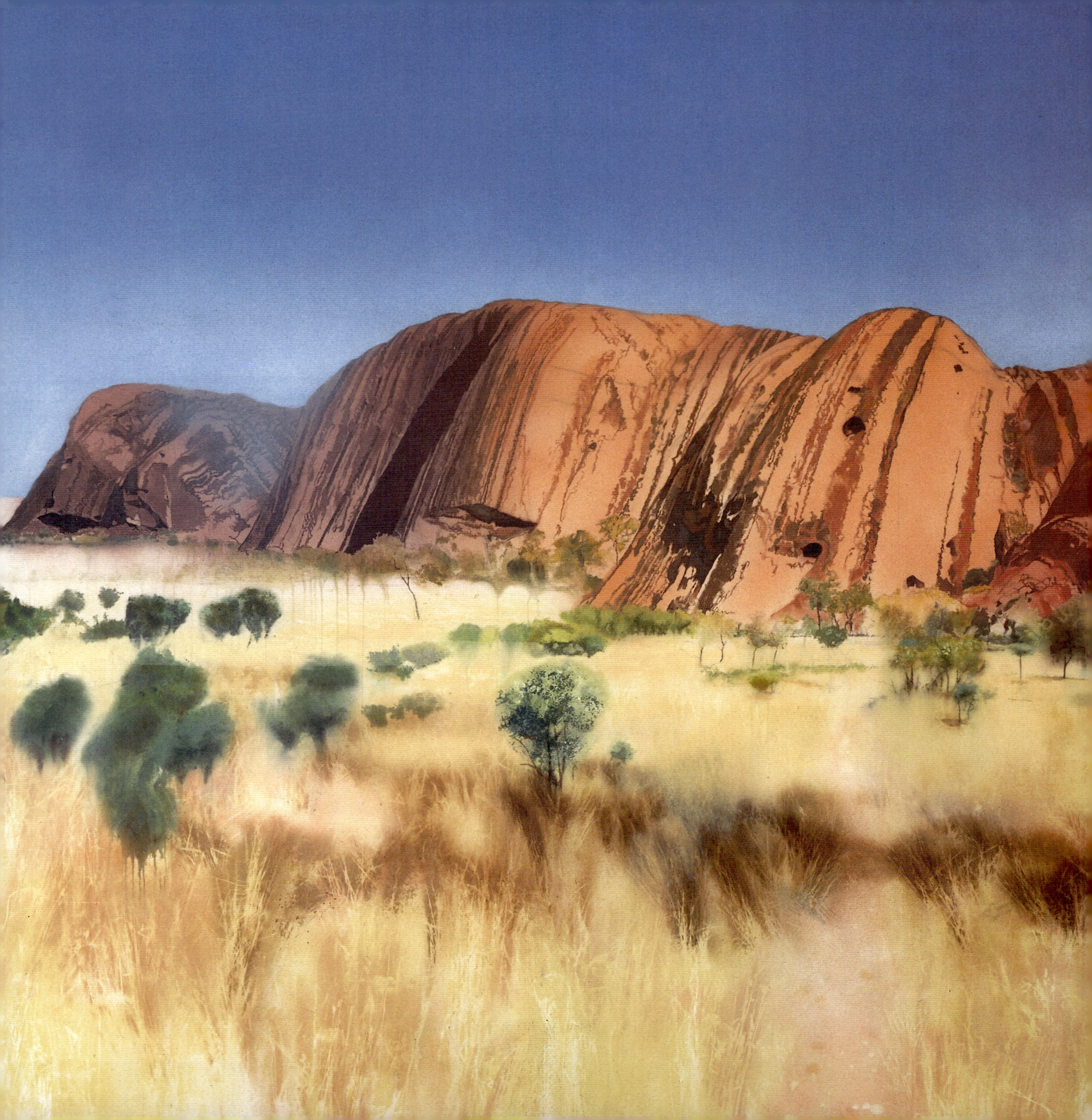

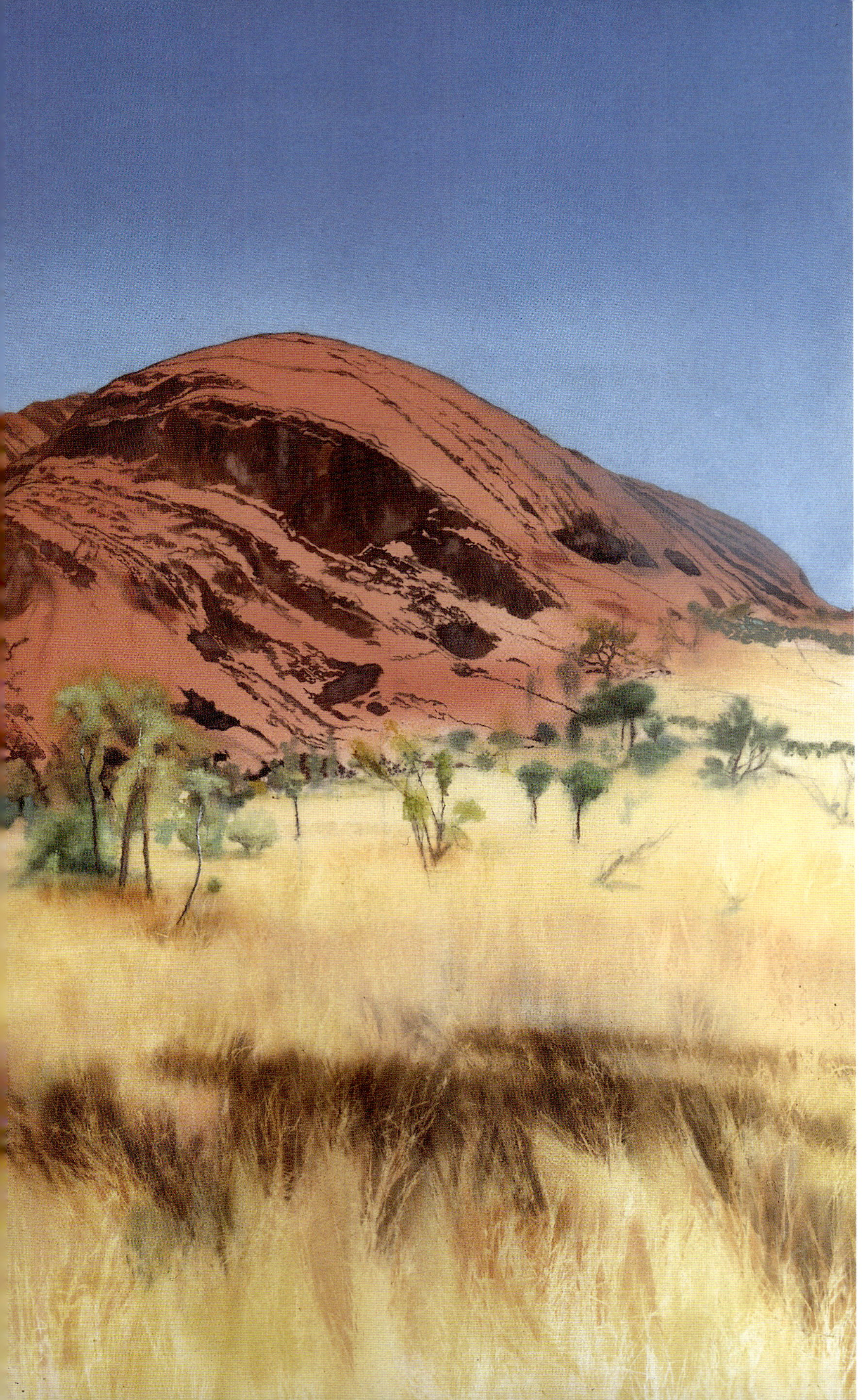

**35. Michael Andrews, *The Cathedral,
The Southern Faces / Uluru (Ayers Rock)*,**
acrylic on canvas, 1987, 244 x 389 cm. Trust
purchase, 1993.

Michael Andrews used a spray-gun and stencils, including dried indigenous grass, to mask and diffuse his paint. He also incorporated small rock fragments in many of the paintings. An elusive, shy and self-effacing man, he worked slowly. Involved in the bohemian life of 1950s Soho, he moved to Norfolk in 1977.

David Nash's *Ash Dome* (fig. 36) is a drawing, dating from 2000 in charcoal, crayon and chalk on paper, which was bought by the Derek Williams Trust together with another charcoal drawing as well as photographs (fig. 54) relating to the creation of a living-tree sculpture of that title. The sculptor, who has lived and worked in Blaenau Ffestiniog since 1967, exhibits internationally and his work featured in an exhibition at the museum in 2019.[ii] Other work by the artist is discussed on pages 109 and 113.

Nash's main concern is with the material, cultural and symbolic essence of trees and their environment. He is also interested in works that relate to a specific place and to issues of time and space. While helping to plant some trees near his home he realised that a space could be created by growing a group of them. He was attracted to local dome-shaped hills and mountains at Cae'n-y-Coed and, in 1977, decided to grow an equivalent form from twenty-two ash trees planted, as saplings, in a thirty-foot diameter ring. His intention was to encourage the trees, through techniques like grafting and pruning, to grow in a particular way over a period of thirty years to create such a space. Essentially a living sculpture, it would change with the seasons and passing years. A place for meditation and collaboration with nature, originally planted for the future, some have found its controlling of nature to be unnerving.

Pamela Rawnsley's 2006 *Cwm Cwareli Vessels* (fig. 37), a pair in silver with gold attachments, stand around ten centimetres high. These were gifted to the museum by

36. David Nash, *Ash Dome,* charcoal, crayon and chalk on paper, 2000, 117 x 188 cm. Trust purchase, 2000.

Nash's main concern is with the material, cultural and symbolic essence of trees and their environment.

---

ii   Nicholas Thornton ed., *David Nash: Two Hundred Seasons at Capel Rhiw*, Amgueddfa Cymru – National Museum Wales, 2019

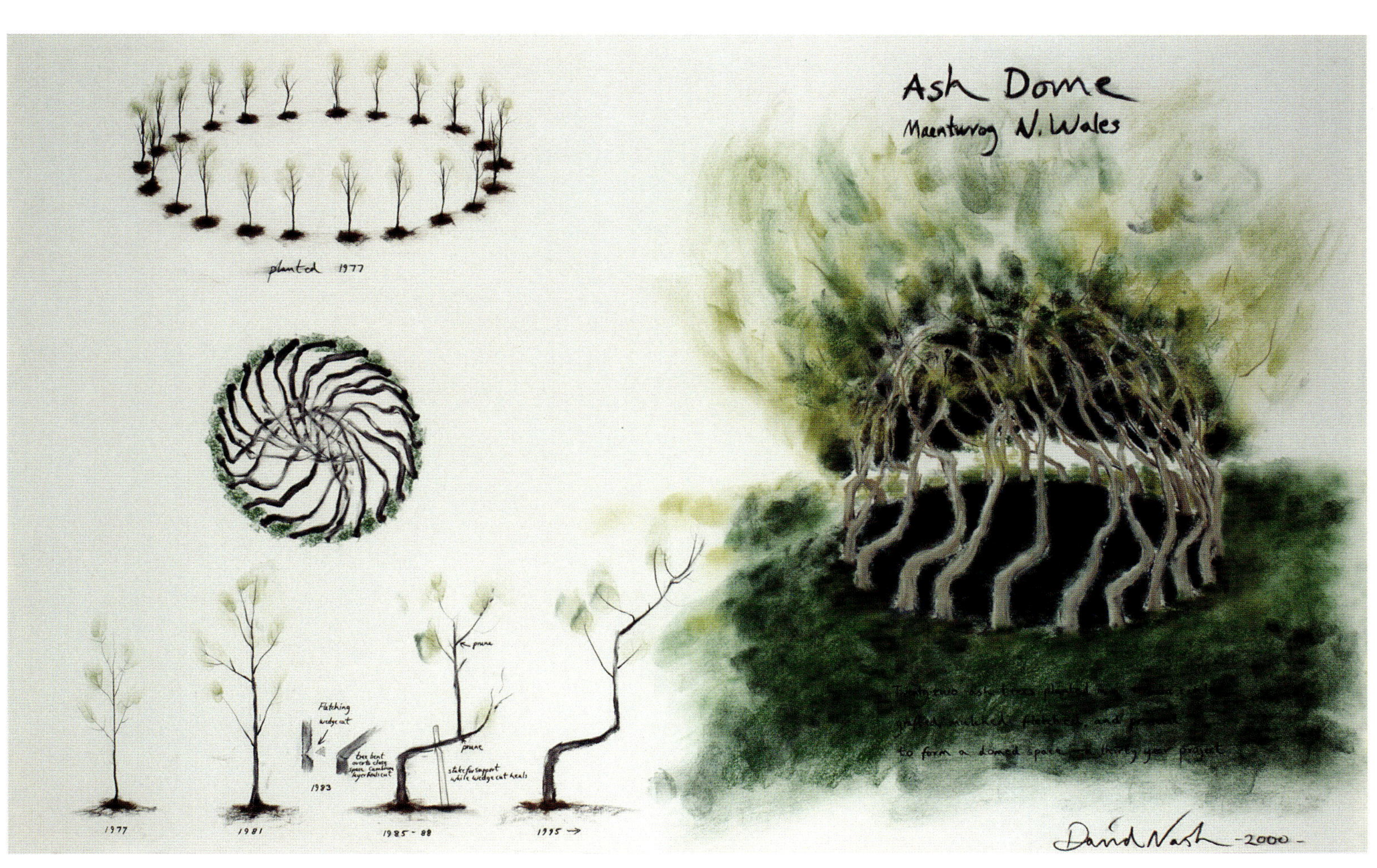

Ash Dome
Maentwrog N. Wales
planted 1977
1977
1981
1985 - 88
1995 →
David Nash -2000-

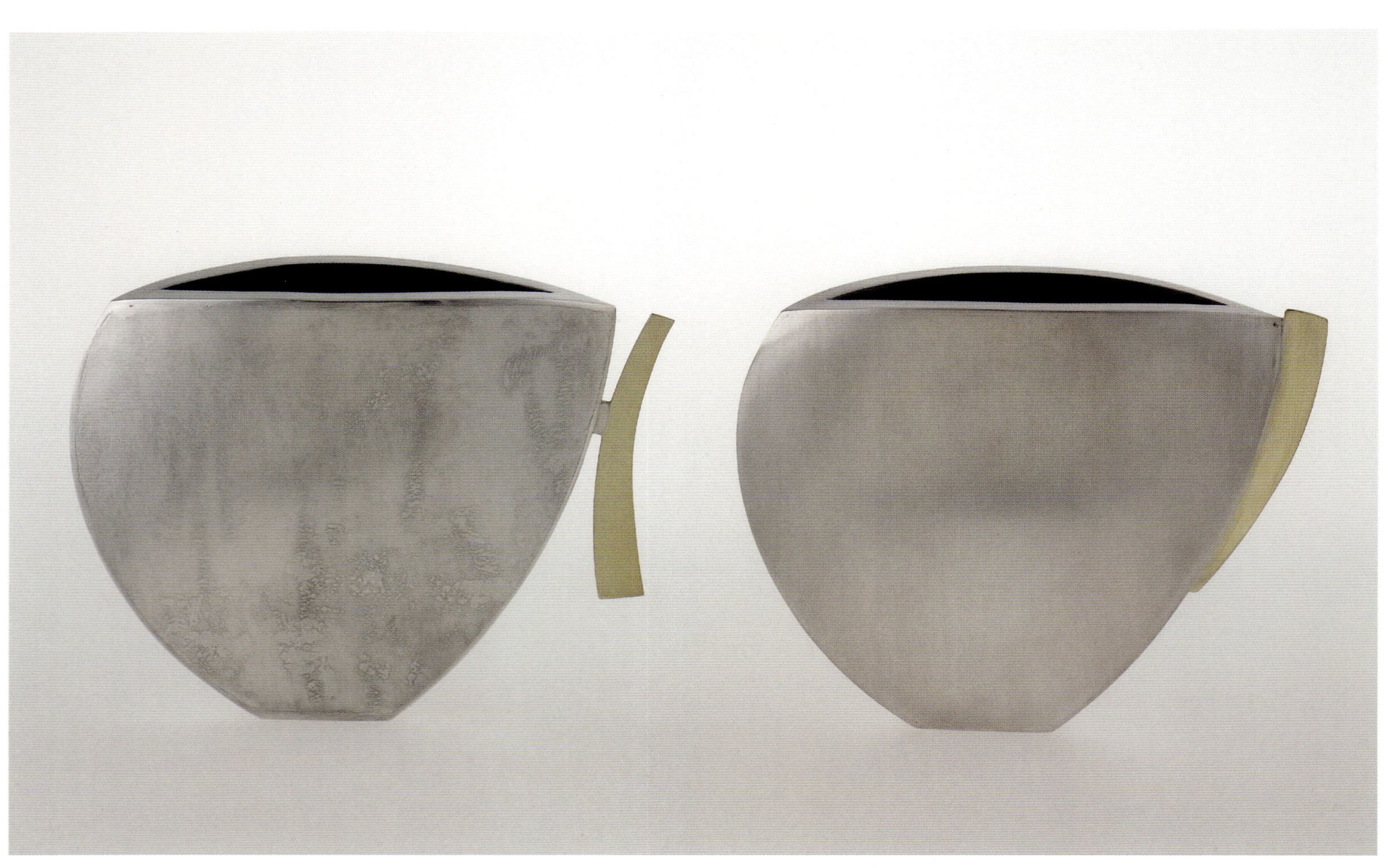

*The silver vessels,
constructed from sheets with
sparing decoration, were
often made in series.*

the trust with funding from Rita Plowman in memory of her parents Jack and
Dolci Josephson.

Rawnsley who, sadly, died relatively young, drew inspiration for these delicately
textured vessels from the dramatic mountains, ice-sculpted from Old Red Sandstone,
around her home near Llanfrynach in the Brecon Beacons. There she would walk
regularly, even in winter, making notes and quick sketches encompassing exposed
ridges, paths, light and weather changes. These would, later, remind her of a fleeting
atmosphere and also provide a sense of timelessness which she would strive to
evoke in her work. Initially she might make monoprints and aluminium and paper
maquettes.[iii]

Pamela Rawnsley, who was supported by Ruthin Craft Centre, had originally studied
glass and ceramics but developed an interest in making jewellery at Hereford College
of Art. Later she became interested in making non-utilitarian hollow silver ware and
some of her motifs were also used in jewellery. The silver vessels, constructed from
sheets with sparing decoration, were often made in series. While not depictions
of landscape they do suggest its outlines, rather in the manner of theatrical flats.
Colours are pared-down on matt and semi-matt surfaces with oxidation and gilding
in green, yellow and black. Many are composite and include, as a visual counterpoint,
smaller attached forms. Sequences of vessels may signify repeat visits to the same
place, the basic shape remaining constant while an attached component might be
changed to reflect a particular memory.

iii   Philip Hughes ed., *Pamela Rawnsley: Shape-Shifting*, Ruthin Craft Centre, 2008

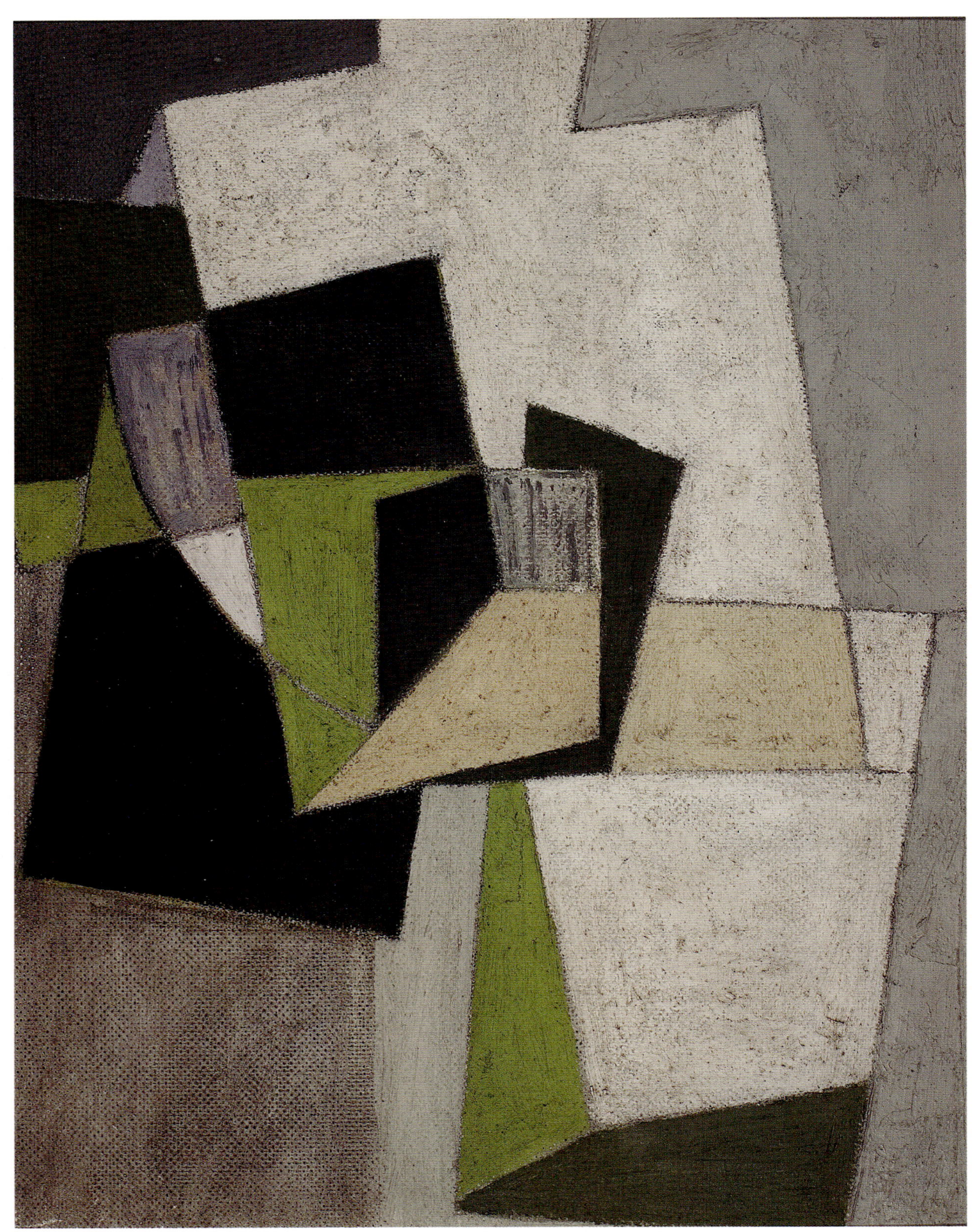

9. THE ENDURANCE OF BRUSH AND PAINT

38. Adrian Heath, *Interlocking Forms,* oil on board, 1950, 46 x 36 cm. Trust purchase, 2010.

Painting has received prominent support from the trust despite challenges to its perceived art-world status from video, installation, photography and performance art. While these media and, notably, sculpture and ceramics, have certainly not been overlooked, this chapter examines a selection of approaches to painting as illustrated by some of the trust's acquisitions. Those discussed are oil or acrylic paintings. Watercolours may be found elsewhere in this book.

Adrian Heath's 1950 oil on board *Interlocking Forms* (fig. 38), acquired by the trust in 2010, dates from a significant transitional period in the evolution of post-war art in Britain. He was a member of a circle of artists interested in the ideals of constructed abstraction which included Terry Frost, Roger Hilton, Kenneth and Mary Martin and, prominently, Victor Pasmore. Heath (1920-1992) arranged exhibitions of, and wrote about, abstract art. He exhibited in the influential 1956 exhibition This is Tomorrow at London's Whitechapel Art Gallery. Concerned particularly with the process of development in a painting, rather than the attractions of any particular form or colour, he created energy and tension from reconciling a desire for order with a deeply held need for conflict. Later, he adopted a more intuitive and less constructed approach and became concerned with conciliating geometric shape with organic form. A senior fellow in fine art at South Glamorgan Institute of Higher Education, Cardiff, from 1977 until 1980, he exhibited at that time with 56 Group Wales.[i]

Although largely abstract, Joe Tilson's dazzling 1964 acrylic-painted wood construction *Ziggurat II* (fig. 39), bought by the trust in 2013, is permeated with significance and relates to pop art. Resembling a stacked toy, it was shown in the 1964 Venice Biennale. Believing that strong form and meaning are linked, Tilson has used a ziggurat, the form of an ancient Mesopotamian stepped pyramid connecting heaven and earth, to

---

i   Jane Rye, *Adrian Heath*, Lund Humphries, 2012

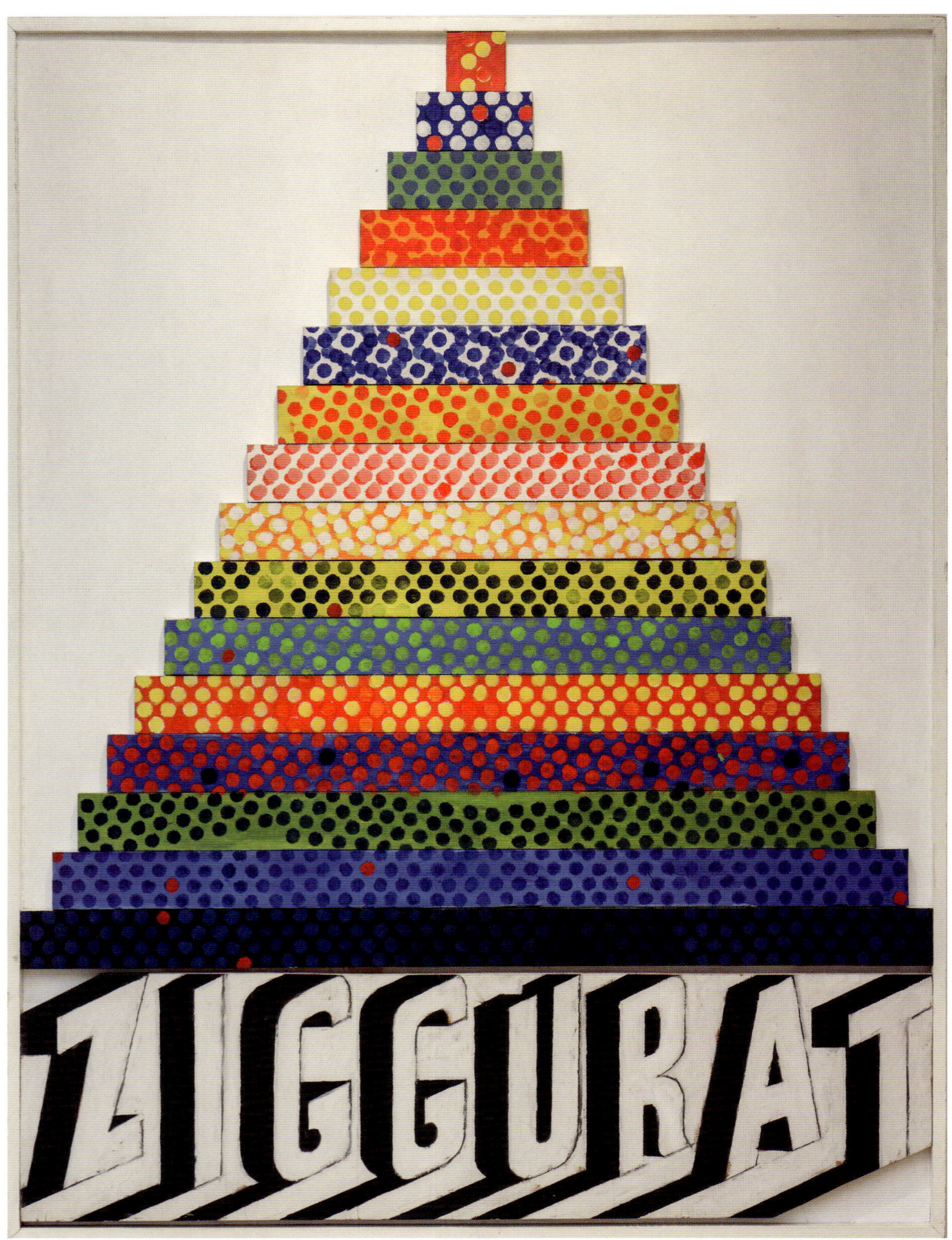

ZIGGURAT

Tilson has used a ziggurat, the form of an ancient Mesopotamian stepped pyramid connecting heaven and earth, to stimulate the viewer's curiosity.

stimulate the viewer's curiosity. Reflecting the artist's anti-hierarchical social views, the freely expressed use of coloured dots on each level, probably stencilled, was a frequent pop art technique derived from those used in colour printing. This also features in the artist's celebrated printmaking.[ii]

Tilson, born in London in 1928, worked in cabinet making before studying at St Martin's and the Royal colleges of art. Lying between painting and sculpture, his work is characterised by home-crafted wood reliefs and a physical and metaphorical use of geometry. He uses modular structuring devices and universal symbols such as alphabets, ladders and labyrinths. His themes transcend time, drawing upon antiquity, as well as cutting across cultures and embracing mythology and magic.

Shani Rhys James's remarkable 2003 oil on linen *Black Cot and Latex Glove* (fig. 40) coincided with her being awarded the prestigious Jerwood Painting Prize that year. Acquired by the trust in 2006, it is a large figurative work, over three and a half metres high, in a restricted palette. Depicting a young child holding the side of a cot while staring, challengingly, at the viewer, it suggests a traumatised caged animal. The single latex glove lying beneath the cot, to the uninitiated, reinforces a sense that this scene is one to be feared. Additional layers of meaning occur, however, when it is known that Rhys James's father, separated from her mother when the artist was a child, was a surgeon and that, while painting, she wears latex gloves for protection.[iii]

Born in Melbourne, Australia, in 1953 to a Welsh father and Australian actor mother, Shani Rhys James arrived in the United Kingdom with her mother in 1963 and studied at Loughborough College of Art and St Martin's School of Art. After living in London, she moved to Wales in 1984. Psychologically intense, her paintings frequently reference memories of her own unsettled upbringing behind the scenes in the theatre world and, pertinently, there is a strong element of theatricality about them. They are also much concerned with the physicality and vitality of her chosen medium and many

ii   Michael Compton and Marco Livingstone, *Tilson*, Thames and Hudson, 1994

iii   Eve Ropek ed., *Shani Rhys James: The Black Cot*, Aberystwyth Arts Centre / Gomer Press, 2004

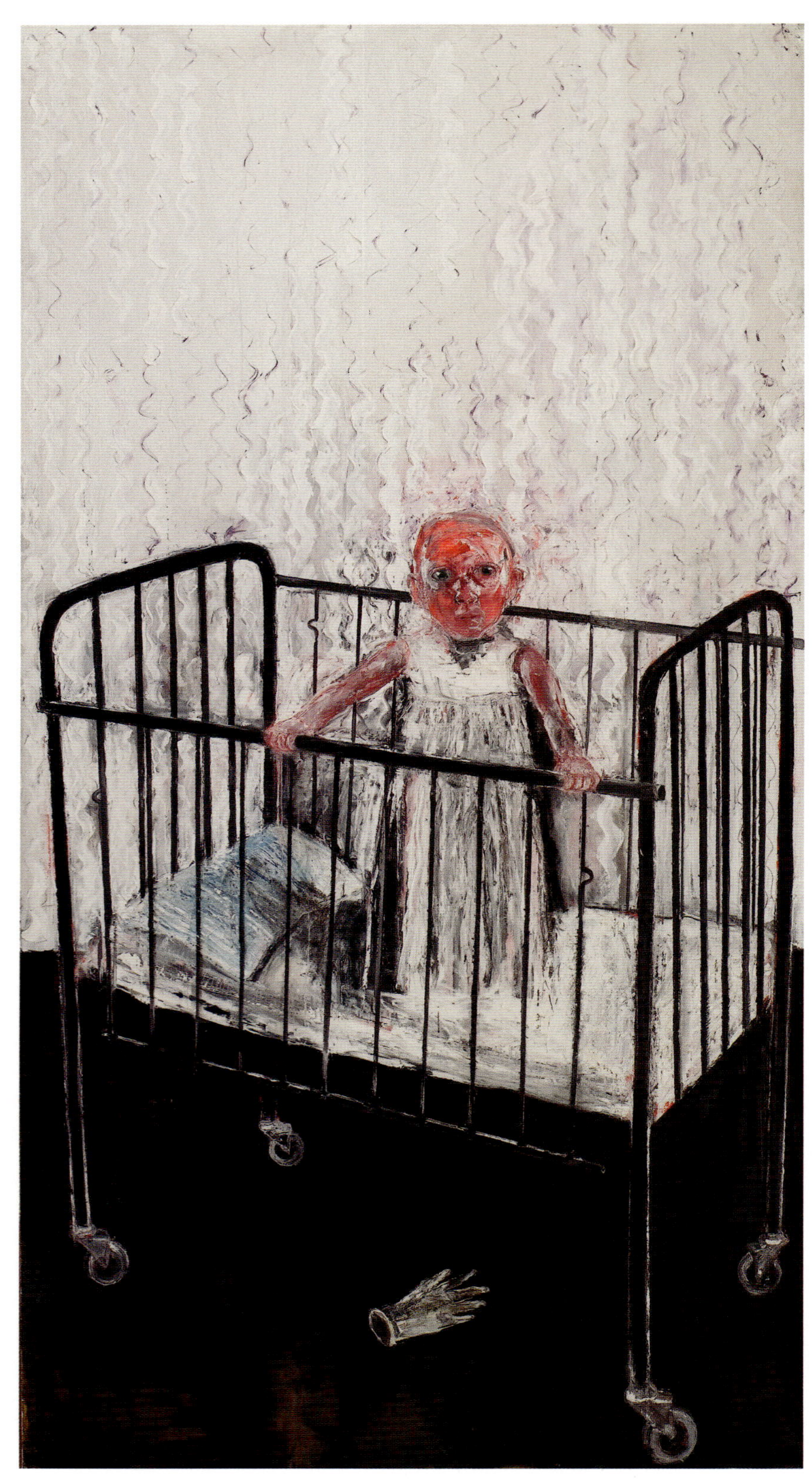

40. Shani Rhys James, *Black Cot and Latex Glove*, oil on linen, 2003, 360 x 180 cm. Trust purchase, 2008.

contain art-historical references. She received the gold medal for fine art at the 1992 National Eisteddfod of Wales and an MBE in 2006.

Ernest Zobole (1927-1999), a very different painter who lived in Wales, was the son of Italian immigrants. He lived for most of his life in Ystrad, Rhondda Fawr, the setting for his lyrical and internalised work. Together with fellow art students who travelled daily by train to Cardiff College of Art, he is associated with what became known as the Rhondda Group. Inspired to become a painter by German expatriate Heinz Koppel, he became a lecturer at Newport College of Art and a founder member of 56 Group Wales. Influences included Chagall and expressionism but his own vision was distinctive and original. *Painter and Subject Matter* (fig. 41), dating from 1996-97, is a trust purchase which, characteristically, features personal memories embedded in a nocturnal world of multiple viewpoints in a restricted palette. A late work, it seems to reach outwards to eternity.[iv]

Another painter of great sensitivity and imagination who exhibited with 56 Group Wales was John Selway (1938-2017). Raised in Abertillery and a contemporary of Hockney at the Royal College of Art, Selway lectured at Newport. His 2002 oil on canvas *'As I rode to sleep', Fern Hill series* (fig. 2) was a 2011 trust purchase deeply informed by the poetry of Dylan Thomas.[v]

A recent acquisition by the trust is a striking 1957 black and white abstract oil and charcoal on board, *Line and Space* (fig. 42), by Heath's associate Victor Pasmore (1908-1998). Short straight or curved lines are played off against each other within a containing oval. Involved in a Bauhaus-influenced revolution in art teaching at the University of Durham in Newcastle-upon-Tyne, Pasmore helped to develop Peterlee New Town, County Durham, the designs for which influenced this work.[vi]

---

iv   Ceri Thomas, *Ernest Zobole: A Life in Art*, Seren, 2007
v   Jon Gower, *Vigilant Imagination: Encounters with John Selway*, H'mm Foundation / Three Imposters, 2018, 130-32
vi   Anne Goodchild *et al.*, *Victor Pasmore: Towards a New Reality*, Lund Humphries / Djanogly Gallery, 2017

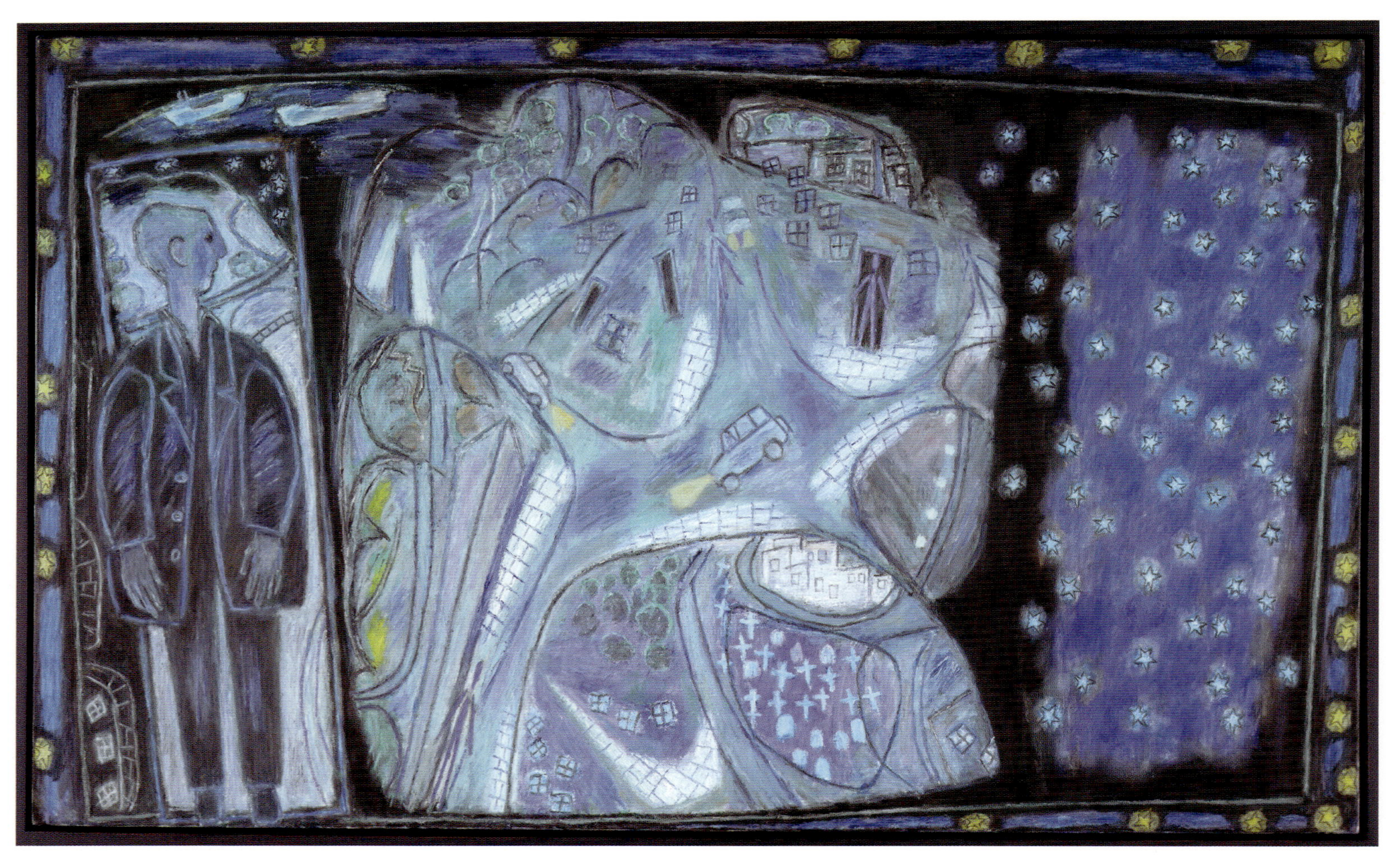

41. Ernest Zobole, *Painter and Subject Matter,*
oil on canvas, 1996-97, 115 x 189 cm. Trust
purchase, 1998.

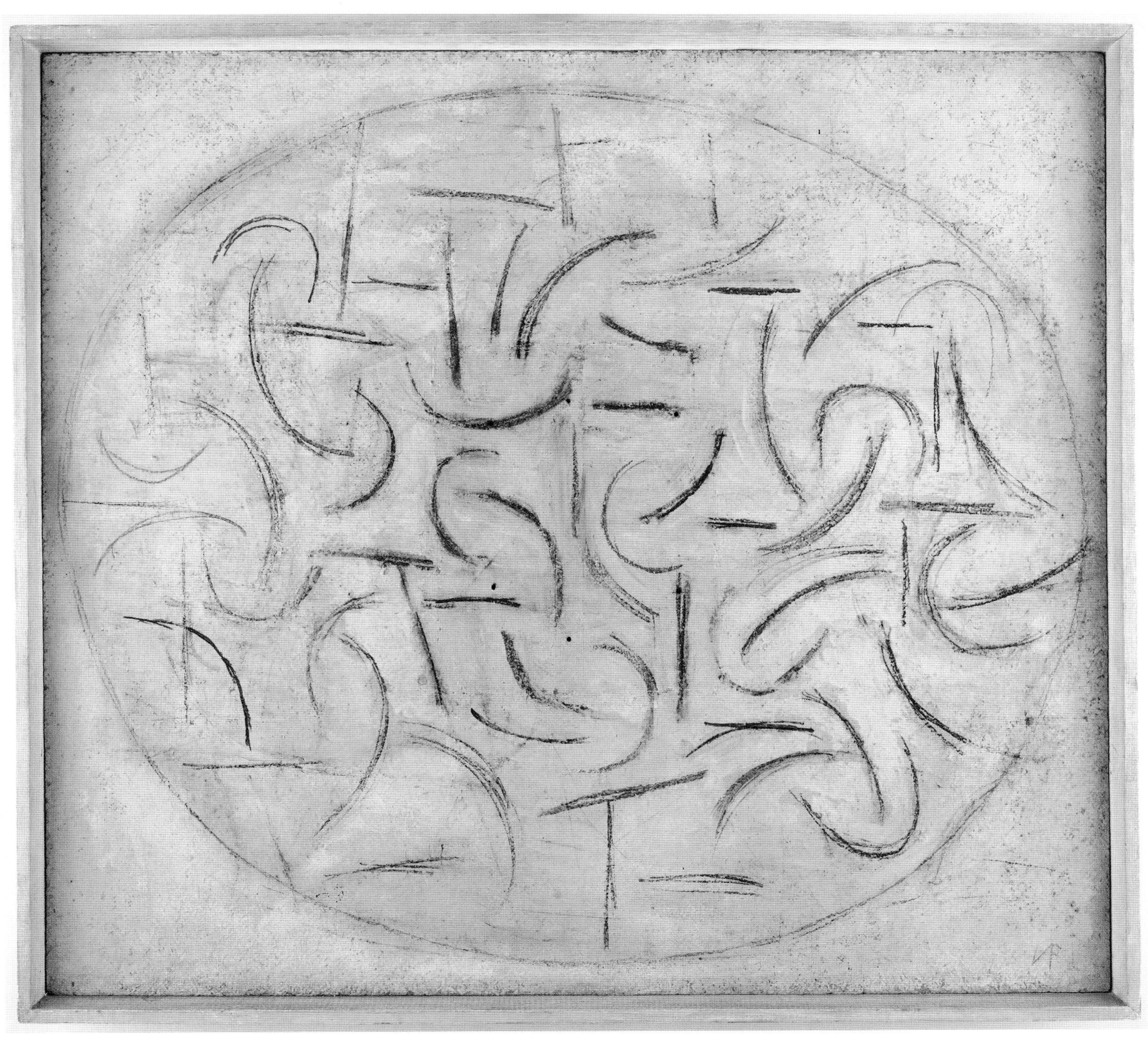

42. Victor Pasmore, *Line and Space*,
oil and charcoal on board, 1957, 69 x 79 cm.
Trust purchase, 2019.

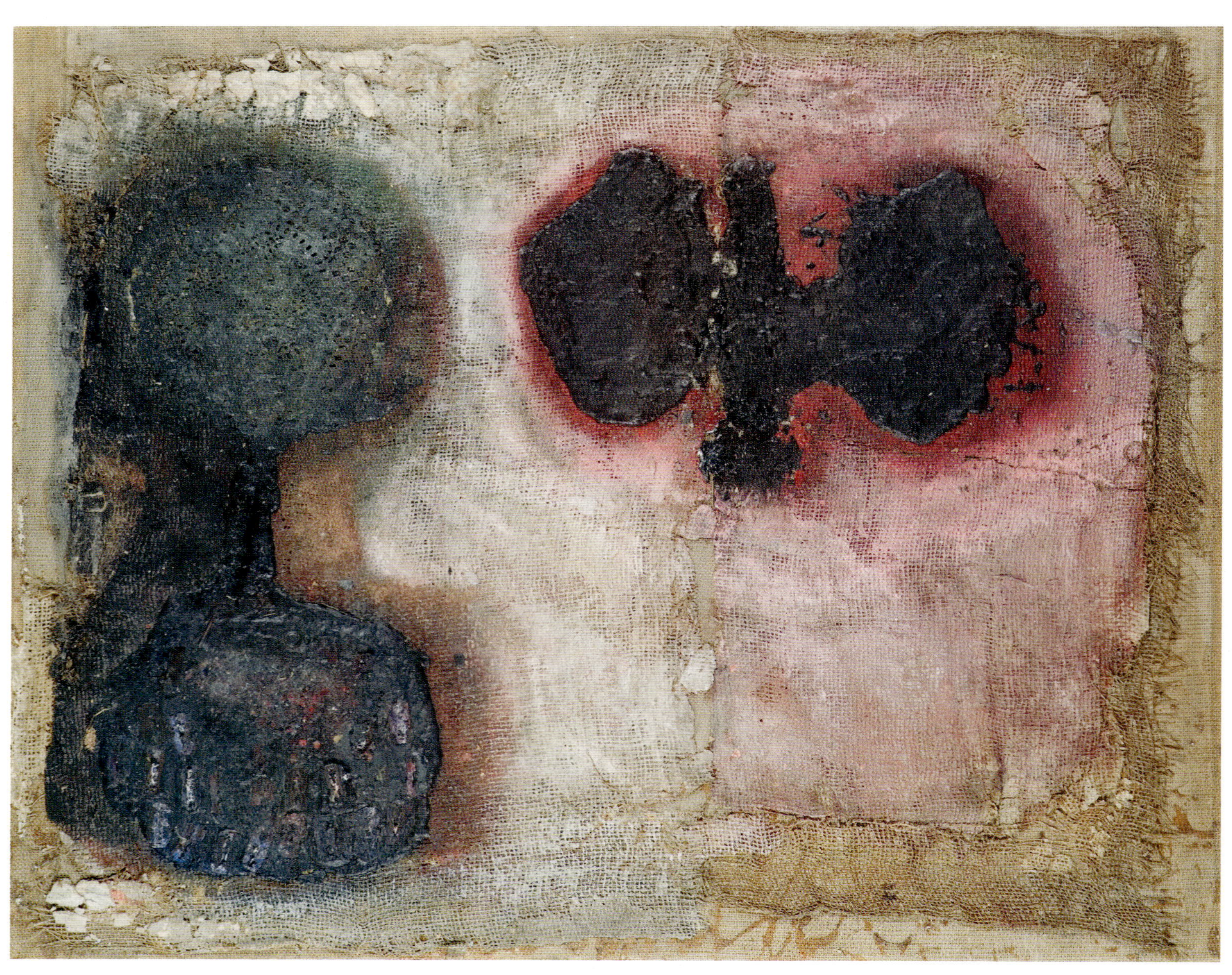

10. WELSH ARTISTS EXPLORING THEIR IDENTITY

43. Ivor Davies, *Prefiguration – Eryr*, mixed media on hessian, 1956-61, 94 x 122 cm. Trust purchase, 2009.

At the centre of certain Welsh artists' work is the exploration of issues relating to their culture, language and identity and, in some cases, with issues of cultural identity in a global context. This chapter explores artists who have been brought up in a traditional Welsh-speaking environment and are driven by a need to highlight specific features of place, culture and memory.

The trust acquired two paintings by Ivor Davies (born 1935), *Caethni*, a 1996 oil on canvas, in 1999 and *Prefiguration – Eryr* (fig. 43), a 1956-61 mixed-media work on hessian, in 2009. The latter was included in Silent Explosion, a recent show at the museum examining the artist's long-term fascination with the role of destruction in art.[i]

Inspired by an accidental inkblot, the left-hand image in *Prefiguration – Eryr* was copied and enlarged onto hessian in charcoal powder mixed with glue. Paper doylies and razor blades were embedded in its surface, introducing tension. The bird-like shape on the right and, indeed, the work's title, evoke the well-known Mabinogi tale of Lleu Llaw Gyffes transforming into an eagle on being struck by a spear thrown by Gronw Pebr as he stood with one foot on the side of a trough and the other on a goat. Such shapeshifting, often involving magic or divine intervention, is, of course, a prevalent motif in mythology and folklore.

Other densely pigmented and layered works by the artist from a period when he studied in Lausanne, Switzerland, also have heavily distressed surfaces suggesting collapse and destruction which, for him, are in a continuous cycle with creation. With indistinct forms and use of materials like dirt and discarded materials, these works are reminiscent of *art informel*, a continental form of abstract expressionism

Other densely pigmented and layered works by the artist from a period when he studied in Lausanne, Switzerland, also have heavily distressed surfaces suggesting collapse and destruction which, for him are in a continuous cycle with creation.

---

i   Heike Roms gol./ed., *Ffrwydrad Tawel: Ifor Davies a Dinistr Creadigol / Silent Explosion: Ivor Davies and Destruction in Art*, Occasional Papers, 2015, 59

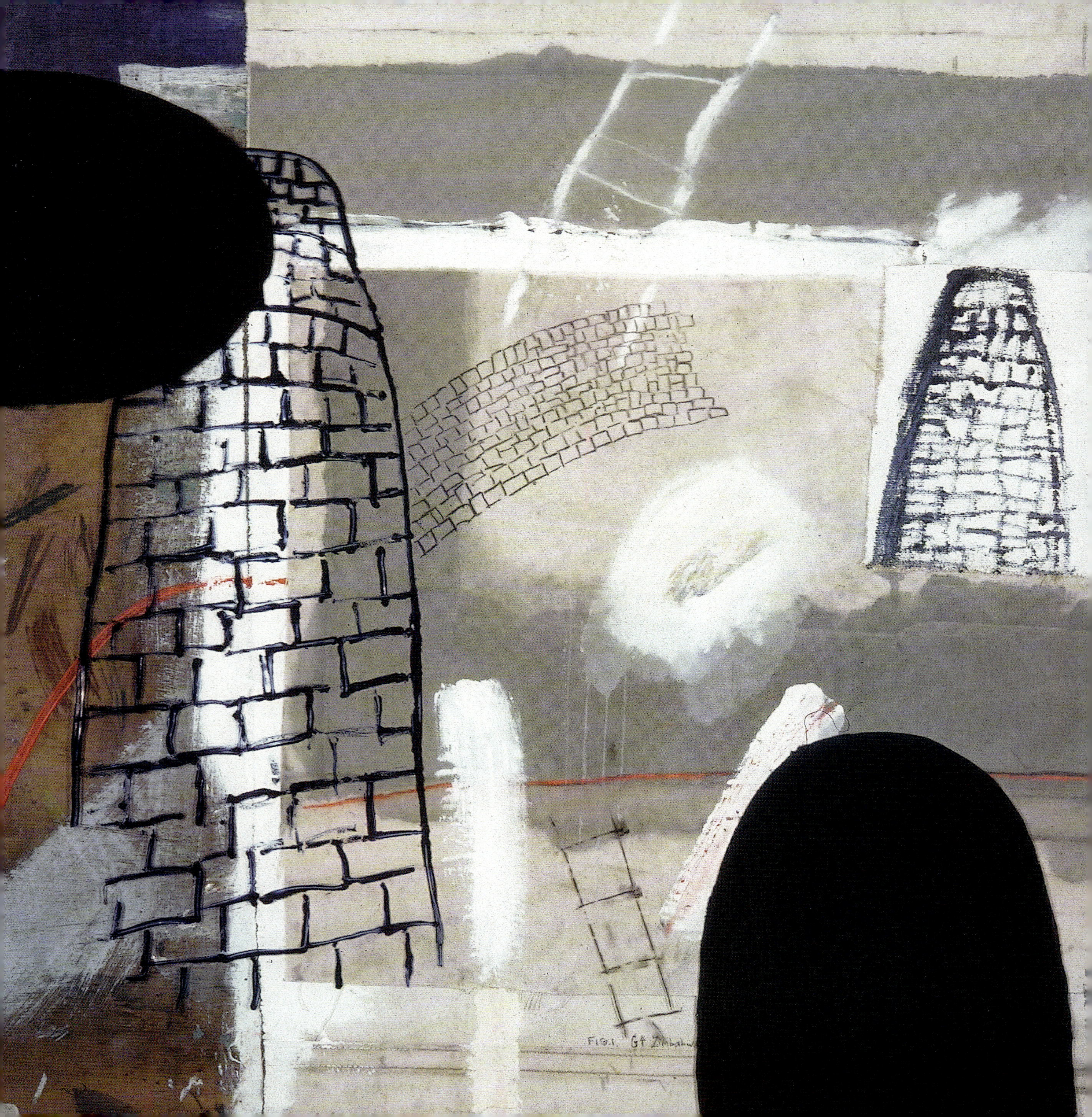
FIG.1. Gt Zimbabw

The Derek Williams Trust has also bought five paintings by Iwan Bala, born in 1956, all of which, in different ways, explore issues of cultural identity in a global context.

characteristic of artists such as Antoni Tàpies and Alberto Burri.

Davies returned to *Prefiguration – Eryr* later in the 1960s, having cut it in half, stitched it back together and placed it on a new hessian ground. This kind of preservation, whether in writing, fragments, discarded objects or memories, destroyed, reanimated or reinterpreted, is central to his ideas. The changing of both form and identity are also associated with concern about the erosion of the Welsh language and its communities.

The Derek Williams Trust has also bought five paintings by Iwan Bala, born in 1956, all of which, in different ways, explore issues of cultural identity in a global context. This has also evolved out of his inheritance, a deep involvement in, and apprehension about the future of, the Welsh language, its culture and communities.[ii]

His 1992 mixed-media *Raise High Your Ruins* (fig. 44), bought in 1998, emerged out of a four-month residency at the National Gallery of Zimbabwe in Harare. The majestic dry-stone ruins of the ancient capital of Great Zimbabwe – as well as contemporary stone sculpture rooted in Shona religion, myth and culture – had a profound effect upon him. Built between the eleventh and fifteenth centuries by the Shona civilisation, this former city and trading post with its palace and striking central conical tower became a symbol for the Republic of Zimbabwe, created in 1980. Its African origins had, however, been censored during much of the 1960s and 1970s under the white minority government in Rhodesia. For two years after his residency, Bala's work dealt with the dislocation he experienced on returning to Cardiff. Imagery associated with the central tower emerged in his painting as he connected a concern for Welsh identity with a broadening awareness of post-colonial issues.

Four more 2005 works by Iwan Bala were acquired in 2007, all mixed media on paper, exploring in distinctive and cartographically-rich imagery the ever-changing

---

ii   Iwan Bala, *Offrymau + Ailddyfeisiadau / Offerings + Reinventions*, Seren / Oriel 31, 2000

relationship between cultural identities globally. Recurring motifs are included. A Janus double-head, inspired by Romano-British carving with one profile facing the past while the other looks to the future, alludes to the ambiguous complexity of national identity. A stylised black boat, reminiscent of the Mabinogi cauldron of rebirth, suggests a process of cultural questioning and reinvention.[iii]

Mary Lloyd Jones's 2007 mixed-media work on paper *Swyn I* (fig. 45) was bought by the Derek Williams Trust in 2008. Born in 1934 she often uses text or ancient writing as part of her visual imagery and as an integral part of landscape painting. Following manuscript research at Llyfrgell Genedlaethol Cymru – National Library of Wales, she selected particular texts to feature in multi-layered works like palimpsests with marks between paint layers. Expressing her Welsh identity, language and culture she has also sought to establish links with a wider Celtic world through the inclusion of early alphabets and symbols derived from Ogham or stone carvings in the prehistoric passage graves of Anglesey and the Republic of Ireland.[iv]

In *Swyn I* she has included a hand-written magic spell, found in family papers, comprising the incantation 'Abracadabra' which was used in folk medicine to cure cattle of illness. This is shown alongside imagery from prehistoric carvings and a Sator Square containing a five-word Latin palindrome to which magic powers are also attributed.

For a number of years the Derek Williams Trust acquired artworks from the visual art exhibitions at the National Eisteddfod of Wales. These have included Ogwyn Davies's mixed-media work *'Mae hen wlad fy nhadau…'*, Lois Williams's textile hanging *A Reconstructed Thing* (fig. 53) and paintings by Terry Duffy and Philip Nicol (fig. 25), photographs by Stuart Lee (fig. 61), turned wood by Steve Howlett and ceramics by Christine Jones (fig. 75).

---

iii   Iwan Bala et al., *Hon, Ynys y Galon*, Gomer, 2007
iv   Mary Lloyd Jones et al., *First Language: Mary Lloyd Jones*, Gomer / Llyfrgell Genedlaethol Cymru – National Library of Wales, 2006

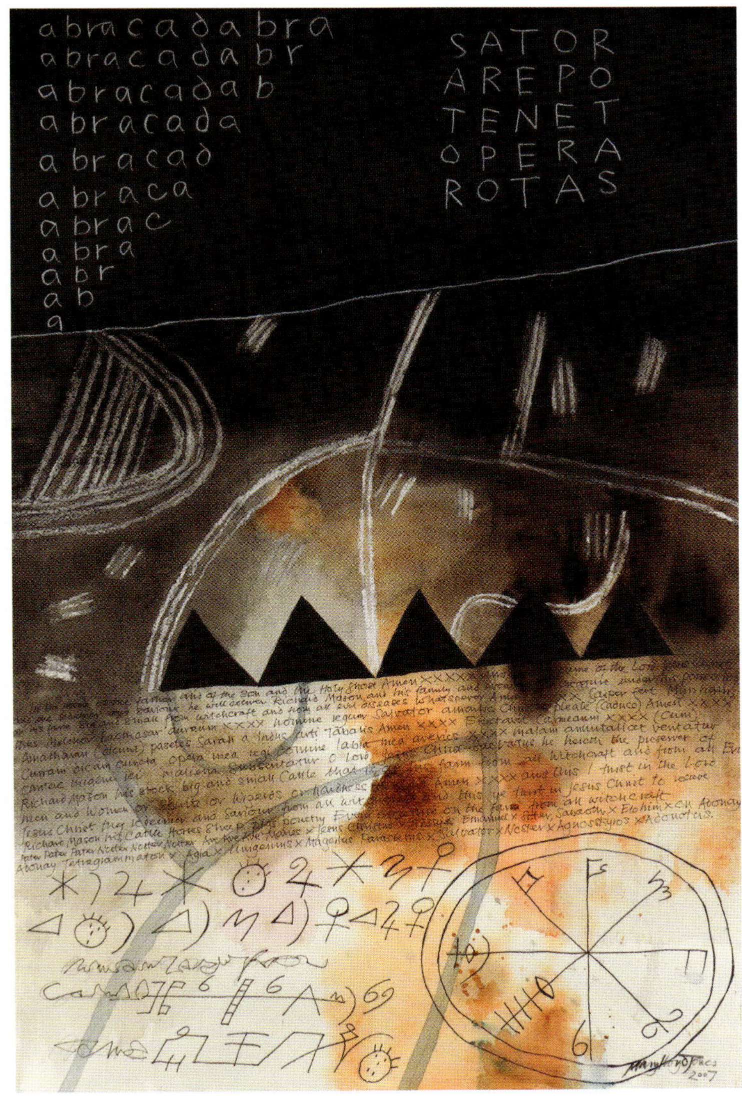

45. Mary Lloyd Jones, *Swyn I,* mixed media, 2007, 69 x 110 cm. Trust purchase, 2008.

Expressing her Welsh identity, language and culture, [Mary Lloyd Jones] has also sought to establish links with a wider Celtic world...

More recently the trust has acquired the 2014 oil on canvas *Loner* by Geraint Evans, depicting a druid standing nonchalantly in the driveway of a modern house. It has also supported the museum in the acquisition of John Meirion Morris's 1997-98 bronze *Cofeb Tryweryn*, commemorating the drowning for a reservoir of the Welsh-speaking village of Capel Celyn (fig. 22), and Tim Davies's 2003 twenty-one part *Postcard Series III – Figures in Landscape*, featuring postcards from which ladies in traditional Welsh costume have, symbolically, been neatly removed. Bedwyr Williams's majestic 2016 video installation *Tyrrau Mawr* (fig. 67) received the Derek Williams Trust's Purchase Prize in *Artes Mundi* 7.

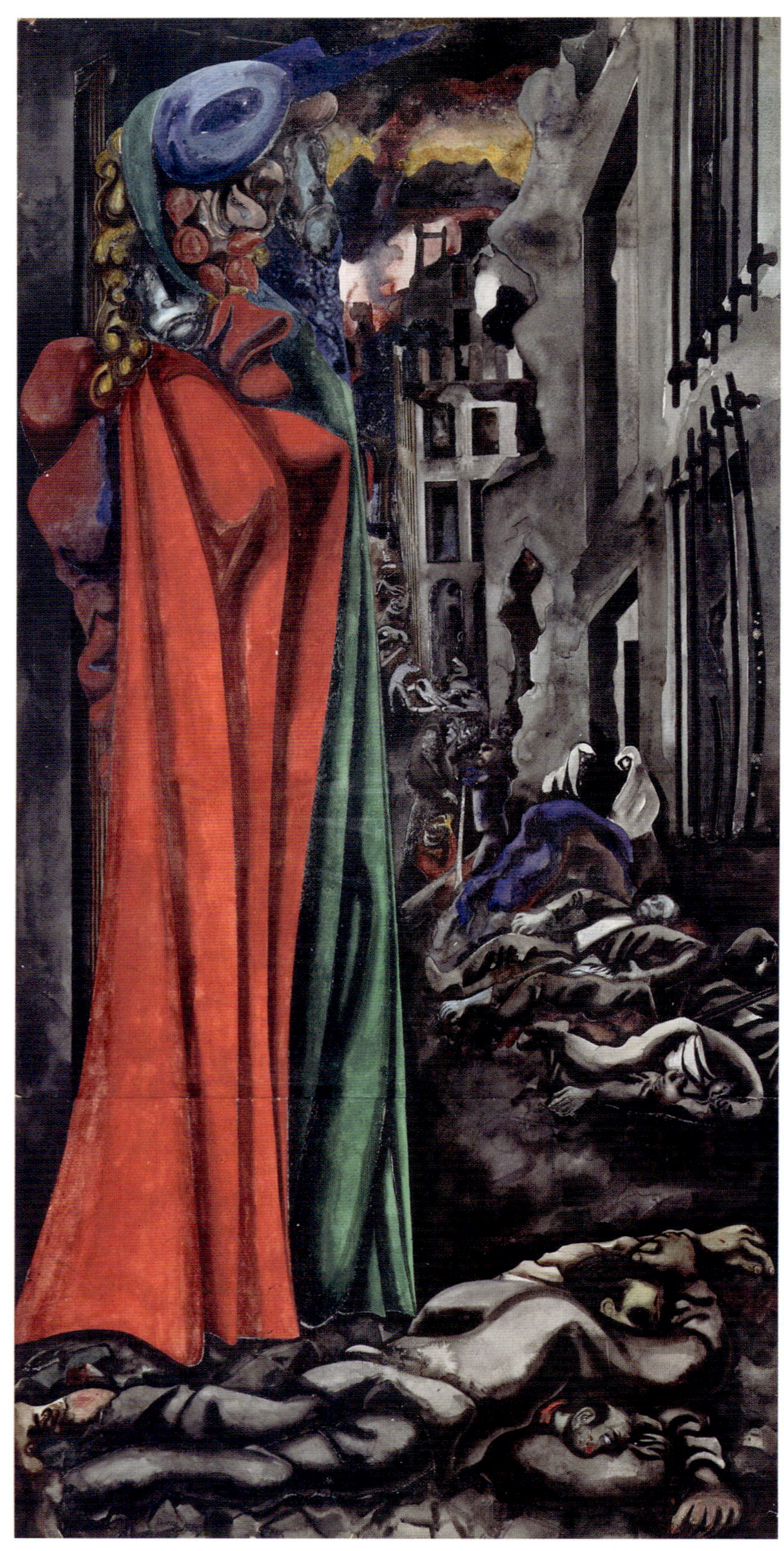

11. ECHOES OF THE UNCONSCIOUS: SURREALIST PERSPECTIVES

46. Edward Burra, *The Red Cloaked Figure,* watercolour on paper, 1936, 112 x 57 cm. Trust purchase, 1994.

Surrealism originated in the anarchic Dada movement, itself a response to disillusionment after the First World War, when techniques such as collage and the reuse of found materials were adopted.

By its nature complex and diverse, surrealism was particularly concerned with the expression of imagery and thoughts associated with the unconscious mind. Closely linked to the development of psychoanalytic theory, the writings of Sigmund Freud on the interpretation of dreams had been influential. Unsurprisingly, many surrealist works featured the language of dreams and took a contemporary view of both sexuality and violent events.

André Breton, a French writer and poet, produced the first surrealist manifesto in 1924. France would remain the main centre for surrealism until the Second World War. The movement embraced painters, sculptors, photographers, film-makers, writers and poets, many of whom adopted it as a state of mind. Its visual imagery varied greatly from the detailed, yet irrational, figurative paintings of Salvador Dalí and René Magritte to more abstract works by Max Ernst and André Masson that had been achieved with techniques to suppress conscious control and awaken the unconscious. Surrealist artworks included incongruous and chance combinations of objects which could be disturbing and, often, shocking.

Between 1936 and 1937 surrealism established itself in Britain. Artists Eileen Agar, John Banting, Roland Penrose and Julian Trevelyan had returned from Paris. They would exhibit, alongside Paul Nash, Merlyn Evans and Henry Moore, in the influential and well-attended 1936 International Surrealist Exhibition at New Burlington Galleries, London. Opened by André Breton, it included significant figures from the continent.[i]

By its nature complex and diverse, surrealism was particularly concerned with the expression of imagery and thoughts associated with the unconscious mind.

---

i   Michel Remy, *Surrealism in Britain*, Lund Humphries, 1999

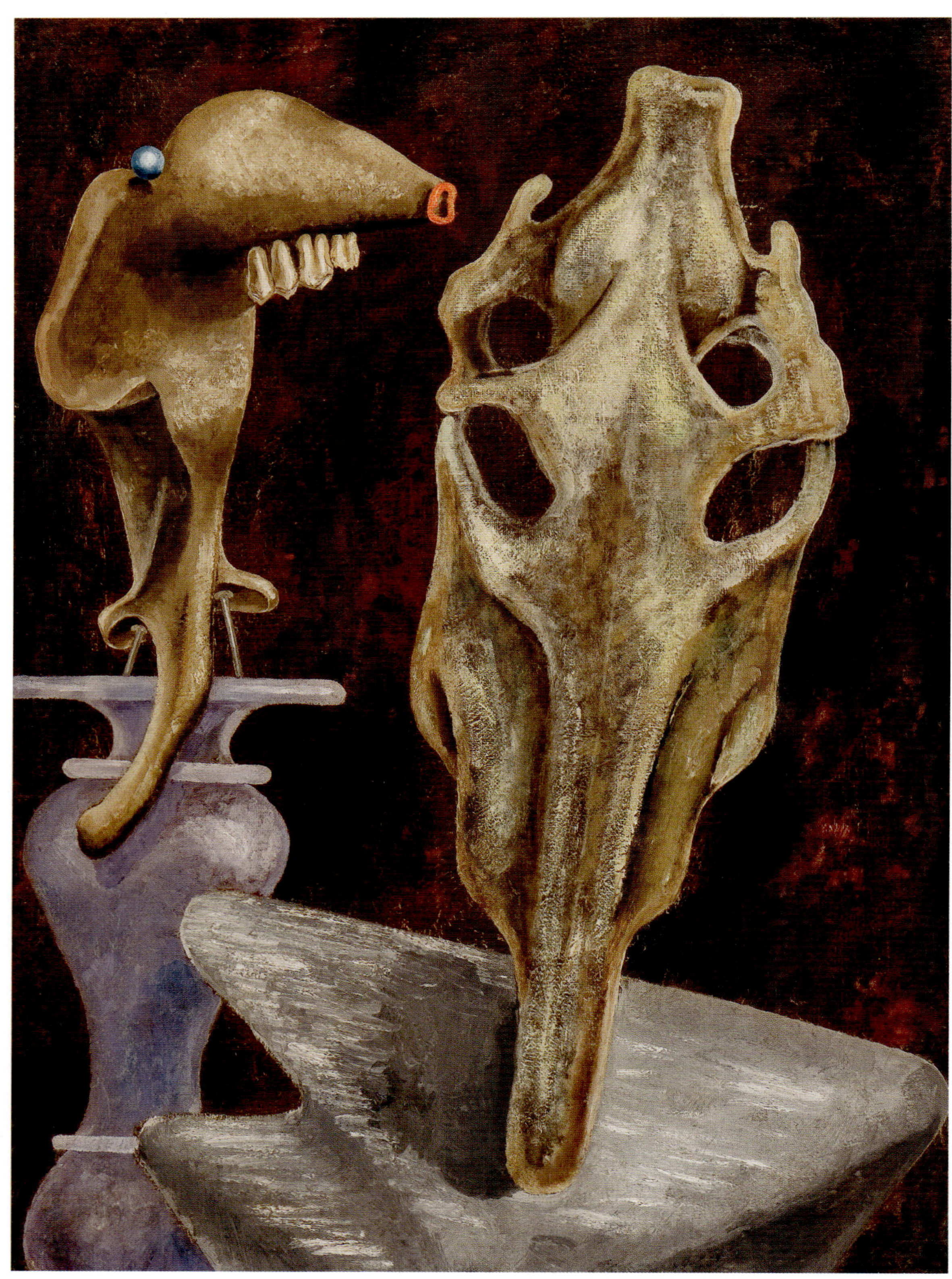

Edward Burra's 1936 watercolour *The Red Cloaked Figure* (fig. 46) was purchased by the Derek Williams Trust in 1994. Burra (1905-76), while being wary of groups and, later, of being labelled a surrealist, had, in the year of this painting, signed up to the English Surrealist Group. Also that year he exhibited in the International Surrealist Exhibition in London as well as in Fantastic Art, Dada and Surrealism at the Museum of Modern Art, New York. Influenced by Paul Nash, they both experimented with collage. Burra's distinctive style became more liberated. Open to a range of art-historical influences, he mainly painted in watercolour and also designed for the stage. Experiencing much ill health he lived, rather soberly, in Rye, Sussex, but became fascinated by grotesque and fantastic figures in some of the livelier parts of New York, Marseilles and Madrid.[ii]

The Red Cloaked Figure was painted after experiencing, in Madrid, the build-up of hatred in the period immediately before the tragic outbreak of the Spanish Civil War. The sinister, dramatic red-cloaked, bird-masked figure creates a sense of unease as it looms over the scene of a massacre.

John Banting's c.1937 oil on canvas *Mutual Congratulations* (fig. 47) was a 2009 trust purchase. Banting (1902-72) had studied in both London and Paris and attended life classes while working as a bank clerk. He travelled a great deal between London, Paris and the French Riviera. Some of his work was inspired by music although much of it was concerned with a condemnation, as he saw it, of banality and insincerity. In *Mutual Congratulations*, animal skulls suggest conversing male and female figures. If these were people, though, the artist hints that their exchanges would still be superficial. Banting and Ceri Richards, another artist involved in surrealism in the thirties, painted billboards drawing attention to starving children in Republican Spain. Banting would make films for the Ministry of Information during the Second World War.[iii]

---

ii   Simon Martin ed., *Edward Burra*, Lund Humphries / Pallant House Gallery, 2011

iii   Michel Remy, *op cit.*, 215.

Eileen Agar's 1950 oil on canvas *An Exceptional Occurrence* (fig. 48) was another trust acquisition from 2009. Agar (1899-1991), British since a child although born in Buenos Aires, studied with Leon Underwood and then at the Slade School of Fine Art. She was much influenced by her time in Paris where she met Breton. Her surreal paintings, collages and mixed-media objects evolved, in the forties and fifties, into more abstract, gestural, yet still surreal, works. She would also become interested in photography. Nature and organic forms were her primary source of inspiration and she was particularly fascinated by marine objects. She was playful with what shapes might reveal when reduced to essentials. The accidental manifestation of rocks, pebbles and driftwood were, for her, expressions of fertility.[iv]

An Exceptional Occurrence is a rare oil from 1950, a period when she was mainly painting watercolours. It suggests a tense choreography between two standing figures and may be a response to curious volcanic rock formations in Tenerife.

British surrealism was rediscovered in the 1970s and particularly since a 1982 exhibition in Paris. The movement has certainly, at times, influenced artists in Wales including, notably, Ceri Richards and, more recently and to varying degrees, Ivor Davies (fig.43), Sally Moore (fig. 79) and Alan Salisbury. It is also central to the work of John Welson whose, often, startling images seem to be continually metamorphing.

An Exceptional Occurrence is a rare oil from 1950, a period when she was mainly painting watercolours. It suggests a tense choreography between two standing figures and may be a response to curious volcanic rock formations in Tenerife.

---

iv   Michel Remy, *Eileen Agar: Dreaming Oneself Awake*, Reaktion Books, 2017

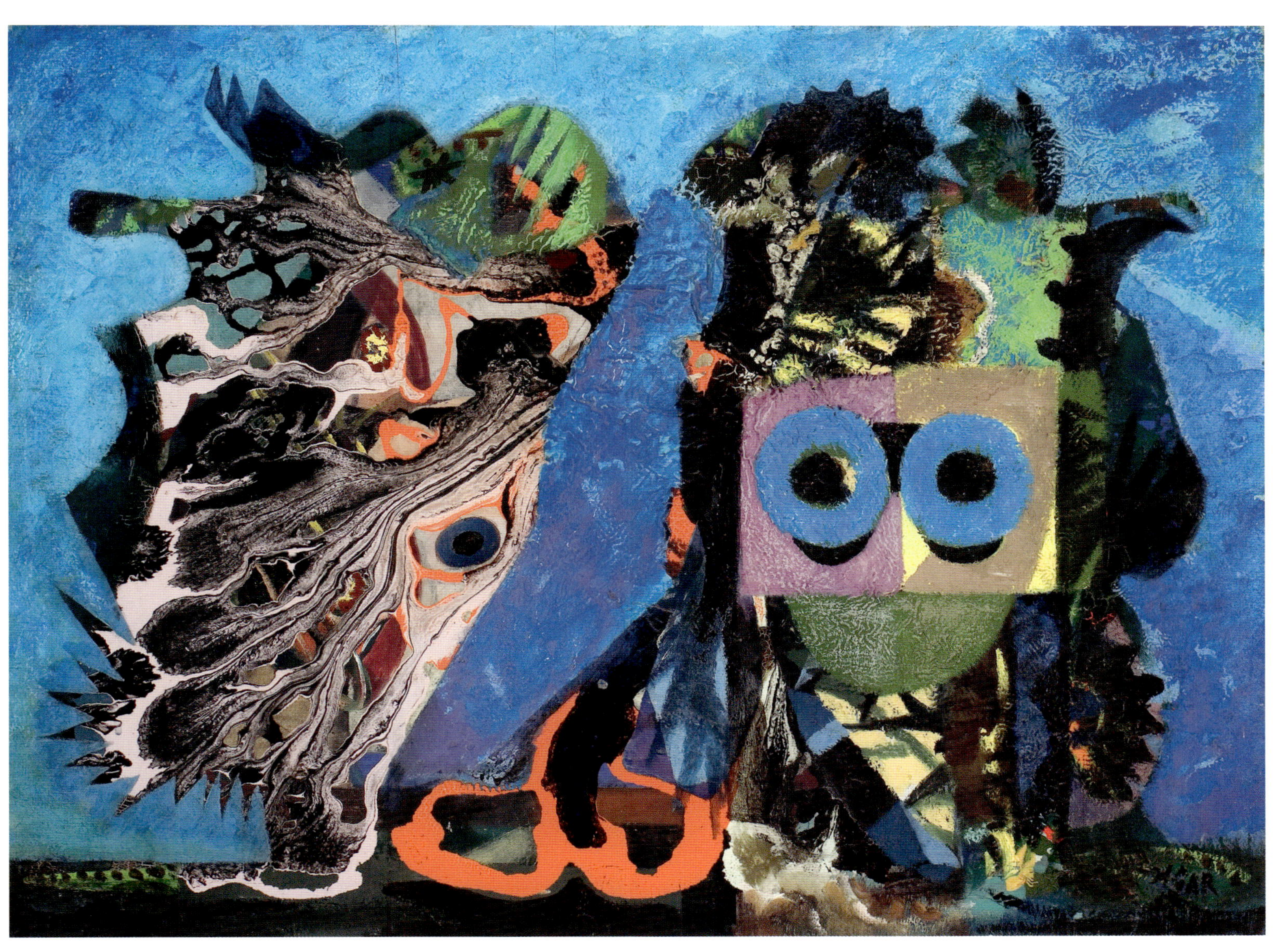

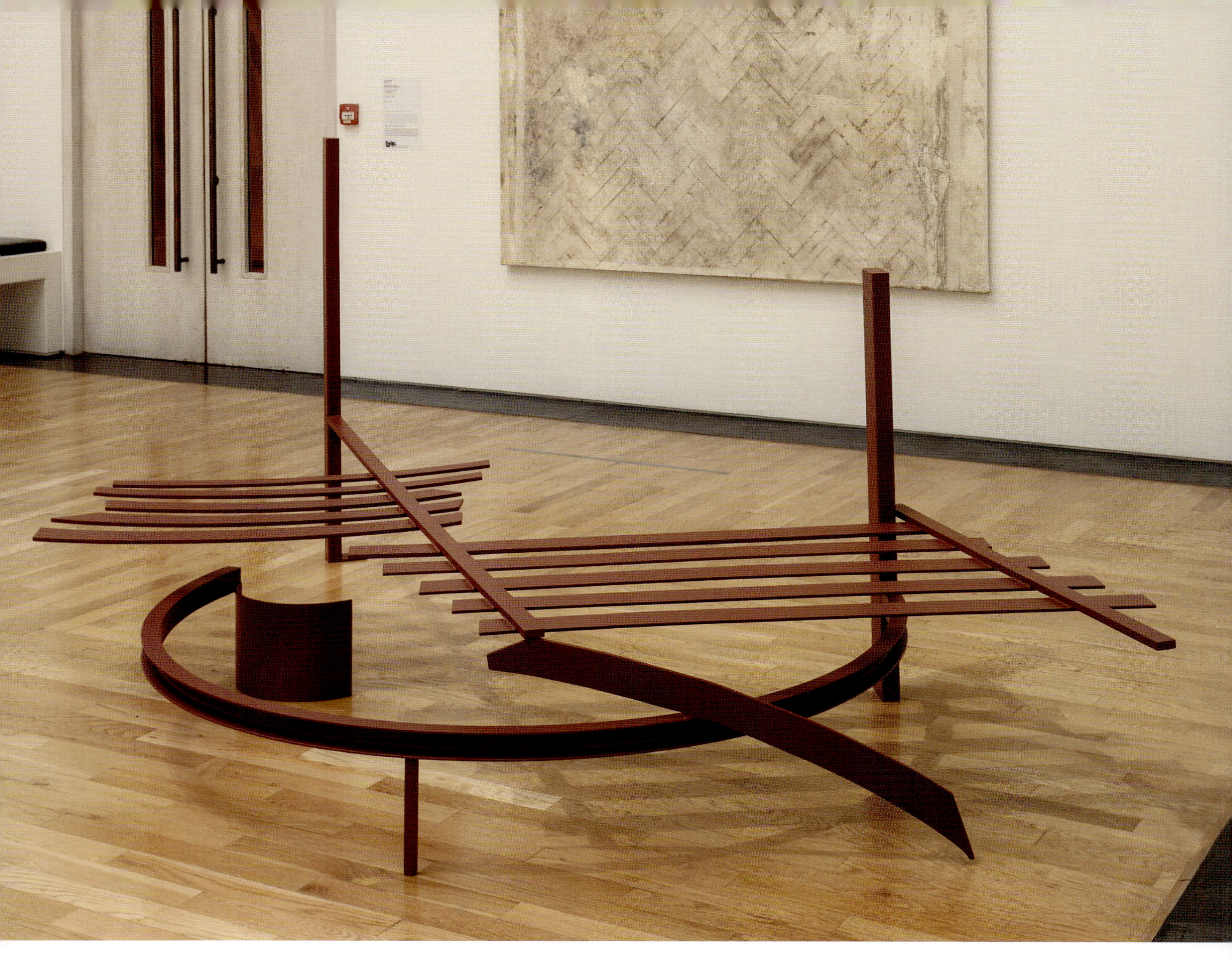

12. ELOQUENCE IN THREE DIMENSIONS: MODERN SCULPTORS

49. **Sir Anthony Caro, *Serenade*, painted steel, 1970-71, 119 x 264 x 229 cm. Trust purchase, 2016.**

The ability to express abstract ideas creatively and eloquently in three dimensions is a rare skill and sculpture is valued highly by the Derek Williams Trust. This chapter focuses on a selection of recent acquisitions by internationally celebrated sculptors associated with significant developments in British sculpture since the late 1960s.

Sir Anthony Caro's 1970-71 painted steel *Serenade* (fig. 49) is a recent important purchase by the Derek Williams Trust of a work which had been in a private collection. 'This sculpture appealed to me,' wrote Hollie Allen, an officer with The Wallich homelessness charity and one of the 2017-18 Who Decides? exhibition's curators, 'because of the flowing lines and how it seems to impose itself on the space.' Using horizontal and vertical components as well as looping and curling forms, this completely abstract work is made from rigid industrial materials and stands directly on the ground. Colour also helps to unify the piece.

Caro (1924-2013) taught sculpture part-time at St Martin's School of Art, London, from 1953 to 1979 and his concern with, for example, improvisation and open-endedness were influential. He was, himself, much influenced by the American sculptor David Smith, who had also used steel extensively. For Caro it was important that sculpture took on architectural qualities and volume was understood by the way in which space was handled. At times he has been regarded as exemplifying a style of formal modernist sculpture that has been overtaken by later sculptors. His work, however, was always more wide-ranging and playful than it has sometimes, in more post-modernist times, been given credit for. It had continued to develop in imaginative ways with reference to other artforms and in collaboration with other artists as well as with architects.[i]

---

i   Peter Murray *et al.*, *Caro in Yorkshire*, Yorkshire Sculpture Park / The Hepworth Wakefield, 2015

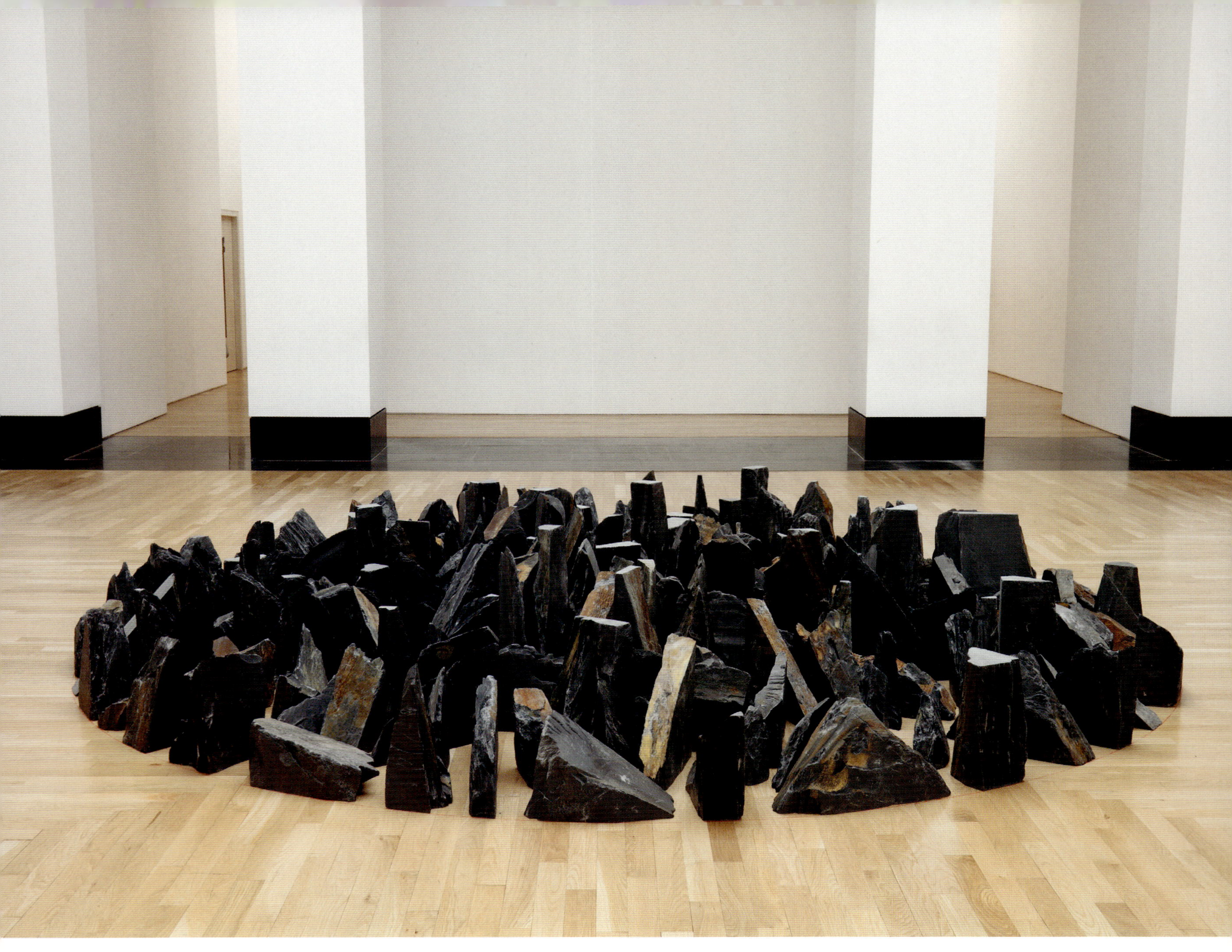

Sir Richard Long's 2011 slate *Blaenau Ffestiniog Circle* (fig. 50) was acquired by the museum with assistance from the Art Fund as well as the Derek Williams Trust in 2012. When it was shown in the Who Decides? exhibition, Mike Pugh, one of The Wallich curators, recalled that 'The stone circle reminds me of Stonehenge, and I react strongly to the colours and the feeling of wilderness.'

Long, born in 1945, began to take an interest in making artistic statements out of his experience of landscape while a student at St Martin's School of Art, London, in the late 1960s. Often categorised as a land artist, much of his work originates in the process of walking. Walks involve making stone structures, sometimes circular ones, taking photographs, film or creating maps or texts drawn from his experiences along the way which mark the passage of time (fig. 6).[ii]

Blaenau Ffestiniog Circle encourages the viewer to walk around it. Influenced by the Italian art movement *arte povera*, or 'poor art', Long uses repeatedly readily-found materials such as stones or pieces of wood. The viewer is encouraged to consider their origin and preparation. Attracted to minimalist structures, the works may, as here, have a monumental quality.

A 1981 mixed-media installation by Bill Woodrow, born in 1948, *The Red Hat* (fig. 51), was purchased by the museum with assistance from both the Derek Williams Trust and the Contemporary Art Society in 2015. The Wallich volunteer and curator Heidi Jones points out that 'One person's junk is another person's treasure. Bill Woodrow makes art from other people's rubbish.'

In the 1980s a new style of British sculpture emerged. Sculptors such as Bill Woodrow and Tony Cragg tended to concentrate upon relatively contained fixed objects often made from found materials, the identity of which was part of the work. Woodrow

'The stone circle reminds me of Stonehenge, and I react strongly to the colours and the feeling of wilderness.'

---

ii   Richard Long ed., *Richard Long: Walking the Line*, Thames and Hudson, 2002

became prominent after showing a series of works in which mass-produced household electrical goods, destined to decay, had their sheet-metal casing roughly cut out to create completely different items. A physical link between the two was often retained, the shape left behind revealing that of the new object. These narratives, made with wit and irony and expressive of the artist's feelings, make gentle fun of the process of making art. They are also metaphors for a make-do-and-mend society. The festive hat in *The Red Hat* brings the metal violin and bow to life.[iii]

Richard Deacon's 1984 galvanised steel, laminated wood and canvas *Tall Tree in the Ear* (fig. 8) was a museum acquisition with assistance from the Derek Williams Trust and a private donor in 2015. Deacon was born in Bangor in 1949. While abstract, the work is also metaphorical and poetic, the viewer being intrigued by a combination of form, materials, process and title. Often his materials, such as galvanised metal, laminated wood or leather only become meaningful in the way he uses them. The works may allude, as here, to parts of the body used for communication.[iv]

51. Bill Woodrow, *The Red Hat*, mixed-media installation, 1981, 78 x 88 cm. Acquired by Amgueddfa Cymru – National Museum Wales with support from the Derek Williams Trust and the Contemporary Art Society, 2012.

These narratives, made with wit and irony and expressive of the artist's feelings, make gentle fun of the process of making art.

---

iii Julia Kelly and Jon Wood, *The Sculpture of Bill Woodrow*, Lund Humphries, 2013
iv Clarrie Wallis *et al.*, *Richard Deacon*, Tate Publishing, 2014

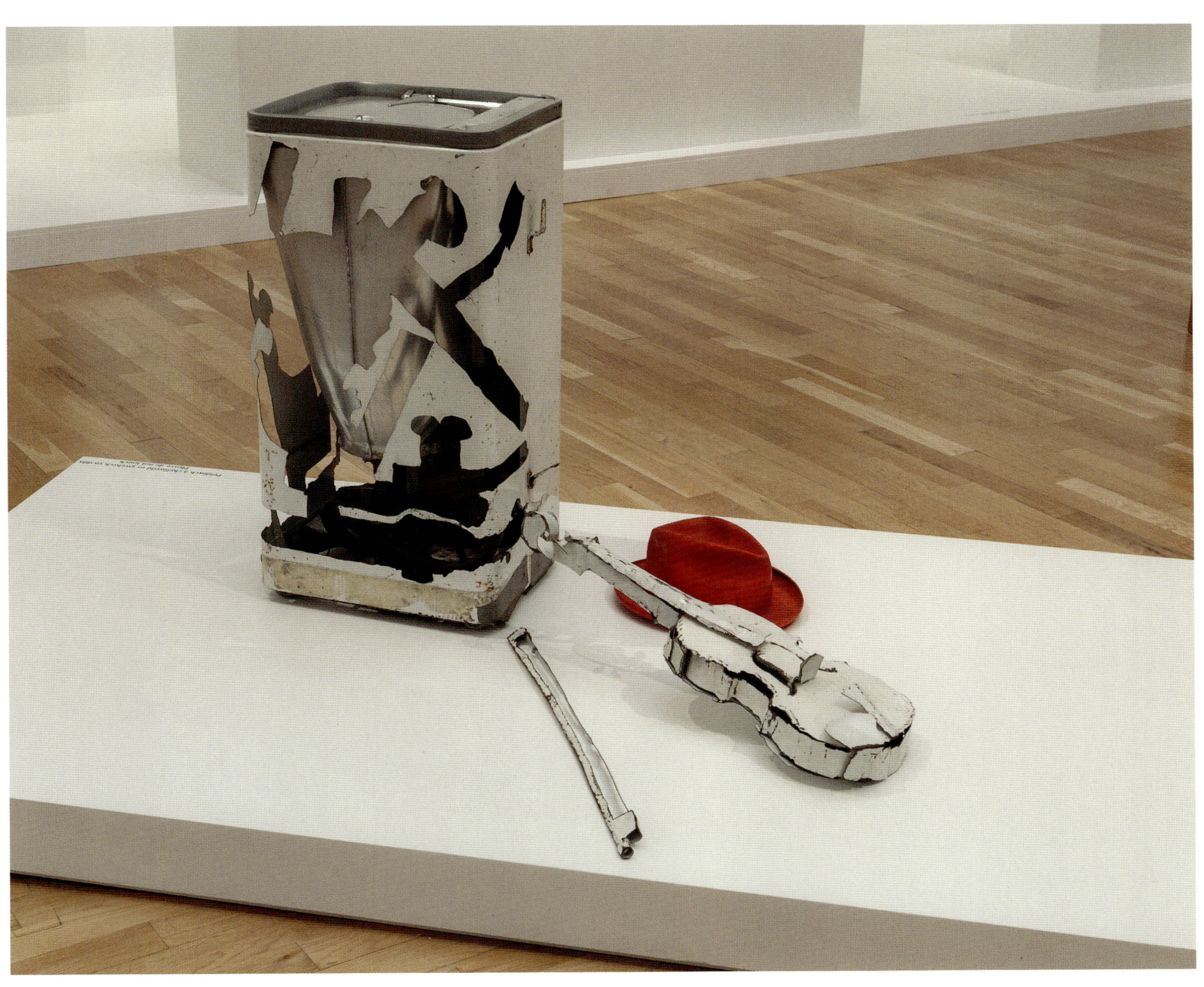

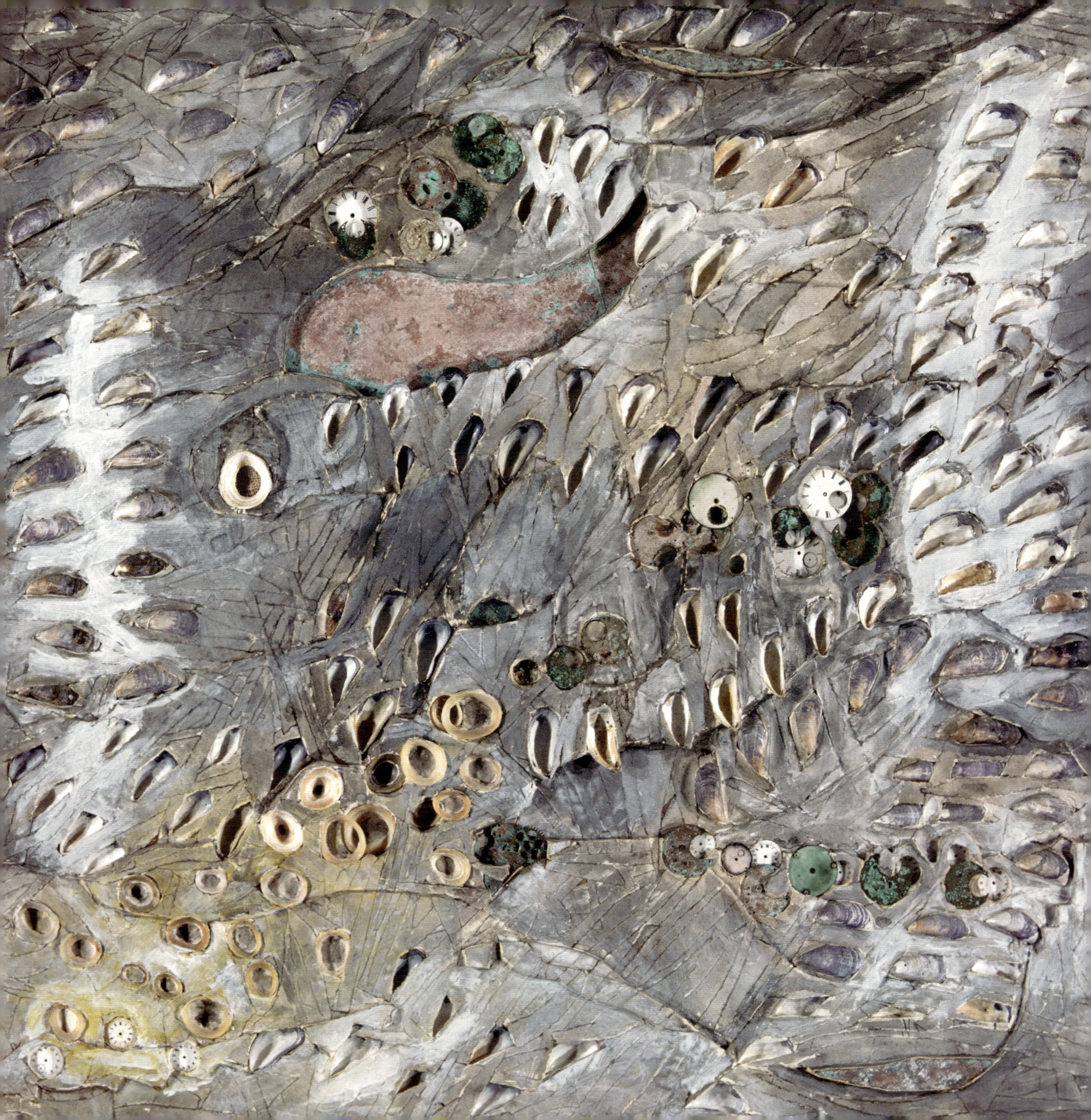

13. DIVERSE SCULPTORS IN WALES

52. Arthur Giardelli, *The Sea's Edge*, mixed-media relief on board, 1990, 92 x 91 cm. Trust purchase, 2001.

Wales has been the home to many significant sculptors and this chapter highlights four of them – Arthur Giardelli, Lois Williams, David Nash and David Garner – whose work has been acquired or grant-supported by the Derek Williams Trust.

Arthur Giardelli's 1990 mixed-media relief on board *The Sea's Edge* was acquired by the Derek Williams Trust in 2001. Giardelli, who died in 2009 at the age of ninety-eight, was a painter, constructed-relief artist and notable art educator. Living first in Pendine, Carmarthenshire, and, from 1969, at Warren, Pembrokeshire, Giardelli's most significant works were, undoubtedly, his abstract constructions from the mid-1950s, of which *The Sea's Edge* (fig. 52) is a good example. Using found materials such as, in this case, shells and watch fragments or, in others, slices of furniture or oars, they reveal a fascination with the sea's rhythms as well as with the enigmatic nature of our relationship with time. He also painted distinguished watercolour landscapes.[i]

Giardelli was a founder member, in 1956, of the high-profile artist exhibiting association 56 Group Wales. Influenced by international movements in art, its original members were frustrated by limited opportunities to show their work, much of which was concerned with abstraction, and were driven by a desire to exhibit together, promoting member-led selection. Giardelli was the group's determined and visionary chair for nearly four decades. The group celebrated its sixtieth anniversary in 2016.[ii]

Lois Williams's 1994 wool and woven yarn *A Reconstructed Thing* (fig. 53) was acquired by the Derek Williams Trust in 2000. Originally made in response to objects in the collection of Amgueddfa Cymru – National Museum Wales, this is a fragile and ambiguous work which embodies the notion of preservation, reconstruction

---

i   Derek Shiel ed., *Arthur Giardelli – Paintings, Constructions, Relief Sculptures: Conversations with Derek Shiel*, Seren; 2001; David Moore, *Arthur Giardelli, Obituary*, The Guardian, 12 November 2009
ii   David Moore, *A Taste of the Avant-Garde: 56 Group Wales, 56 Years*, Crooked Window, 2012

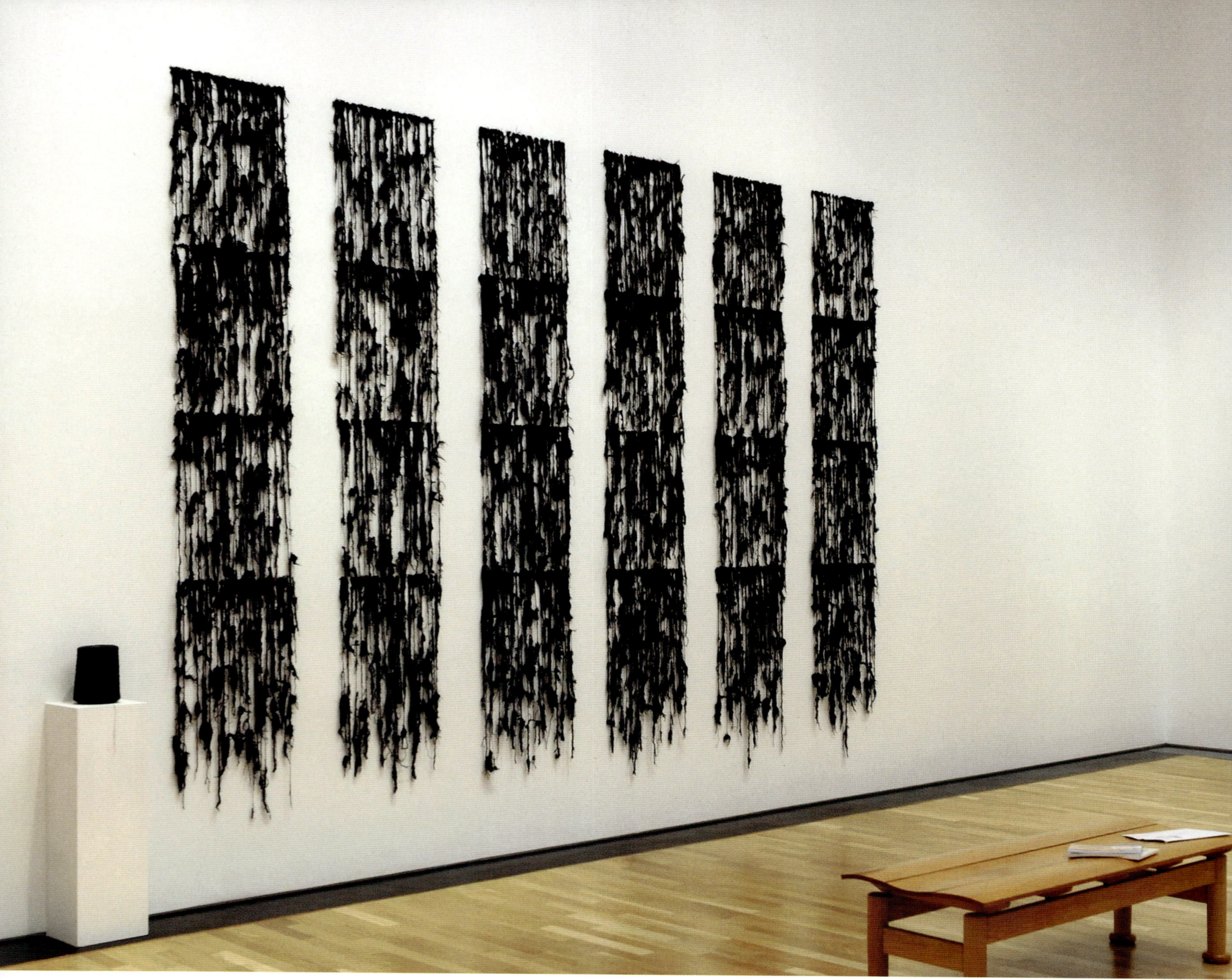

53. Lois Williams, *A Reconstructed Thing*,
wool and woven yarn, 1994, 280 x 850 cm.
Trust purchase, 2000.

Much of her understated sculpture, concerned with narratives and symbolism relating to sewing, weaving and clothes, relates to broader sculptural practice.

and presentation. Made from one thread of spun wool, it has been unravelled, or deconstructed, and may be seen as presenting a sequence of evidence for the evolution of the woollen industry itself, although, like a curtain, the work conceals as much as it reveals. It has a presence that art historian Michael Tooby has described as 'testimony to the female energy released when the skills and understanding of making are realised in new purpose.'[iii]

The artist, born in north Wales in 1953 and brought up on a farm, has an instinctive feel for animals, regeneration and material objects. She celebrates local traditions alongside her sense of the world. Much of her understated sculpture, concerned with narratives and symbolism relating to sewing, weaving and clothes, relates to broader sculptural practice.

David Nash's 2000 beech *Multi-Cut Column* (fig. 55) was acquired by the Derek Williams Trust in 2000. This wood-cut sculpture is a development from the artist's earlier columns in that its facets run in many directions, reminiscent of changing patterns in rock strata near his home in north Wales.

Nash, who was born in 1945, has lived and worked in Blaenau Ffestiniog since 1967 and is much influenced by its dramatic landscape. Many of his works, which have been exhibited in museums and galleries all over the world, are made with a chainsaw, the resulting forms reflecting the local geology and landscape. With a strong concern for the environment, he uses gifted wood or that from well-managed woods. Unseasoned, the many resulting saw cuts accelerate the drying-out of the wood and lead to the

iii   Michael Tooby, 'Lois Williams: Storytelling, Female, Welsh, Torn, Artist' in Susan Daniel and Martin Barlow eds., *From the Interior: Lois Williams, Selected Sculpture, 1981-1995*, Oriel Mostyn / Wrexham Library Arts Centre, 1995; Iwan Bala, 'The simplest aid to looking at Wales: Communications with Lois Williams', in Iwan Bala ed., *Certain Welsh Artists: Custodial Aesthetics in Contemporay Welsh Art*, Seren, 1999

54. David Nash, *Ash Dome*, Twelve black and white board-mounted photographs, 2000, 117 x 162 cm. Trust purchase, 2000.

55. David Nash, *Multi-Cut Column*, beech, 2000, 241 x 76 x 77 cm. Trust purchase, 2000.

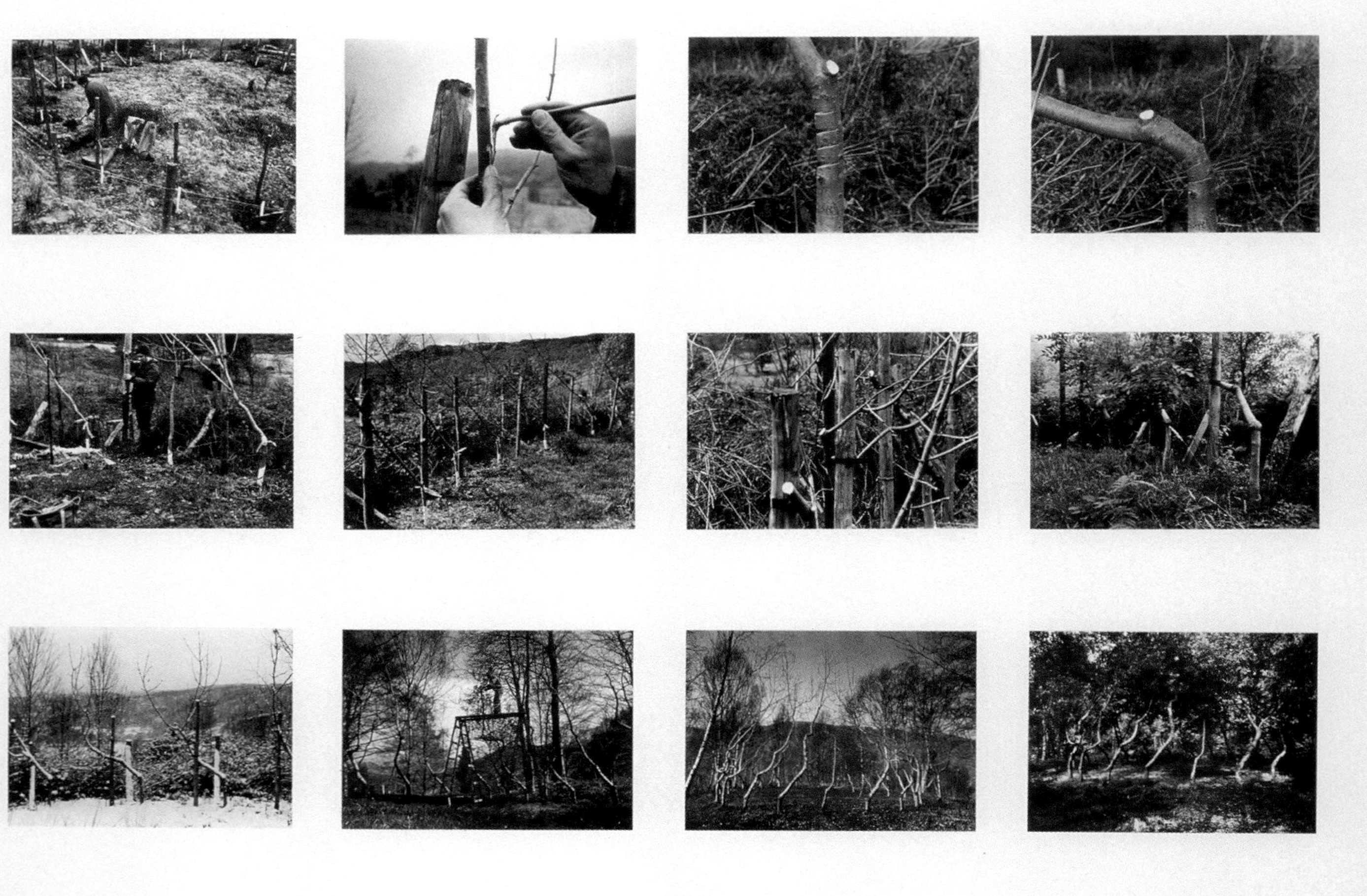

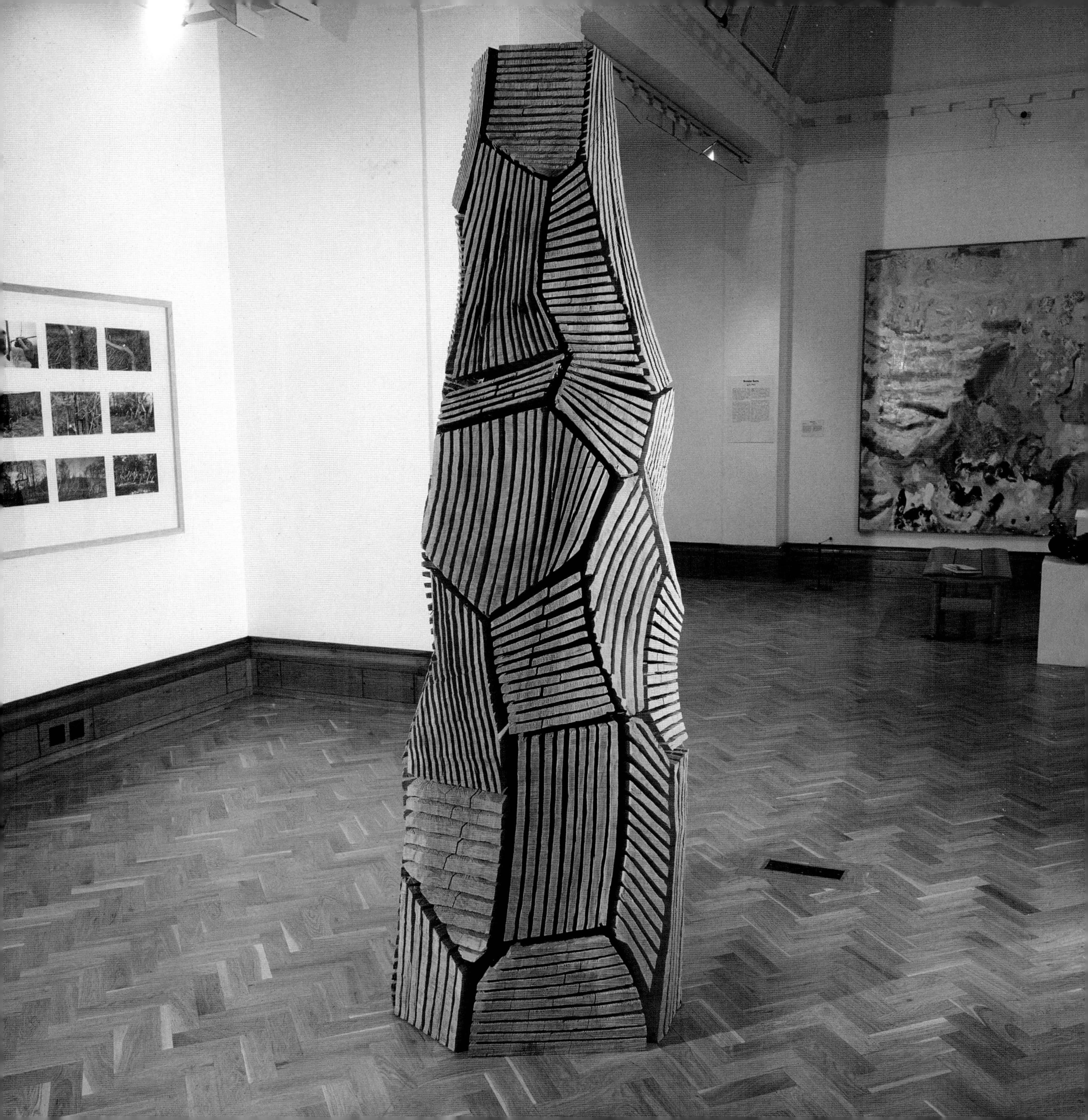

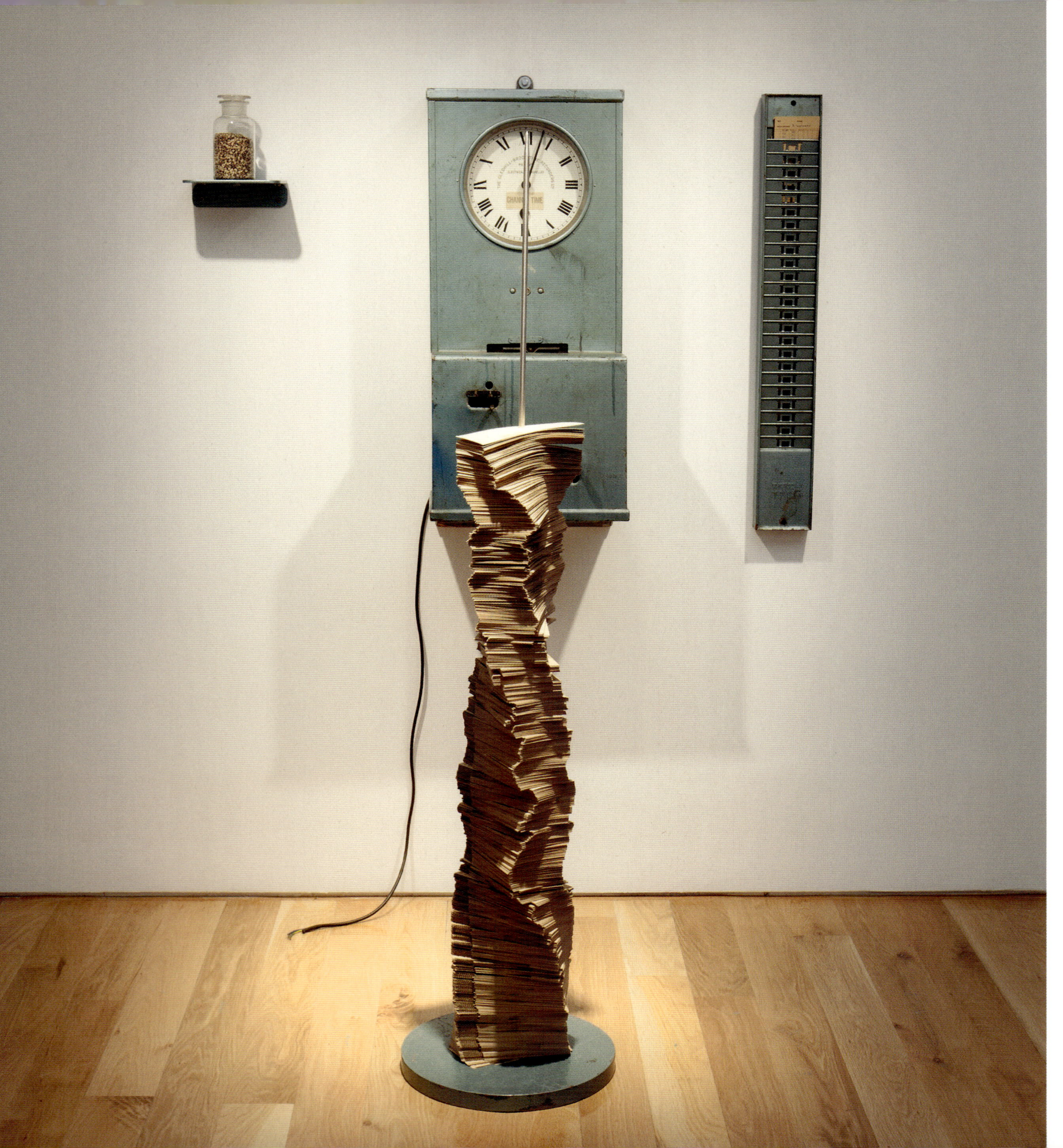

Born in 1958, Garner is a highly political artist, much concerned with labour and class narratives, who, after attending art college in London, returned to live in the eastern Welsh valleys in the mid-1980s.

characteristic warping and cracking in his work.[iv]

Nash is, perhaps, best known for two well-documented interventions in the natural environment. His living-tree sculpture in north Wales, *Ash Dome*, is discussed on page 76 in the chapter exploring landscape into art. The trust acquired drawings and photographs, dating from 1999-2000, which reveal aspects of this artwork's creation and appearance (figs. 36 and 54). The trust also purchased a portfolio of work recording, between 1978 and 2003, the unpredictable movement of the sculptor's *Wooden Boulder*. Sculpted from oak and placed in the River Dwyryd, Gwynedd, its subsequent movement was, remarkably, traced and often with great difficulty.

David Garner's 2009 mixed-media installation *Last Punch of the Clock* (fig. 56) was acquired by the museum with assistance from the Derek Williams Trust in 2015. The 1950s clock and cardholder suggest the entrance to an industrial workplace. On an exaggerated desk spike are a lifetime's clocking-in cards, symbolically reaching the height of the artist's father, who had experienced the repetitition of this daily working ritual in the mines. Clippings from the cards are presented in a small jar. It marks not just the end of one person's hard working life but also that of a whole community.[v]

Born in 1958, Garner is a highly political artist, much concerned with labour and class narratives, who, after attending art college in London, returned to live in the eastern Welsh valleys in the mid-1980s. He has responded to major change in the coal-mining industry and to its communities as well as, in later works, to the persecution of refugees and to the demonisation of Muslims. His conceptual and poetic sculpture and installations are a dialogue with ordinary lives through, as in the coal industry, re-using in his work everyday items such as working clothes.

iv   Michael Tooby, *David Nash: Chwarel Goed / Wood Quarry*, Canolfan Celfyddydau / Centre for Visual Arts, 2000; Nicholas Thornton ed., *David Nash: Two Hundred Seasons at Capel Rhiw*, Amgueddfa Cymru – National Museum Wales, 2019

v   David Garner *et al.*, *David Garner: Future Tense*, Aberystwyth Arts Centre, 2012

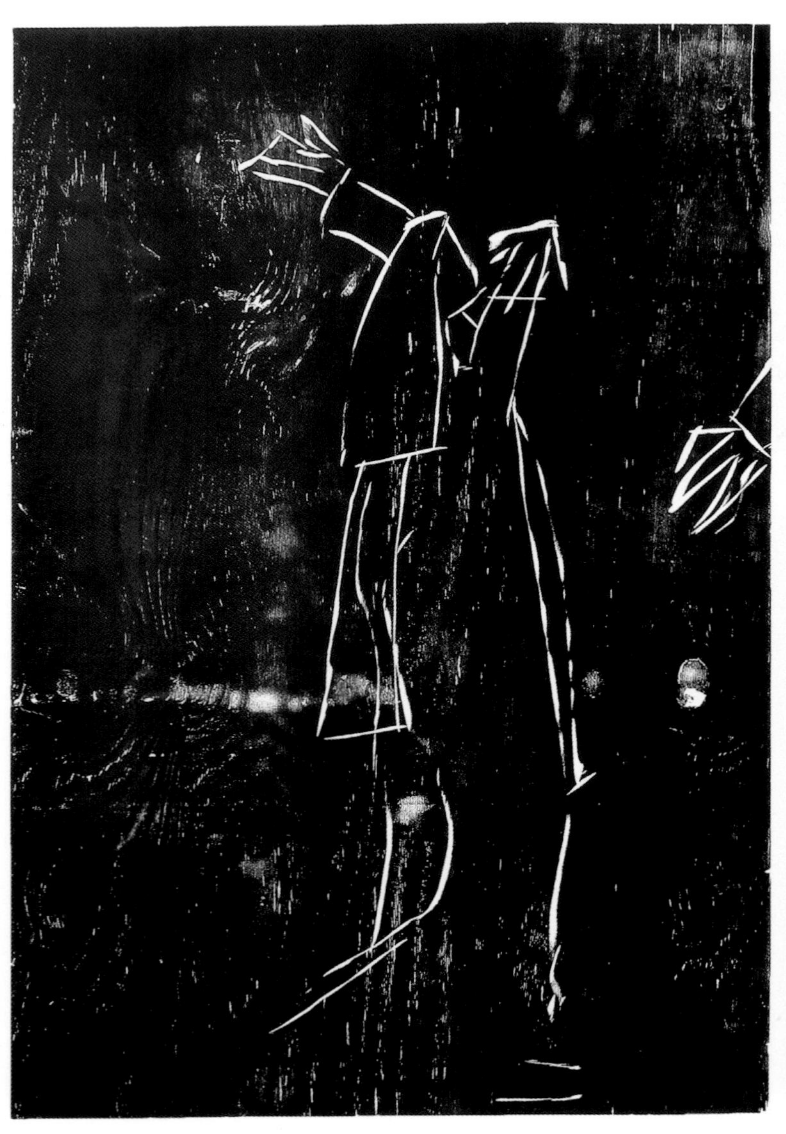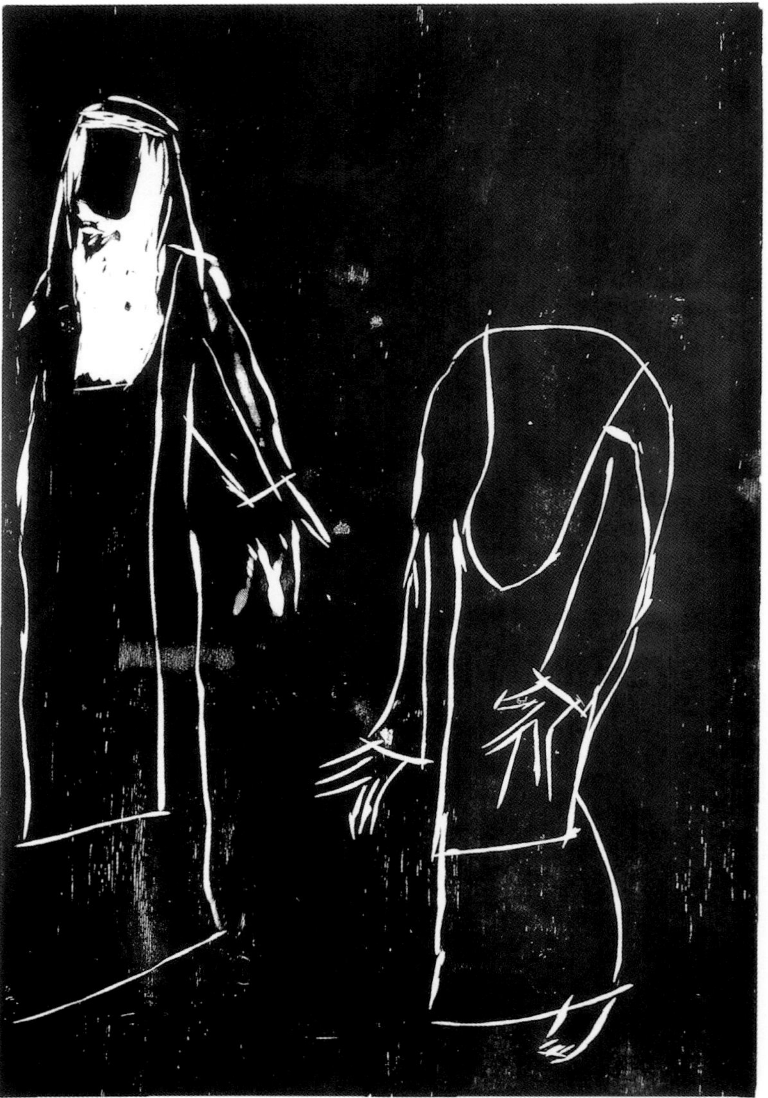

14. ARTISTS IN PRINT: WIDER-REACHING IMAGES

Multiple copies of artworks may be created by a wide range of fine-art printing techniques and some of these are extremely complex and inventive. Only a few relevant techniques are explored here. Often more affordable to buy than a painting by the same artist, they facilitate the wider reach of an image. Common traditional hand-forms are relief, intaglio, lithography and screenprinting, although, in recent decades, forms of digital print are also used.

With relief prints, such as woodcuts and wood engravings, areas of a wood block are left untouched after cutting with a tool. These areas are inked and used to convey an image onto paper. Woodcuts, cut *along* the grain, became widespread from the fourteenth century for the mass distribution of religious images but, eventually, other techniques became more prominent. The technique was revived in the early-twentieth century by German expressionists. Wood engravings, cut *across* the grain of hard wood, enabled finer work to be achieved such as that perfected by David Jones in the 1920s.

Derek Williams Trust grant-funded prints at the museum include Andrea Büttner's large 2007 two-panel woodcut *Dancing Nuns* (fig. 57), which also received funding from the Contemporary Art Society. It conveys a sense of liberation, joy and movement. Her woodcuts, made since the 1990s, are characterised by simplicity of line, the use of black and white or monochrome and a significant relationship with flat colour. The blocks are made from plywood, a material in the spirit of *arte povera*, and often feature Christian iconography and subjects such as monks, saints and beggars.

Conceptually Büttner strives for a sense of amateurism in her work in contradiction to expectations that art should look sophisticated or skilled. She is much concerned with behaviour and ethical questions related to dignity, shame, self-consciousness, vulnerability, emancipation and value. Religious communities are of particular

Her woodcuts, made since the 1990s, are characterised by simplicity of line, the use of black and white or monochrome and a significant relationship with flat colour.

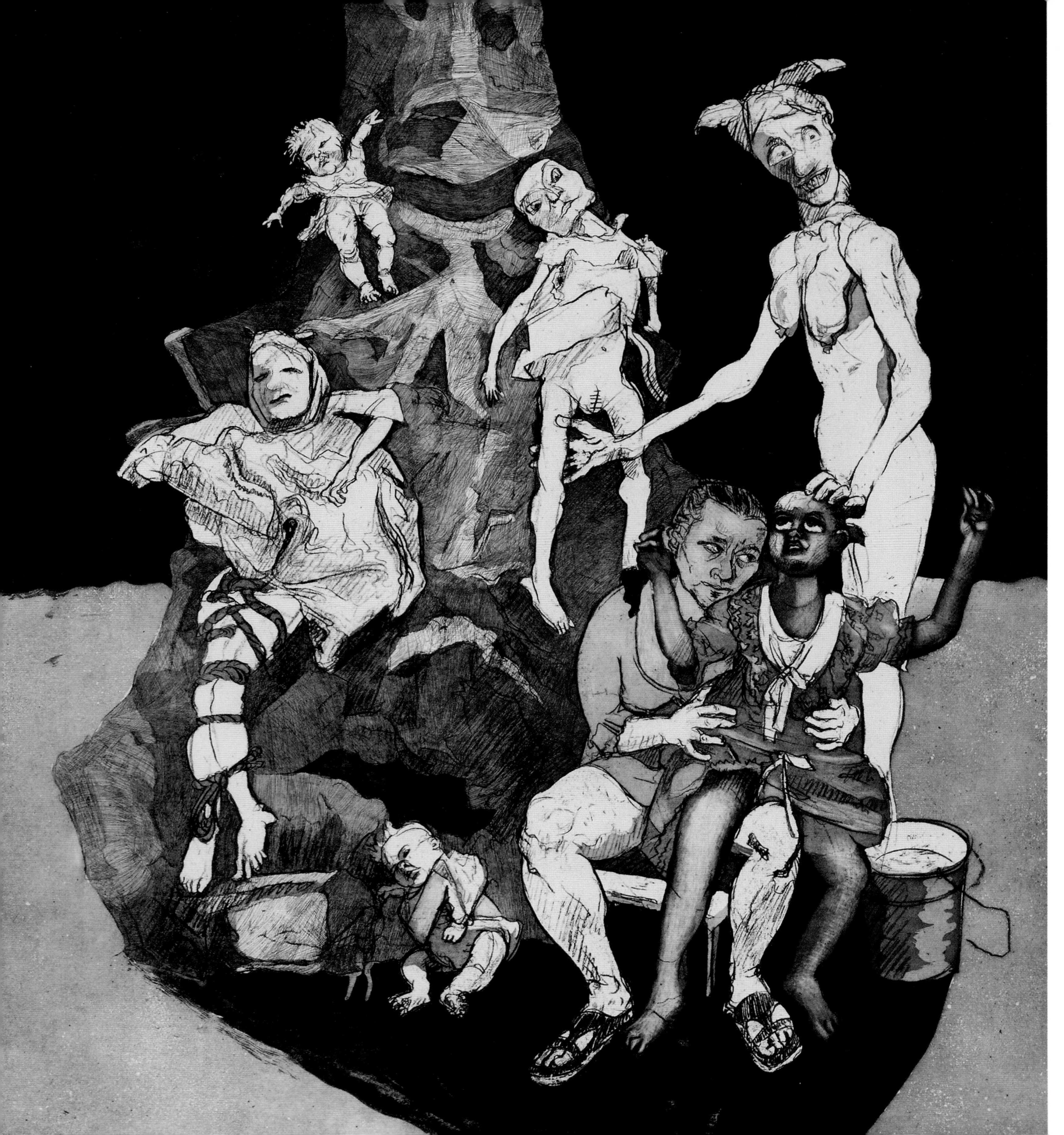

Feminism and, often, provocative dark humour underlie all her work with this series exploring a sinister side to family relations and sexuality.

interest. Poverty, she feels, is one reason people feel shame.[i]

Büttner, born in Stuttgart in 1972, works in both Frankfurt and London. Winner of the Max Mara Art Prize for Women at Whitechapel Art Gallery in 2011 and short-listed for the Turner Prize in 2017, she also makes films and installations. Her five films, *Little Works*, also acquired with support from the trust, resulted from giving a Carmelite nun a camcorder to film inside her convent. They show nuns in their free time making objects such as lavender bags or small religious icons. Educated herself at a convent, where, intriguingly, she was taught woodcut by a nun, she studied art history and philosophy and obtained a doctorate on the subject of shame in art.

Intaglio prints include engravings, made from incising a metal printing plate with a sharp point, or etchings, which permit acid, selectively through a ground, to etch an image into a plate. Other types are aquatints and carborundum prints. A 1927 still-life etching by a renowned exponent of that medium, Bolognese artist Georgio Morandi (1890-1964), was recently acquired by the Derek Williams Trust (fig. 1).

Another grant-funded acquisition at the museum is Dame Paula Rego's exuberant, if startling, 2009 *Female Genital Mutilation Series* (fig. 58) comprising six etchings with aquatint entitled *Lullaby*, *Night Bride*, *Circumcision*, *Stitched and Bound*, *Mother Loves You* and *Escape*. Many of Rego's prints are based on a narrative with one image leading to another. Feminism and, often, provocative dark humour underlie all her work with this series exploring a sinister side to family relations and sexuality. These large, highly-praised etchings, printed by Paupers Press, are her way of championing the rights of many girls and women who are profoundly discriminated against in parts of Africa, the Middle East and Asia. A practice caused by complex cultural, social and religious factors can have serious health consequences. Her etchings, intended to shock, are a way of communicating her concerns more widely. The illustrated etching *Stitched and Bound*,

i   Susanne Gaensheimer and Anthony Spira eds., *Andrea Büttner*, Koenig Books, 2013

has been described as 'a kind of unlit funeral pyre of damaged children'.[ii]

The approach to etching of Rego, who was born in 1935 in Portugal and attended the Slade School of Fine Art, suits her passion for drawing. She draws into a hard ground of warm wax or bitumen. Acid is allowed to etch through the line to a copper plate below. Once the ground is removed, the plates are inked, then cleaned, ink remaining in the etched lines. Damp paper, when pressed against the plate, draws out the ink from the lines. Aquatint is used to create areas of different tone. With this technique a fine layer of rosin powder, derived from solid resin, is fused to the plates and then etched in acid, the immersion period determining the amount of tone.[iii]

The Derek Williams Trust recently bought three prints by abstract artist Gillian Ayres (1930-2018). Printmaking was intrinsic to her practice and as part of a major exhibition of her paintings at the museum in 2017 a room was dedicated to work on paper including prints. Brought up in London, she attended Camberwell School of Art, where she was taught lithography by Edwin La Dell and Michael Rothenstein. When teaching at Bath Academy of Art, Corsham, in the early 1960s she met Jack Shirreff, a technical master of printmaking, who introduced her to carborundum etching. He had learned about it from Joe Tilson. Ayres lived for a time on the Llŷn Peninsula and, latterly, in north Devon.

Myrrh of Marib (fig. 59), one of the recent acquisitions, resulted from an early experimental project in 1998 in which Shirreff and Ayres collaborated. A complete edition of it was funded by Alan Cristea Gallery. It was a carborundum etching with acrylic hand painting. Carborundum, a carbon and silicon compound, was ground into various grades of powder, mixed with synthetic resin or varnish to become a paste and painted onto a printing plate. It dried hard and could then be inked with

59. Gillian Ayres, *Myrrh of Marib*, carborundum etching with acrylic hand painting on paper, 1998, sheet size 80 x 102 cm. Trust purchase, 2018.

When teaching at Bath Academy of Art, Corsham, in the early 1960s she met Jack Shirreff, a technical master of printmaking, who introduced her to carborundum etching.

---

ii   T.G. Rosenthal, *Paula Rego: The Complete Graphic Work*, Thames & Hudson, 2012 edition, 247
iii   Paul Coldwell in T.G. Rosenthal, *ibid.*, 337-40

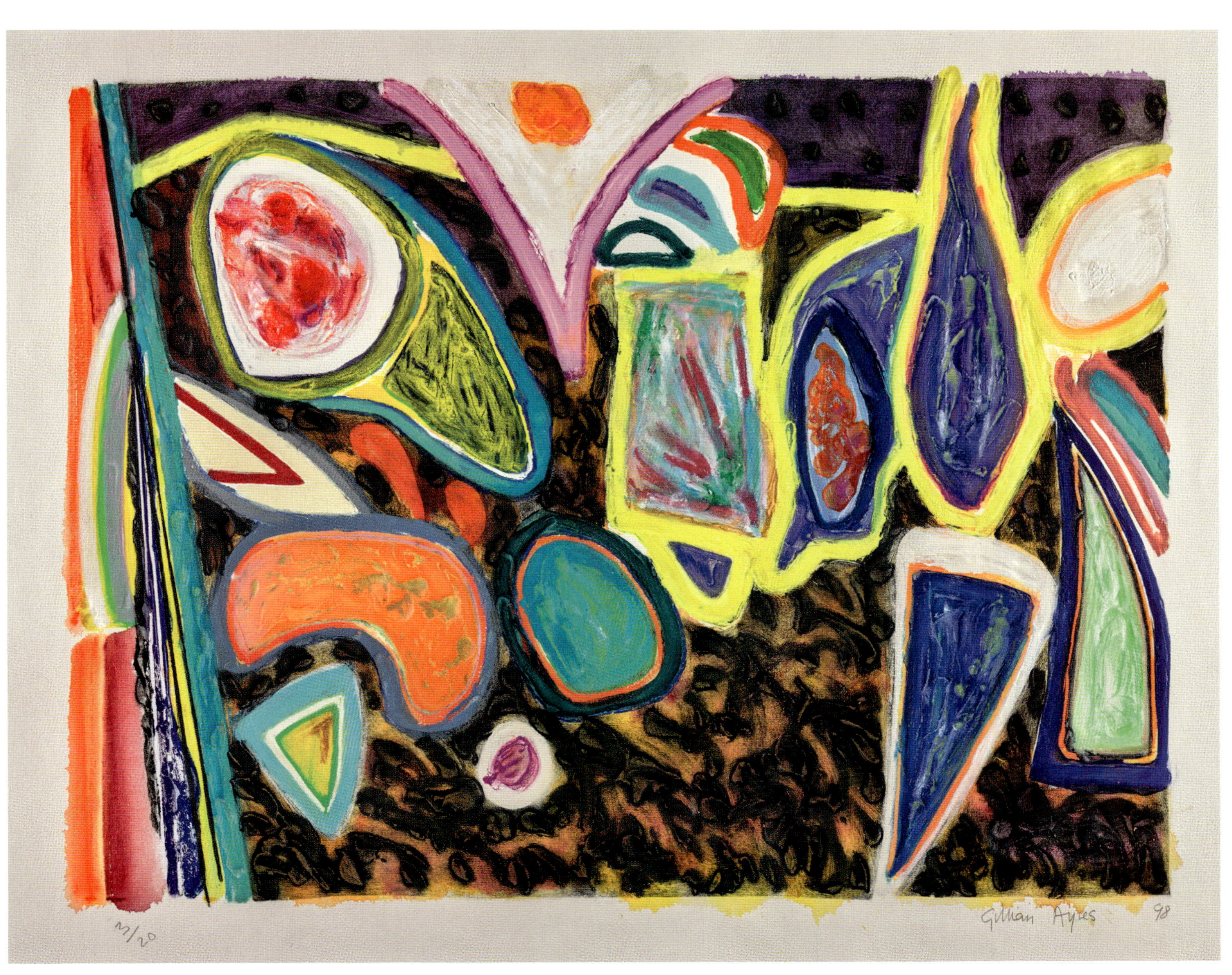

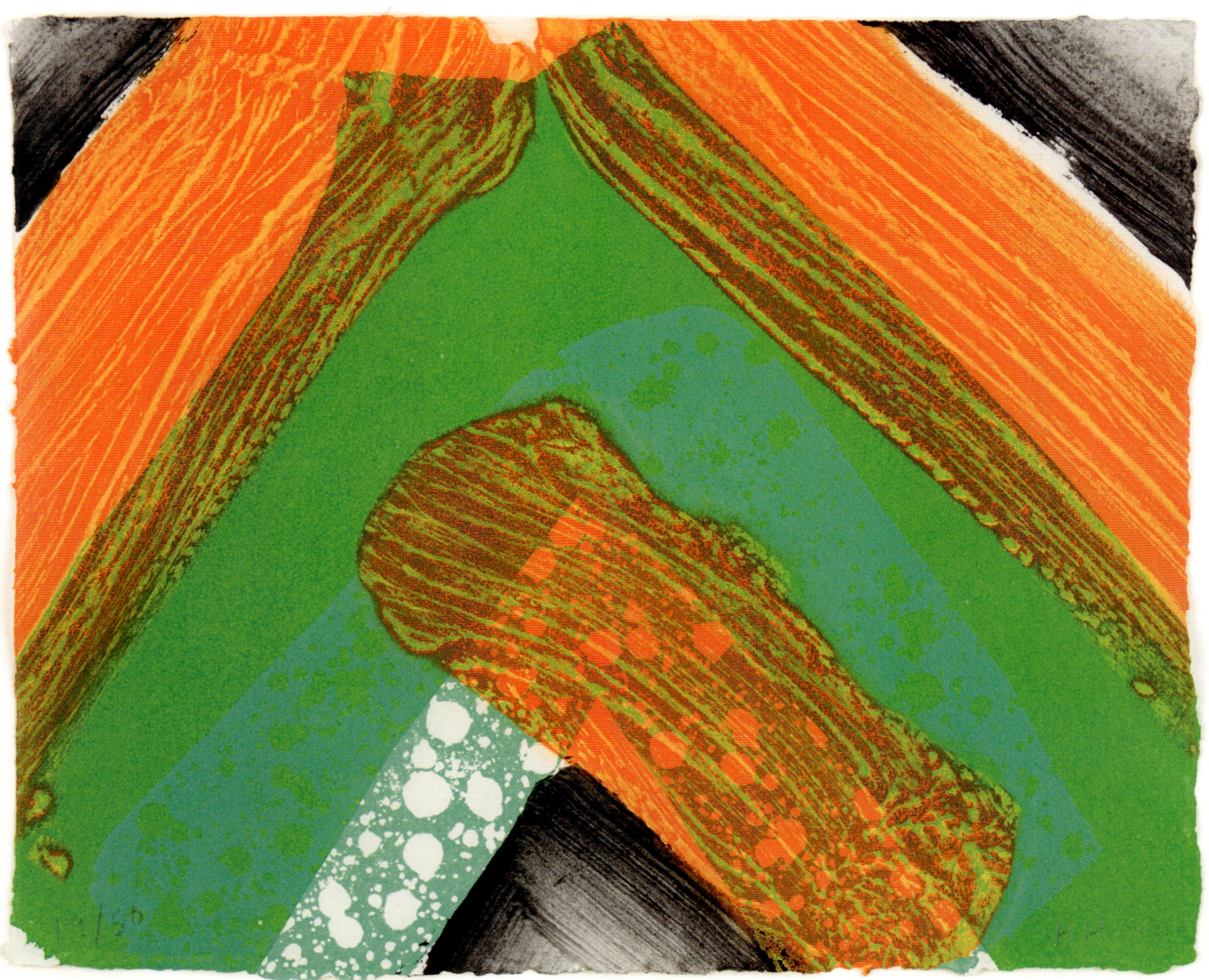

Two copper plates were used together with carborundum from an acrylic plate. Lift-ground etching (or sugar lift) enables the artist to draw directly and spontaneously onto a copper plate with a solution of sugar and ink.

multiple colours for printing together. The resulting intense painterly textures greatly suited Gillian Ayres's way of working. Hand-finishing in acrylic blurred the boundaries between printmaking and painting.[iv]

Another of Ayres's prints acquired by the trust, a late work from 2017, is a luminous woodcut on Japanese paper entitled *Thuban* (fig. 30). While some parts were pressed from one block, additional carefully-aligned blocks were also used. Reflecting sparser colour application in the artist's painting, she had became interested in single-hued organic shapes.

Sir Howard Hodgkin's 2001 hand-painted lift-ground etching with aquatint *You Again* (fig. 60) was a trust purchase from 2011. A simple triangular composition, it was also made in collaboration with Jack Shirreff for Alan Cristea Gallery and combined techniques perfected over many years. Two copper plates were used together with carborundum from an acrylic plate. Lift-ground etching (or sugar lift) enables the artist to draw directly and spontaneously onto a copper plate with a solution of sugar and ink. When dry it is varnished, then washed in warm water. The sugar dissolves and selectively lifts the varnish ready for etching with acid. The gestural prints of Hodgkin (1932-2017), who lived for most of his life in London, were as much a vital part of his practice as his paintings.[v]

Although screenprinting was invented at the start of the twentieth century, it did not come into its own until pop artists explored it in the 1960s, when it was often combined with photography. The museum acquired a trust-supported portfolio of twelve prints commissioned for the 2012 London Olympic and Paralympic Games. They include screenprints by Sir Michael Craig-Martin, Bridget Riley and Dame Rachel Whiteread and lithographs, involving making a greasy mark in crayon or paint on a limestone slab or metal plate, by Tracey Emin and Chris Ofili.

iv   Mark Gayford and David Cleaton-Roberts, *Gillian Ayres*, Art Books Publishing Ltd., 2017
v   Liesbeth Heenk, *Howard Hodgkin Prints: A Catalogue Raisonné*, Thames & Hudson , 2003

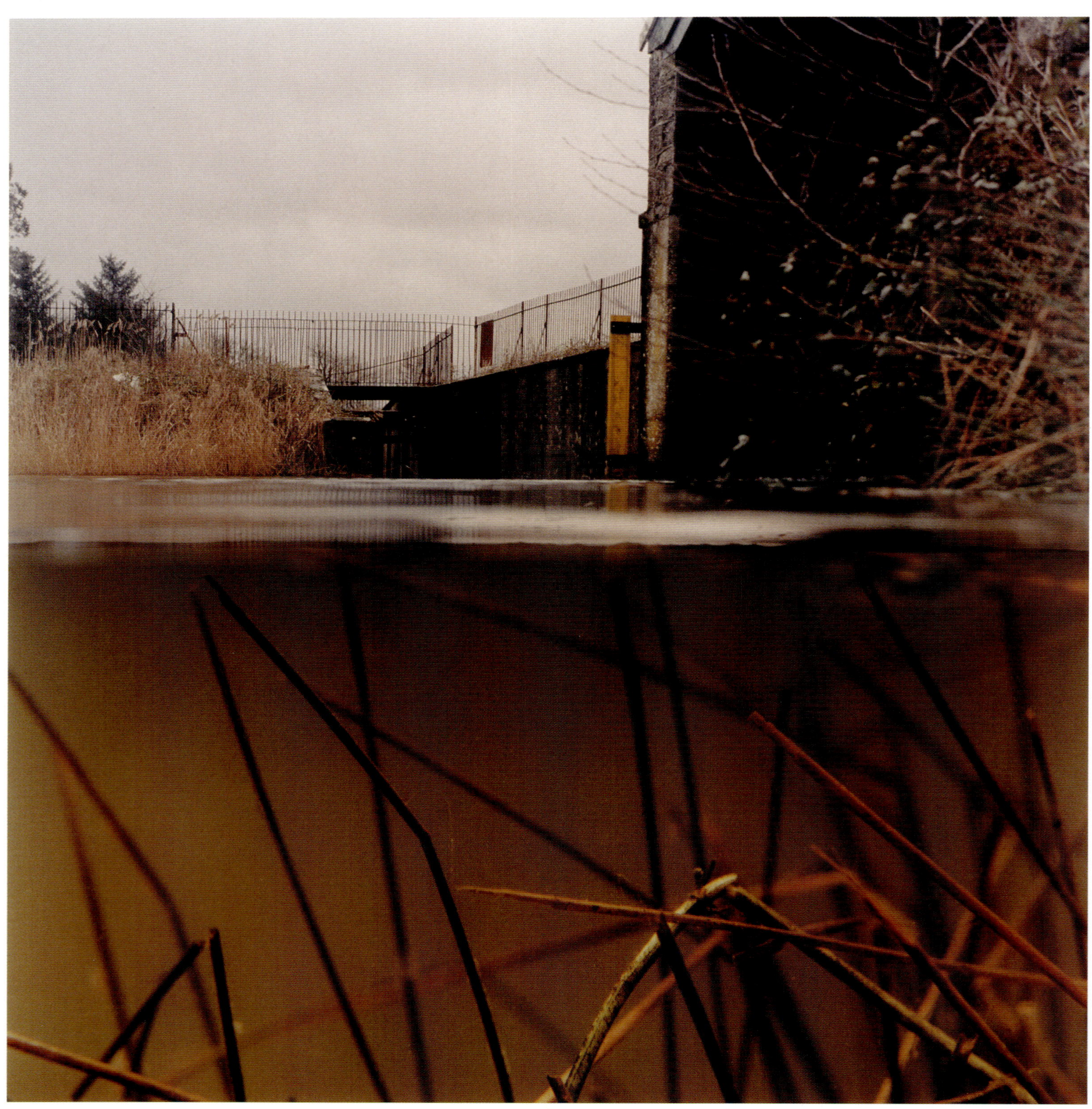

15. LENS-BASED MEDIA: FOCUSING ON PHOTOGRAPHY AND VIDEO

The Derek Williams Trust's principal involvement with photography and video has been through its grant-funding support to Amgueddfa Cymru – National Museum Wales. These media are now well established at the museum but this was not always the case. It was 2000 before the trust bought any photographs and 2005 before it supported a film purchase from the National Eisteddfod of Wales.

Magnum Photos photographer David Hurn, who founded a prominent documentary photography course at Newport College of Art in 1973, gifted to the museum in 2017 fifteen hundred of his own photographs as well as a collection of seven hundred by leading contemporary photographers. Together with the appointment, four years ago, of a dedicated photography curator this has had a substantial impact upon the profile of photography at the museum.

Four of Stuart Lee's 2004 *Water Level Series* colour photographs (fig. 61) were bought by the trust in a scheme linked to the National Eisteddfod of Wales. Lee was the gold-medal winner for fine art that year. Fascinated by the relationship between people and nature, he had observed that 'the closer we attempt to get to nature, the further from nature we become… in wildlife photography the practitioner tries to gain an intimate view of nature, yet must remain at a distance to avoid disturbing his or her subject.'[i] The *Water Level Series* considers bodies of water on the outskirts of urban areas stocked for recreational fishing. In each image a glimpse of pond life below the water line is contrasted with the detached view from above. Lee, born in Slough in 1974, studied documentary photography at the University of Wales, Newport.

Trust purchases include photographs by land artists. Black and white images of David

In each image a glimpse of pond life below the water line is contrasted with the detached view from above.

---

i   Stuart Lee, 'Stuart Lee', *Eisteddfod Genedlaethol Cymru: Casnewydd a'r Cylch – Arddangosfa Celfyddydau Gweledol / National Eisteddfod of Wales: Newport and District – Visual Arts Exhibition*, 2004, 12-13

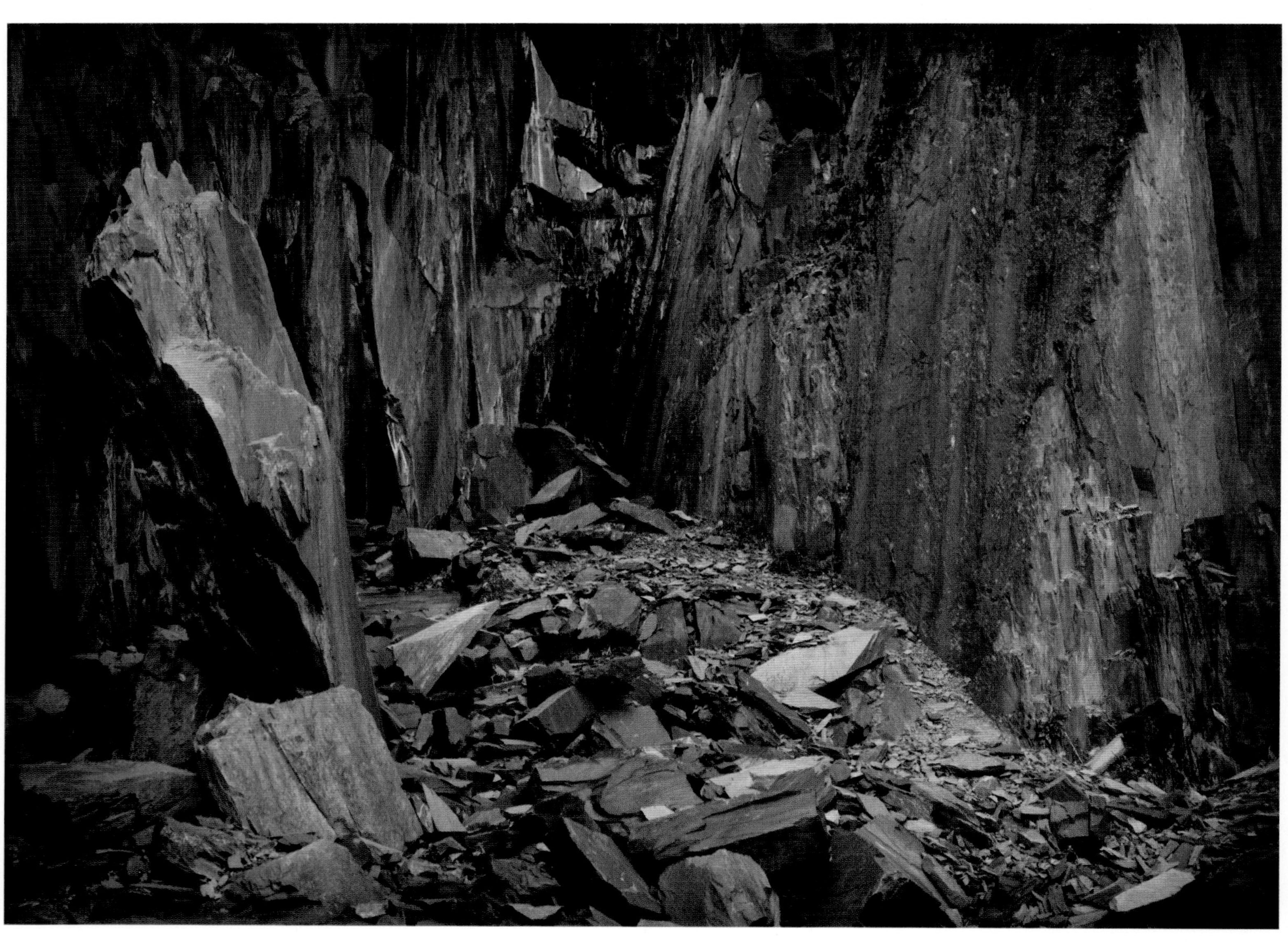

Images form in his mind well before opening the camera's shutter. With this and exposures often taking several minutes, he refers to 'making' rather than 'taking' a photograph.

Nash's *Ash Dome* taken c.2000 (fig. 54) were part of a group of works by the artist, including sculpture and drawings, acquired at that time. Richard Long's 2006 inkjet colour print *Snowdonia Stones (along a five day walk in North Wales)* (fig. 6) was bought in 2010.

Thomas Joshua Cooper's 1992 black and white photograph *A Premonitional Work (Message to Friedrich and Frith), Blaenau Ffestiniog, Gwynedd, Wales* (fig. 62), was acquired by the trust in 2009. Cooper largely uses nineteenth-century photographic techniques including a heavy plate camera and chemical development. His subject is the landscape, often looking out to sea from the extreme edge of landmasses. Rather like land artist Richard Long, Cooper plans walks and selects locations on a map. Images form in his mind well before opening the camera's shutter. With this and exposures often taking several minutes, he refers to 'making' rather than 'taking' a photograph. A notable characteristic of his meditative images is the way they seem to capture a sense of time passing. Born in San Francisco in 1946, Cooper became head of photography at Glasgow School of Art's photography department in 1982. Inspired by early twentieth-century American modernist photographers such as Ansel Adams and Paul Strand, he often dedicates works to pioneering landscape photographers.[ii]

The museum now has a comprehesive collection of film and video artworks. Peter Finnemore's 2005 DVD projection of thirty-five short films, *Base Camp* (fig. 63), awarded the gold medal for fine art at the 2005 National Eisteddfod of Wales and a prize at the Venice Biennale, was an early such acquisition supported by the Derek Williams Trust. The films were part of a long-term project which, in the artist's words, 'explores the possibility of ordinary domestic spaces of home and garden as relevant, challenging and contemporary subject matter.'[iii] Centred around the

---

ii   Duncan Macmillan, 'At the still point of the turning world', in *Point of No Return: Thomas Joshua Cooper*, Haunch of Venison, 2004

iii   Peter Finnemore, 'Peter Finnemore', *Eisteddofod Genedlaethol Cymru: Eryri a'r Cyffiniau – Arddangosfa Celfyddydau Gweledol / National Eisteddfod of Wales: Snowdonia and Surrounding Areas – Visual Arts Exhibition*, 2005, 12

artist's home in the strongly Welsh-speaking community of the Gwendraeth Valley, the films depict, playfully, a microcosm of 'global, political, economic, colonialist and militaristic narratives...' Comic military figures dominate and are intended to 'deflate the machismo associated with this attire'. He is interested in notions of cultural camouflage within a colonised environment. There is also an allusion to the Celtic myth of the Green Man. Born in Wales in 1963, the artist attended Dyfed College of Art, Glasgow School of Art and the University of Michigan and has lectured in photography at Swansea and Newport.[iv]

Helen Sear's DVD projection *Company of Trees* (fig. 64), commissioned by Arts Council Wales and curated by Ffotogallery as part of Wales's contribution to the 2015 Venice Biennale, was also acquired by the museum with trust support. An immersive visual and aural experience, it compels the audience to take an active role. One of many influences was the zoetrope, a cyclical pre-film animation device creating an illusion of motion from a sequence of drawings or photographs. A young woman in a red dress continually circles around trees and is rapidly interrupted, through cutting and editing, by images of branches, woodland and red-painted numbers on trunks signifying that they are to be felled. The imagery and colour have been sensitively digitally manipulated.[v]

Sear explores ideas of vision, touch and representing the nature of experience with a combination of drawing, lens-based media and digital technologies. Born in Banbury in 1955, she moved to Wales in 1984 and has now moved to France. She was a senior fellow at the Centre for Photographic Research in Newport and, more recently, visiting professor at the Royal Academy Schools, London. Challenging, from a feminist perspective, established views of photography, she reconstructs images that

63. Peter Finnemore, *Base Camp,* still from DVD projection of thirty-five short films, 2005. Acquired by Amgueddfa Cymru – National Museum Wales with support from the Derek Williams Trust, 2006.

Comic military figures dominate and are intended to 'deflate the machismo associated with this attire'. He is interested in notions of cultural camouflage within a colonised environment.

---

iv   Peter Finnemore, *Zen Gardener*, Oriel Mostyn Gallery, 2004
v   Steven Connor in David Drake ed., *Helen Sear: '...the rest is smoke'*, Wales in Venice / Ffotogallery Wales Ltd., 2015

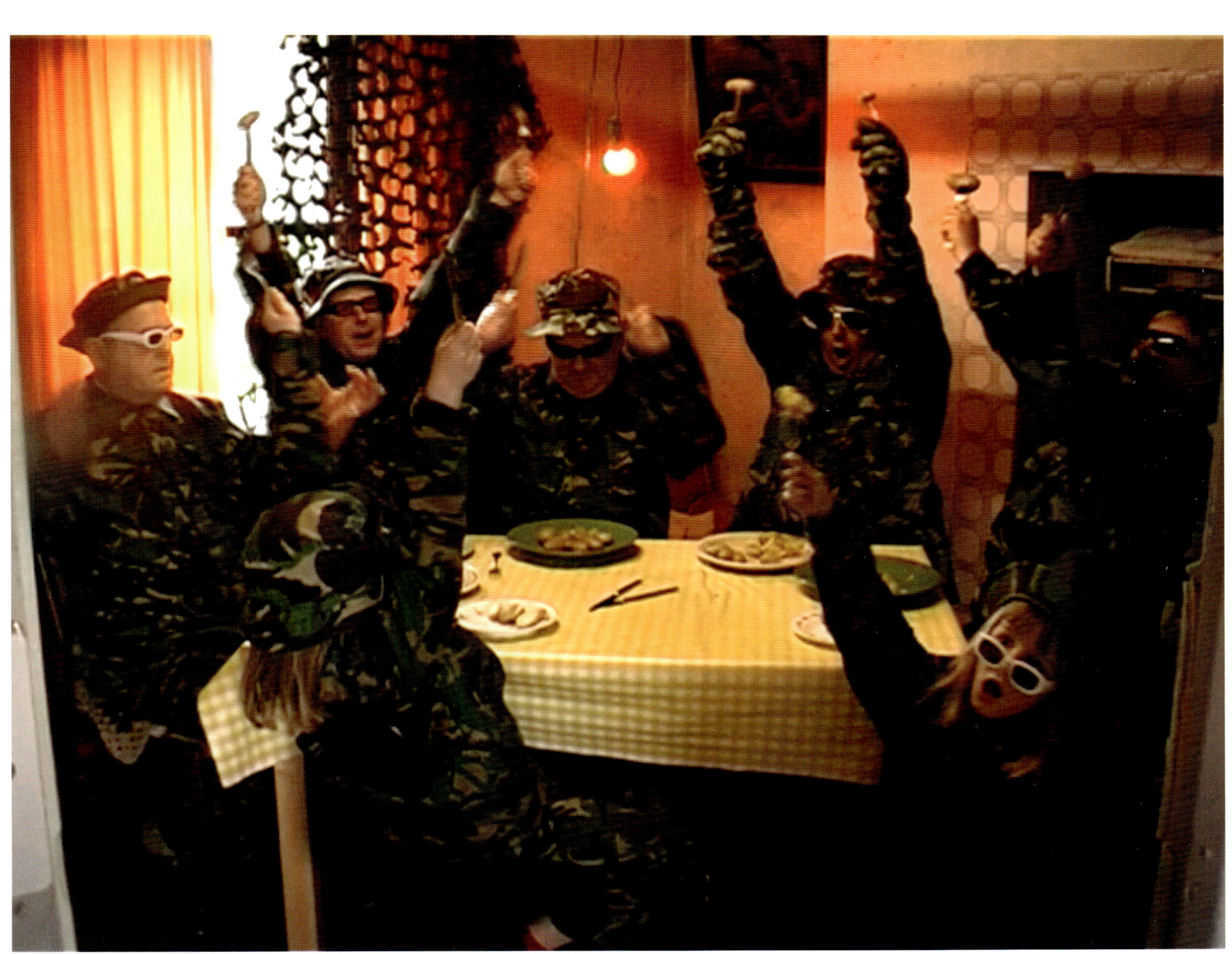

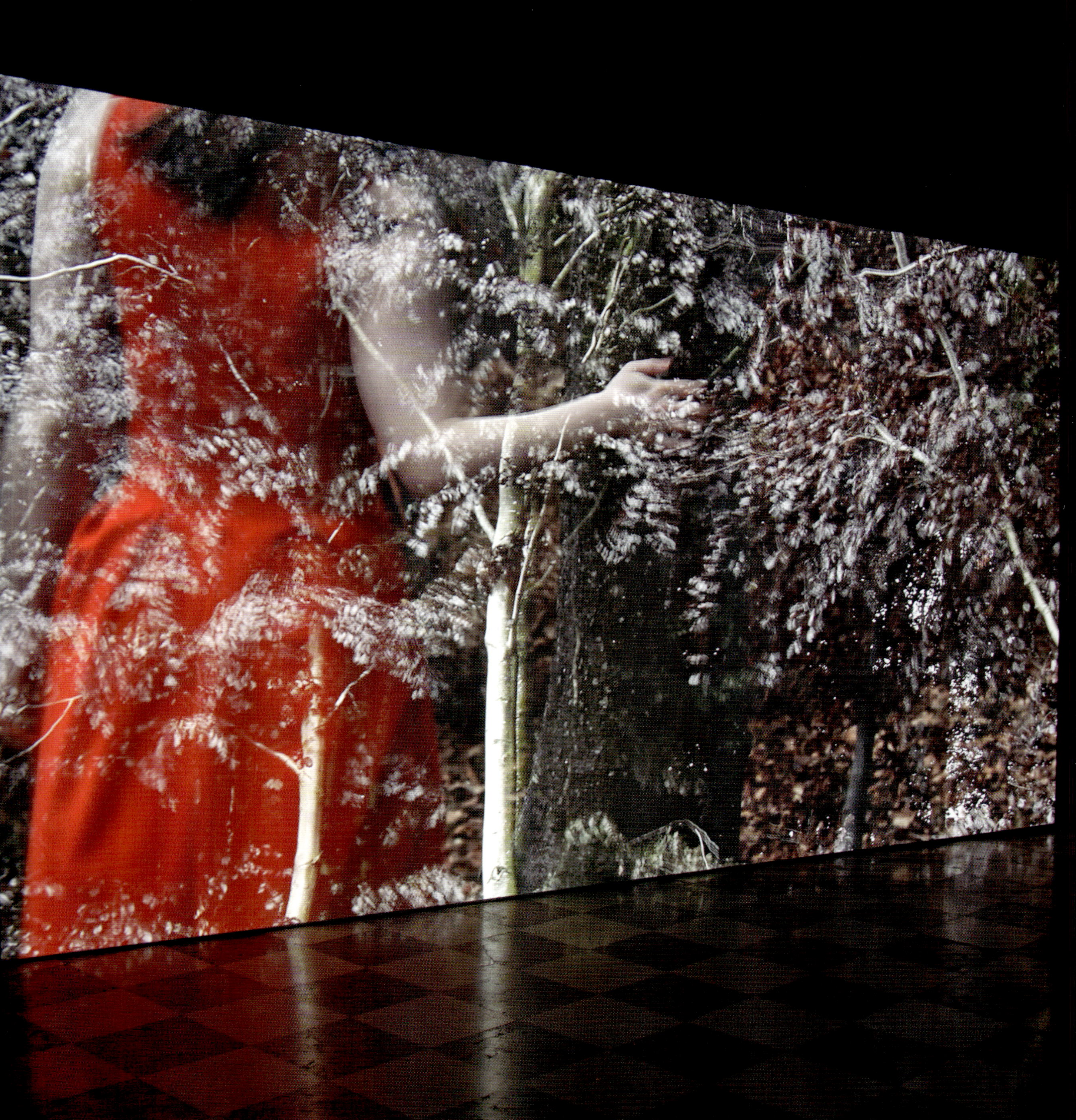

emphasise the physicality and presence of the body.[vi]

Other artists whose lens-based artworks at the museum have been supported by the Derek Williams Trust are photographers Richard Billingham, Martin Parr and Bedwyr Williams. They also include lecturers such as Keith Arnatt and Paul Seawright at the successive institutions concerned with teaching and researching photography and film at Newport. In addition, trust grant-supported DVDs have been acquired from Shimon Attie, Andrea Büttner, David Cushway, Tim Davies and Anthony Shapland. A particularly strong interest in *Artes Mundi* artists and prizewinners leading to the acquisition of video works from a wide international arena is explored in chapter 16.

A young woman in a red dress continually circles around trees and is rapidly interrupted, through cutting and editing, by images of branches, woodland and red-painted numbers on trunks signifying that they are to be felled.

vi   Sharon Morris and David Chandler, *Inside the View: Helen Sear*, Ffotogallery Wales Ltd., 2012

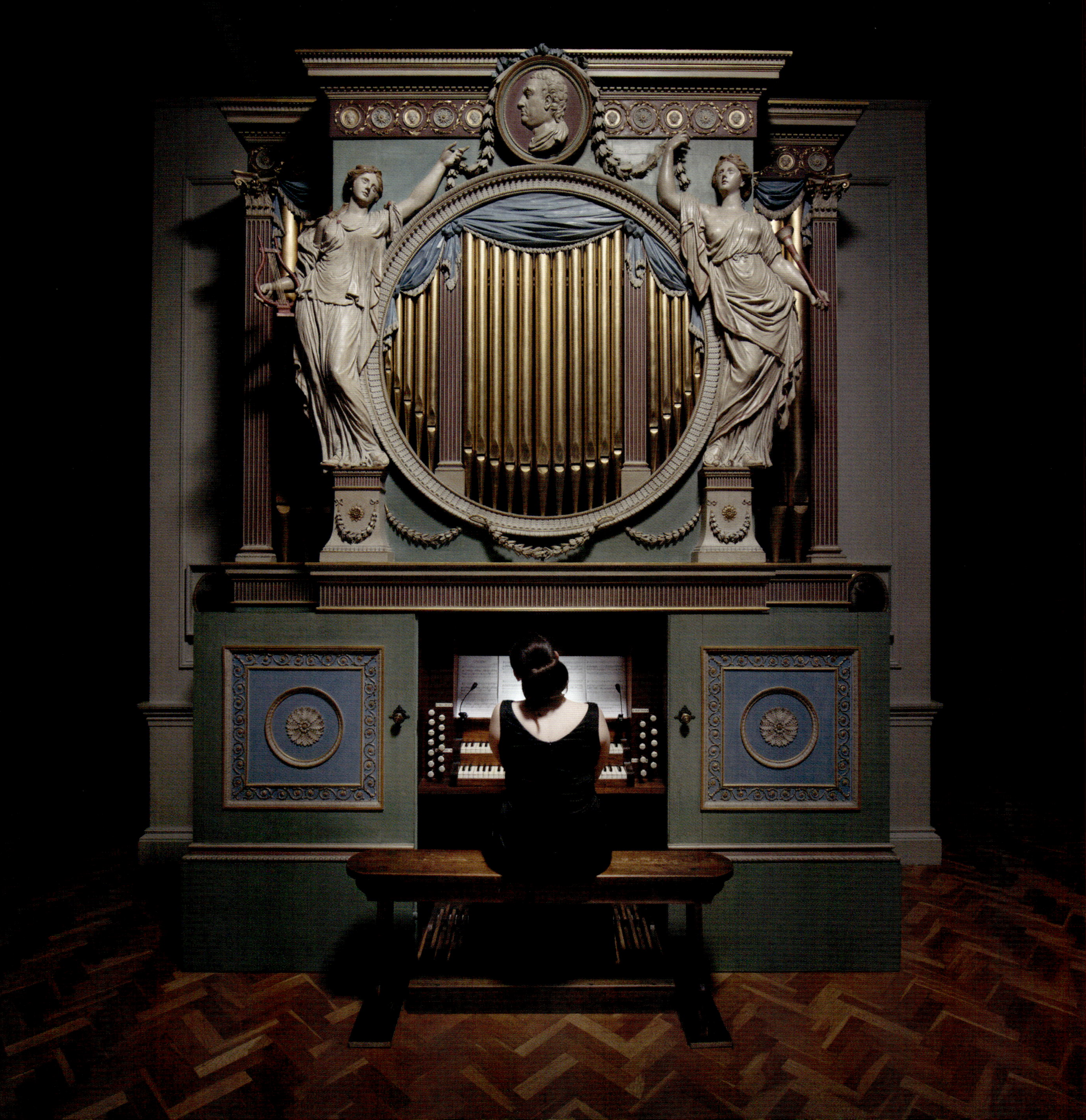

16. VISUAL ART AND THE HUMAN CONDITION: SUPPORTING *ARTES MUNDI*

65. Ragnar Kjartansson, *The Sky in a Room*, installation and performance at the museum, 2018. The organist is playing and singing Gino Paoli's 1960 release *Il Cielo in una Stanza*. Commissioned by Amgueddfa Cymru – National Museum Wales and *Artes Mundi* with Art Fund support after winning the Derek Williams Trust Purchase Prize, *Artes Mundi* 6, 2015.

In early 2018 a big surprise awaited regular visitors to the upper floor of Amgueddfa Genedlaethol Caerdydd – National Museum Cardiff. Eighteenth-century paintings had been removed to leave large areas of ornately-patterned blue wall fabric. A rota of singing organists played continually a song on Sir Watkin Williams Wynn's chamber organ.

This was a site-specific installation and performance by Icelandic artist Ragnar Kjartansson. Shortlisted for the 2014 international art prize and exhibition *Artes Mundi* 6, Kjartansson received the Derek Williams Trust Purchase Award for a film installation *The Visitors*. Sometimes this prize has implied the acquisition by the museum of a work in the exhibition. On this occasion, though, it led to the commission by *Artes Mundi* and the museum, supported by the Art Fund, of a new artwork, a performance entitled *The Sky in a Room* (fig. 65) for which the museum acquired certain rights. Named after an Italian love song, *Il Cielo in una Stanza*, written by Gino Paoli and released in 1960, it alludes to a love so intense that space and time become meaningless with walls and ceiling transforming into forest and sky. The artist has intensified this experience by hypnotic repetition.[i]

The Derek Williams Trust has, since its inception, grant-aided the acquisition of artworks from *Artes Mundi* for Amgueddfa Cymru – National Museum Wales. The trust, indeed, supported the establishment of the prize and its related exhibition at the museum, which was first held in 2004. Originally the idea of artist and cultural entrepreneur William Wilkins, it was conceived and based in Wales as a biennial event to celebrate how visual artists interpret the human condition. With an enticing prize of £40,000 competition has, unsurprisingly, been strong. It showcases artists recognised

A rota of singing organists played continually a song on Sir Watkin Williams Wynn's chamber organ.

i   Massimiliano Gioni, 'Ragnar Kjartansson: Repetita iuvant' in Karen Mackinnon ed., *Artes Mundi 6*, Artes Mundi Prize Limited, 2014, 50-55; Nicholas Thornton *et al.*, *Ragnar Kjartansson: The Sky in a Room*, Artes Mundi / Amgueddfa Cymru – National Museum Wales, 2018

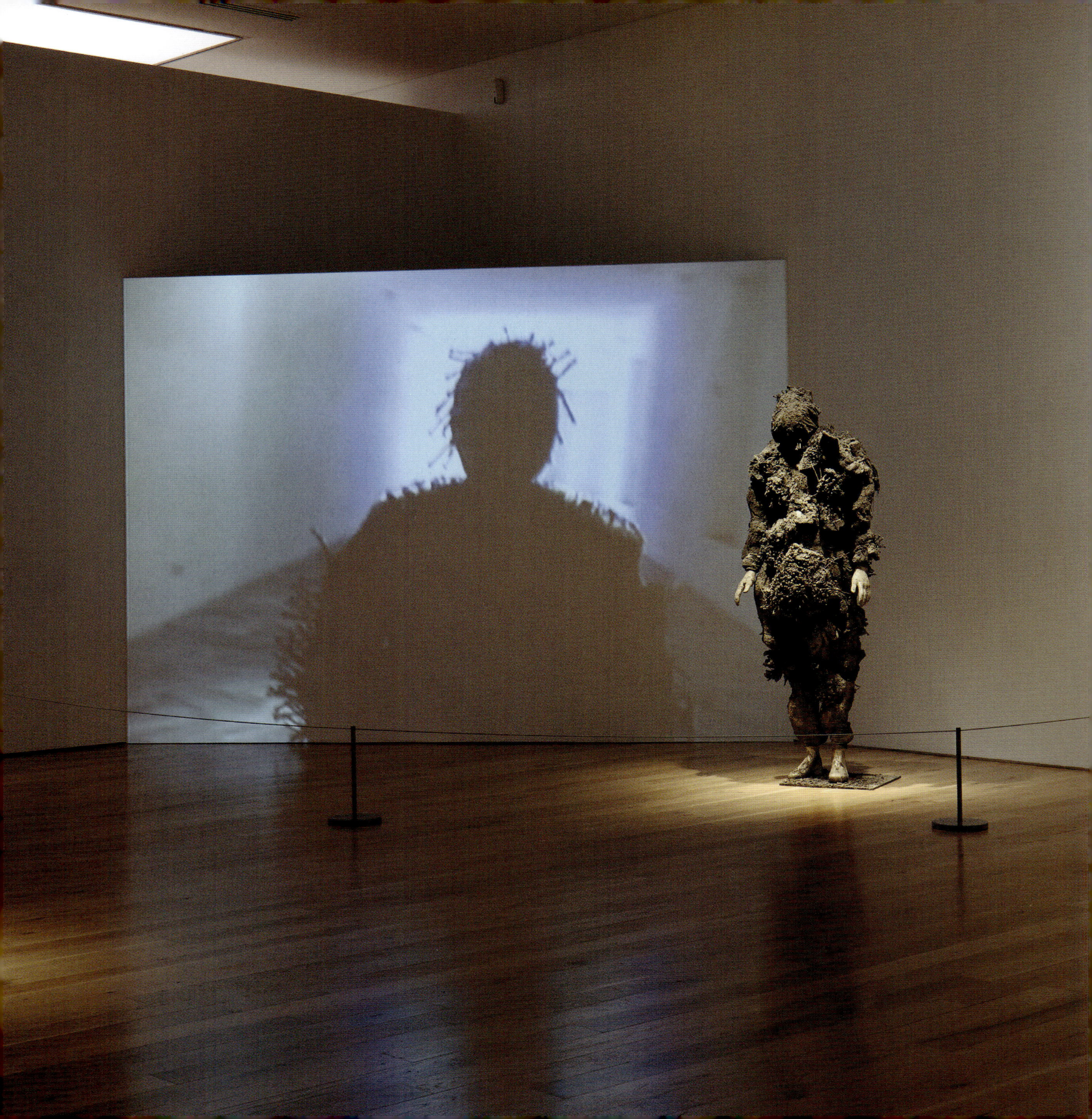

66. Tania Bruguera, *Destierro*,
performance film recording with costume,
1998-99. Acquired by Amgueddfa Cymru –
National Museum Wales after winning the
Derek Williams Trust Purchase Prize, *Artes
Mundi* 5, 2012.

Bruguera's art is concerned with power structures and is an active attempt to influence them. Critical of both art institutions and cultural and political establishments, her social interventions involve the public in exploring self-determination.

in their own country who are emerging internationally.

In its early days the acquisition of works by *Artes Mundi* artists for the museum was less formalised. A significant video installation work was purchased from South African Berni Searle, one of the artists short-listed in the first year. Others were acquired from the partners Brazilian Mauricio Dias and Swiss Walter Riedweg as well as, with Art Fund support, the Finn Eija-Liisa Ahtila, from *Artes Mundi* 2 in 2006, and Afghan-born Lida Abdul, from *Artes Mundi* 3 in 2008. A sculpture by the Romanian Mircea Cantor was, in addition that year, gifted by the artist to the museum.

Moscow artist Olga Chernysheva's seven-minute long 2003 black and white video *The Train* was purchased from the 2010 *Artes Mundi* 4. It portrays in a documentary style a scene from everyday Russian life in the turbulent post-communist era. The video follows a blind beggar as he walks down the central passageway of a train reciting Alexander Pushkin's poem to a school-friend, *A Message to Yudin*. The recitation gives the situation considerable poignancy.[ii]

The acquisition of works from the well-established event became more formalised in 2012 with *Artes Mundi* 5 and the introduction of the Derek Williams Trust Purchase Award of £30,000. That year this was presented to politically-active Cuban performance artist Tania Bruguera. Having been short-listed for *Artes Mundi*, she exhibited her 2009 video *Tatlin's Whisper no. 6 (Havana version)*. The trust award led to the purchase of a film of her 1998-99 performance work *Destierro (Displacement)* (fig. 66) with its related costume in textile, earth, glue, wood and nails of an African Nkisi Nkonde religious fetish. Bruguera's art is concerned with power structures and is an active attempt to influence them. Critical of both art institutions and cultural and political establishments, her social interventions involve the public in exploring self-

---

ii   Charles Merewether, 'Olga Chernysheva: Re-collecting the future' in Tessa Hartog ed., *Artes Mundi 4*,
      Artes Mundi Prize Limited, 2010, 58-65

determination. The much-feared fetish traditionally included relics and granted wishes in return for promises sealed with nails. The maker of an unkept promise was sought out by the spirit. The artist, who wore the costume in Havana, used it allegorically to highlight Cuban Government promises made but never kept.[iii]

Bedwyr Williams's *Tyrrau Mawr (Big Towers)* (fig. 67) was a striking exhibit in the 2016 exhibition for *Artes Mundi* 7. This high-density video installation was projected onto a large wall on a twenty-minute loop. Using cinematic computer-imaging technology, a backdrop in the form of a matt painting is seen for much longer than might normally occur. A potentous voice, that of the artist, reinforced by dramatic rumbling horn music, describes an imaginary scene in which a global city is, bizarrely, built around a lake near Cadair Idris. In gigantic apartment blocks thousands of lights are turned on and off as night and day alternate. Clouds race across mountains and lights twinkle through swirling mist. Like much of Williams's work, it exposes, satirically, the territory between banality and extreme seriousness. It received the Derek Williams Trust Purchase Award and the work entered the collection.[iv]

Many of the works acquired by Amgueddfa Cymru – National Museum Wales from *Artes Mundi* new-media and performance art have particular archival and presentation requirements. They have to be preserved in cool storage and may need to be backed-up regularly. Time-based media vary in their intended scale, complexity and immersiveness. Their presentation may depend upon the retention of obsolete technologies. In 2015 at the museum a 1968 performance work, *Adam on St Agnes' Eve*, was evoked during the exhibition Silent Explosion: Ivor Davies and Destruction in Art using its traces, sound, light and film transferred to DVD. Indeed, the museum has considerable experience in presenting such dynamic art.

67. **Bedwyr Williams,** *Tyrrau Mawr,* still from twenty-minute video installation loop showing at the museum, 2016. Acquired by Amgueddfa Cymru – National Museum Wales after winning the Derek Williams Trust Purchase Prize, *Artes Mundi* 7, 2017

Like much of Williams's work, it exposes, satirically, the territory between banality and extreme seriousness. It received the Derek Williams Trust Purchase Award and the work entered the collection.

---

iii   Kathy Noble, 'Tania Bruguera' in Tessa Hartog ed., *Artes Mundi 5*, Artes Mundi Prize Limited, 2012, 44-49; taniabruguera.com

iv   Ryan Gander and Bedwyr Williams, 'Email Conversation between Ryan Gander and Bedwyr Williams' in Karen Mackinnon ed., *Artes Mundi 7*, Artes Mundi Prize Limited, 2016, 68-77

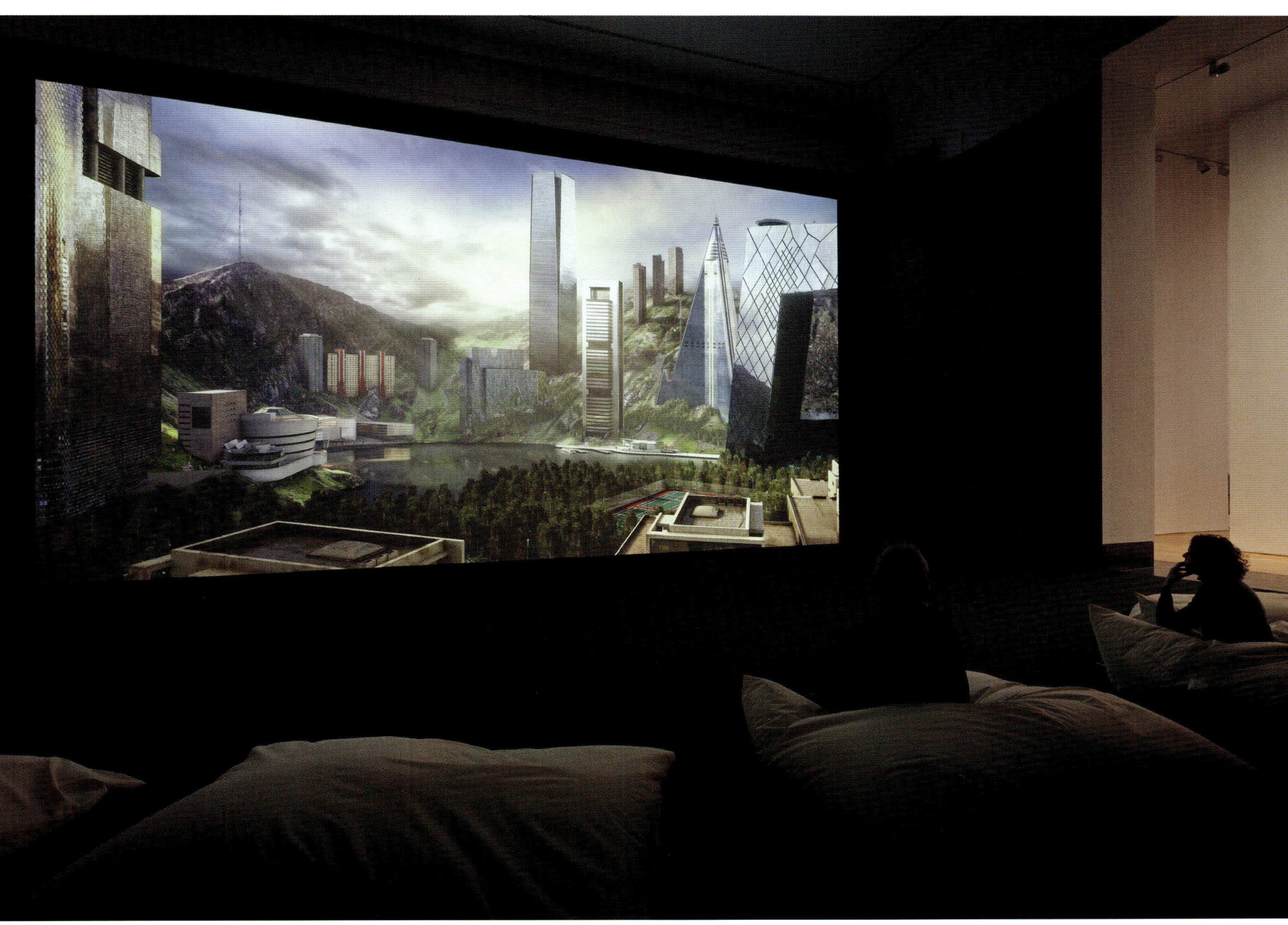

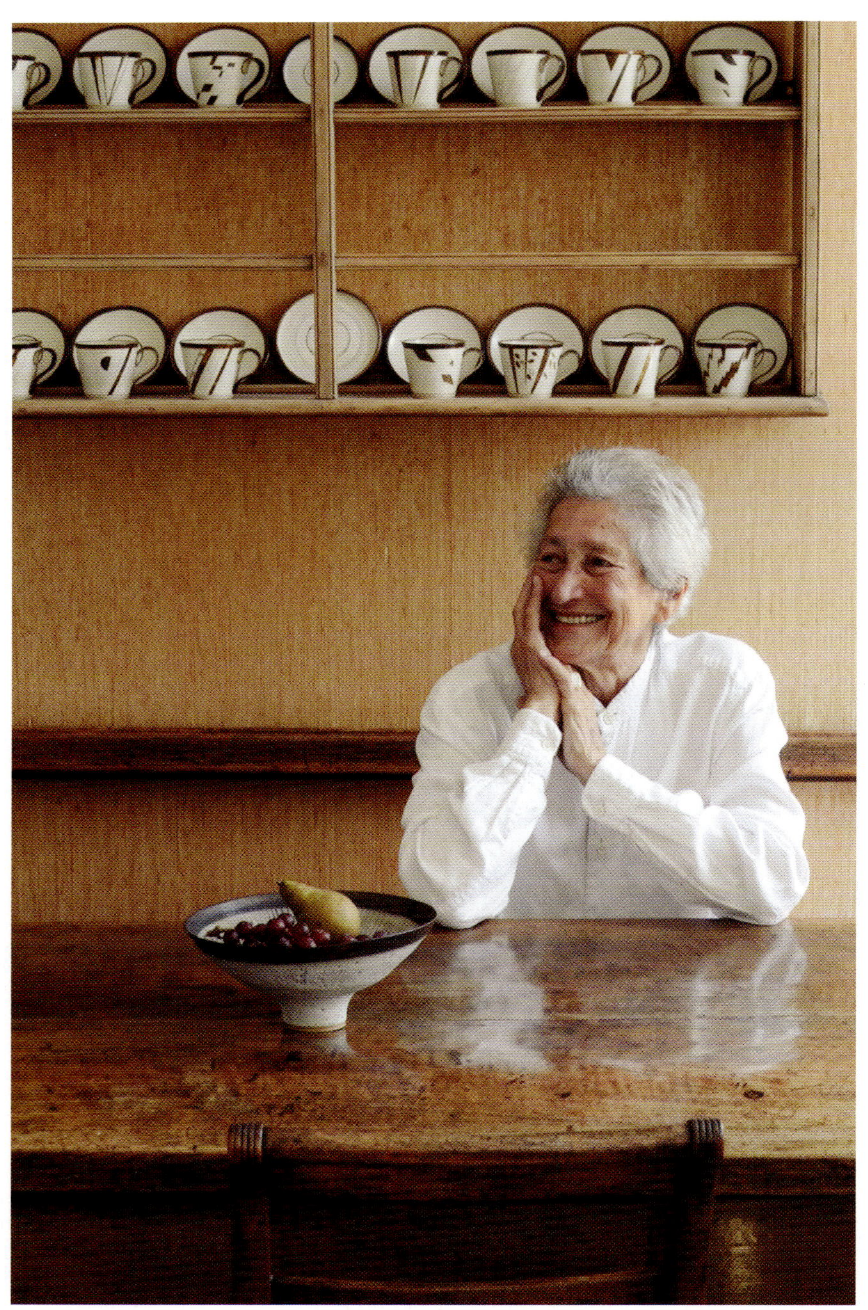

68. Anita Besson in her Hampstead home, 2015.

At the centre of the museum's 2017-18 exhibition Who Decides? Making Connections with Contemporary Art was an impressive display of modern studio ceramics. This was the first complete showing of a major 2015 bequest of seventy-four catalogued items from ceramics dealer Anita Besson's private collection to the Derek Williams Trust.[i]

Anita Besson (1933-2015) opened Galerie Besson at one end of the stylish Royal Arcade off London's Old Bond Street in 1988. Unusually it specialised in ceramics as fine art. It ran until 2011, the opening show featuring Lucie Rie, and showed more than a hundred and fifty artists in over two hundred exhibitions. Besson, born in Zurich to a French-Swiss mother and German-Swiss father, had settled in England in 1956 and, after working as a translator, pursued a career in commercial art galleries.

William Wilkins, Derek Williams trustee and art adviser, has worked closely with Andrew Renton, the museum's keeper of art, and his predecessor Oliver Fairclough and others to build upon its already outstanding ceramics collection. Wilkins, who has a keen appreciation of ceramics himself, first met Anita Besson in 1986. She was impressed with the commitment of the trust to develop and ensure the display of outstanding fine and applied art at Cardiff. Besson invited Wilkins to her Hampstead home to select work from her personal ceramic collection that would complement that in the trust's collection.

'Studio Pottery', a term dating from the 1920s, comes in many forms but tends to refer to ceramics made by hand on a relatively small scale. Originally it was distinguished from 'art pottery' which was produced on a more industrial scale. Influential early practitioners were Bernard Leach (1887-1979) in St Ives, his one-time Japanese

'Studio Pottery', a term dating from the 1920s, comes in many forms but tends to refer to ceramics made by hand on a relatively small scale.

---

i   William Wilkins *et al.*, *Anita Besson: The Derek Williams Bequest*, Erskine, Hall & Coe for the Derek Williams Trust in association with Amgueddfa Cymru – National Museum Wales, 2016; David Whiting, 'Anita Besson obituary', *The Guardian*, 1 November 2015; galeriebesson.co.uk; A complete list of items in Anita Besson's bequest may be found in Appendix IV

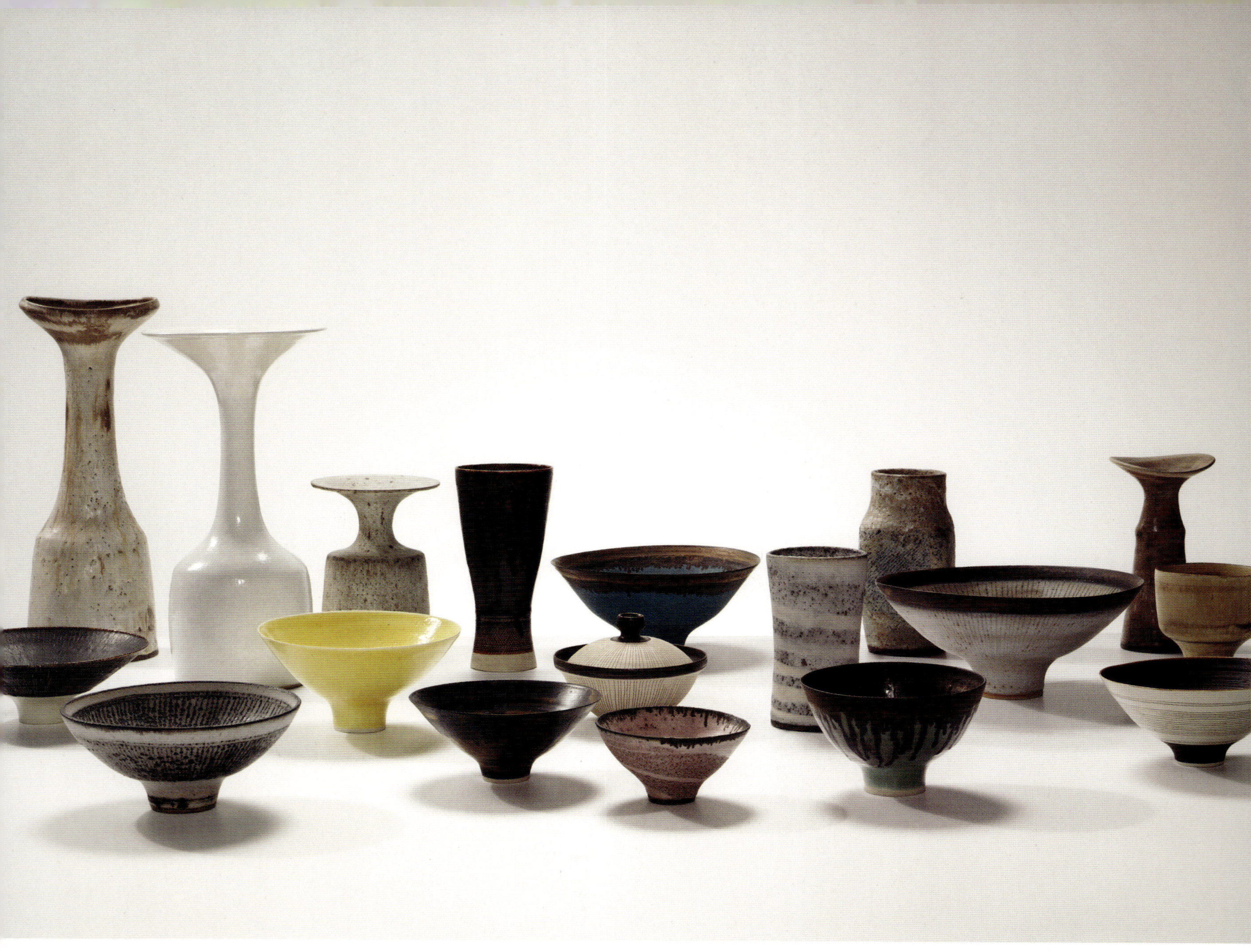

Tenacious and single-minded, her innovative, distinctive and elegant wheel-turned pots, bowls and vases were minimalist, exploring materials, flowing form, surface texture, sgraffito decoration, colour, layered slips and glazes.

colleague Shōji Hamada (1894-1978) and Leach's pupil Michael Cardew (1901-83). Another was William Staite Murray (1881-1962), head of ceramics at the Royal College of Art, who rejected even the need for functionality in his pots. Nevertheless, Leach, Hamada and Staite Murray were all steeped in eastern philosophies and regarded ceramics as a fine art and spiritual pursuit. Cardew, though, was rather more focused upon making large quantities of functional slip-decorated wares.[ii]

It is, however, Lucie Rie (1902-95) and Hans Coper (1920-81), whose work Anita Besson had known since childhood, who are most strongly represented in her bequest. As cultured refugees in 1930s London from, respectively, Austria and Germany, both made forms which stretched convention in British studio pottery.[iii]

Lucie Rie, a friend of Leach, was a private person who worked from a Paddington mews studio. Tenacious and single-minded, her innovative, distinctive and elegant wheel-turned pots, bowls and vases were minimalist, exploring materials, flowing form, surface texture, sgraffito decoration, colour, layered slips and glazes (fig. 69). Ceramicist Alison Britton has succinctly described her pots as 'a poised combination of daring and restraint.'[iv]

Rie, internationally recognised, has had a huge influence upon modern ceramics and in raising the status of the studio potter. She taught in the 1960s at Camberwell School of Art. Her work, already evolving in pre-war Vienna, relates to European modernism and to interior design and architecture generally.

After the war Hans Coper assisted Rie in making fashionable ceramic buttons. She encouraged him to become a potter. He, in turn, restored Rie's confidence and encouraged her to pursue the modernist forms first seen in her pre-war work. Theirs

---

ii   Oliver Watson, *Studio Pottery*, Phaidon / Victoria and Albert Museum, 1993

iii   Margo Coatts ed., *Lucie Rie and Hans Coper: Potters in Parallel*, Barbican Art Gallery, 1997

iv   Alison Britton, 'Lucie Rie – Urban Idyll/Ideal' in Emmanuel Cooper ed., *Lucie Rie*, Ceramic Review, 2002, 40-50

was a vital collaboration and friendship. They shared a small London workshop for twelve years and jointly produced tableware. Coper was less interested than Rie in colour and more in sculptural, often totemic, compound shapes in stoneware.

In the 1970s and 80s new approaches to ceramics emerged. A hand-building tendency opened up the wider possibilities of sculptural form in clay although it never entirely displaced the tradition of wheel-thrown, subtly-glazed pottery.

Another potter well represented in the Besson bequest is Ian Godfrey (1942-1992). Rie regarded him as her best student at Camberwell. His intensely-felt work was decorated with incised patterns and a distinctive vocubulary of whimsical animal forms and archaeological references.[v]

Ewen Henderson (1934-2000) challenged traditional notions of ceramics by making energetic, expressive sculptural forms with complex textures. He was much inspired by visits to the museum in Cardiff as well as by leading art-educator Harry Thubron at Barry Summer School. Later, in London, he studied with Coper and Rie.[vi]

Catalonian potter Claudi Casanovas, born in 1956, builds up layers, like geological strata, of different clays in a single work. Interested in texture and colour, he uses materials such as sand, sawdust and straw to represent landscape-making processes. He was encouraged by Japanese potter Ryoji Koie, born in 1938, to find his own voice by developing the confidence and freedom to learn from mistakes. Koie himself makes teabowls which have a found rather than thrown quality.[vii]

Anita Besson's bequest to the trust greatly enhances a significant and expanding collection of international ceramics at Amgueddfa Cymru – National Museum Wales.

70. Hans Coper, *Large Thistle*, stoneware, c.1965, 32 x 24 cm. Anita Besson bequest to the Derek Williams Trust, 2015.

71. Claudi Casanovas, *Rectangular Wall Plate*, stoneware and porcelain, 1989, 100 x 87 cm. Anita Besson bequest to the Derek Williams Trust, 2015.

In the 1970s and 80s new approaches to ceramics emerged. A hand-building tendency opened up the wider possibilities of sculptural form in clay although it never entirely displaced the tradition of wheel-thrown, subtly-glazed pottery.

---

v   David Whiting, *An Enchanted Landscape: Ian Godfrey*, Oxford Ceramics Gallery, 2019

vi   Anon., 'Ewen Henderson, Obituary', *The Times* 30 November 2000

vii Geraint Roberts, 'Filling the Silence: Towards an Understanding of Claudi Casanovas' Blocks' in Jo Dahn and Jeffrey Jones eds., *Interpreting Ceramics: Selected Essays*, Wunderkammer Press, 2013

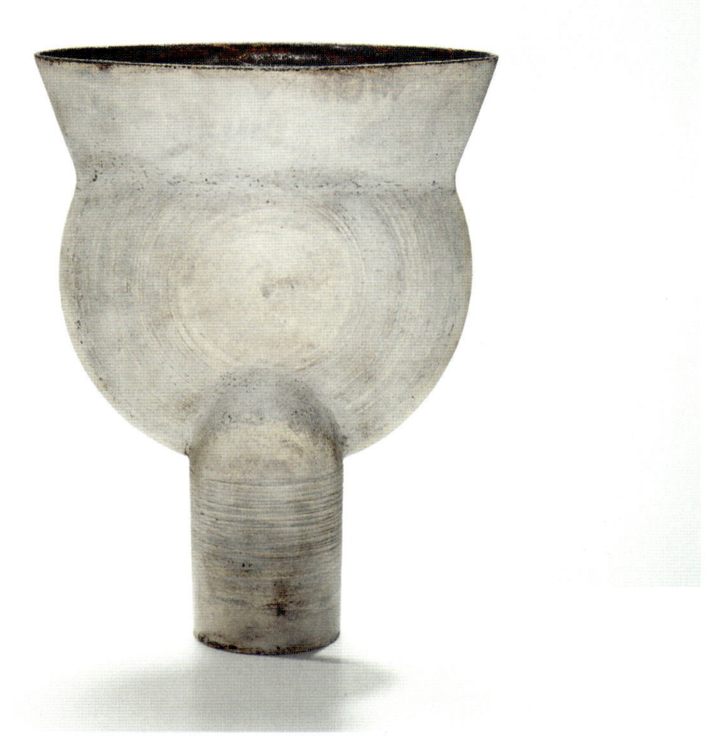

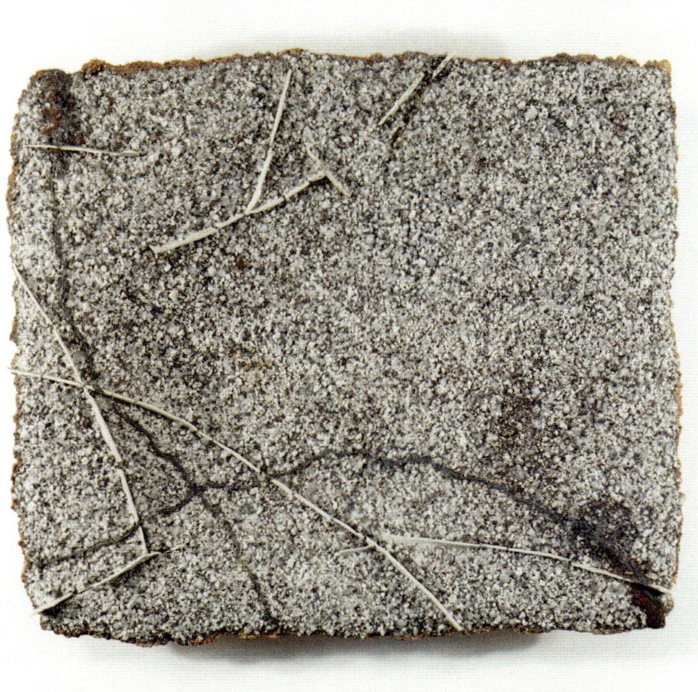

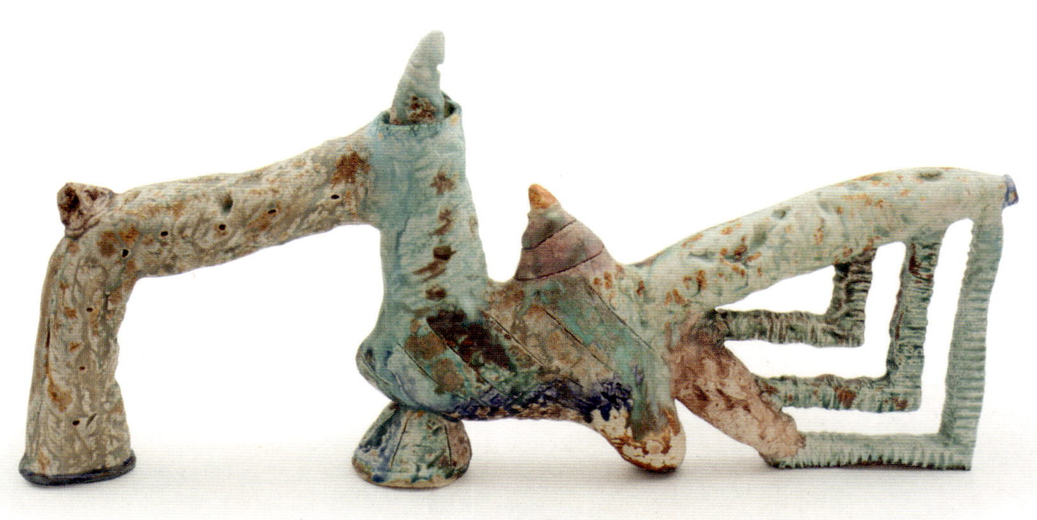

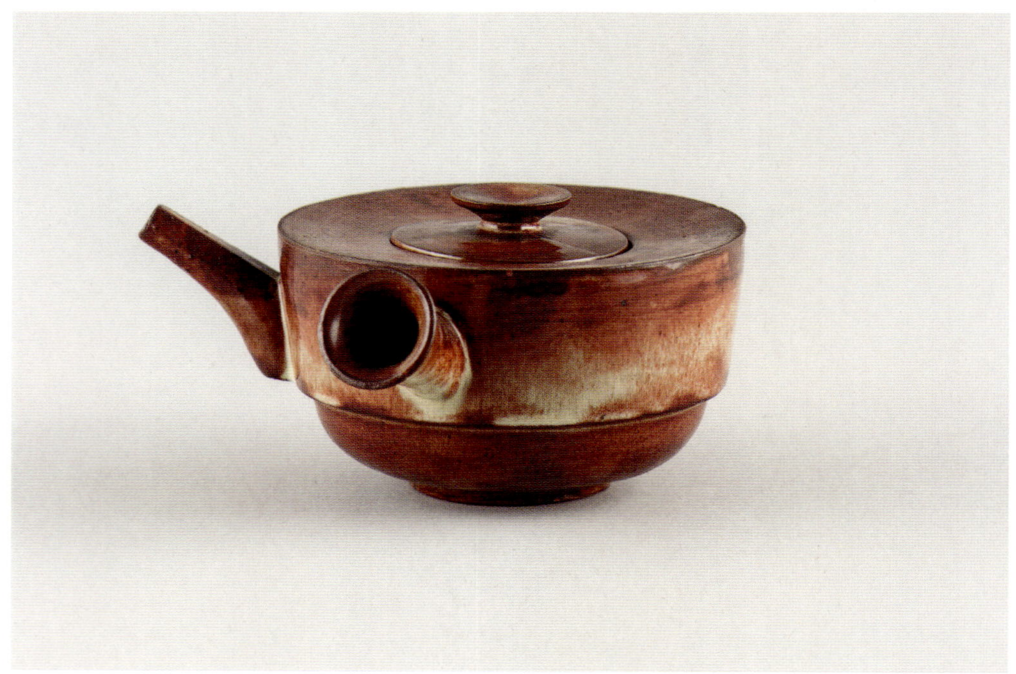

18. MODERN AND CONTEMPORARY CERAMICS: FOR UTILISATION OR CONTEMPLATION?

72. Angus Suttie, *Extended Teapot*,
Stoneware, c.1991, 260 x 560 x 60 cm.
Acquired by Amgueddfa Cymru – National
Museum Wales with support from the
Derek Williams Trust, 2018.

73. Theodor Bogler, *Combination Teapot*,
(Bauhaus Ceramic Workshop, Dornburg),
stoneware with a tin glaze, cast and
assembled, 1923, 16 x16 cm.
Trust purchase, 2018.

Bogler's teapot, a model for teaching and future mass production, was radical at the time although, due to its subsequent wide influence, this may not be apparent to modern eyes.

Ceramics are a major area of collecting by the Derek Williams Trust, reflecting not only its own interests but also those of recent keepers of art at Amgueddfa Cymru – National Museum Wales. This chapter explores a selection of internationally significant modern and contemporary ceramics either purchased or supported by the trust.

A recent acquisition by the trust is a 1923 cast stoneware and tin-glazed *Combination Teapot* by Theodor Bogler (fig. 73). Bogler (1897-1968) was a member of the innovative and practical Bauhaus Ceramic Workshop, Dornburg, Germany, part of the nearby influential Bauhaus school of art and design in Weimar.

The school, founded in 1919 by architect and designer Walter Gropius, was fundamentally concerned with breaking down artificial divisions between the fine and applied arts. Handicrafts were at the root of its teaching and its teachers included famous artists such as Paul Klee and Wassily Kandinsky. Bogler joined the ceramic workshop in 1921 and trained with craft master Max Krehan and form-design master Gerhard Marcks.[i]

Bogler's teapot, a model for teaching and future mass production, was radical at the time although, due to its subsequent wide influence, this may not be apparent to modern eyes. It demonstrated how a limited number of standardised cast parts could be assembled in numerous ways. To the main body shape a variety of handles, spouts and openings were added. Subtly-coloured monochrome glazes added character.

The short-lived ceramics workshop closed when the Bauhaus moved to Dessau in 1925. The Bauhaus itself was eventually dissolved in 1933 under pressure from the National Socialists or Nazis.

i   Magdalena Droste, *Bauhaus, 1919-1933*, Bauhaus-Archiv / Taschen, 2006, 68-72

In complete contrast, yet also focusing upon a conventional ceramic subject, Scotsman Angus Suttie's freely-expressive hand-built stoneware 1991 *Extended Teapot* (fig. 72) is one of three of his ceramics recently acquired by the museum and supported by the Derek Williams Trust. They were bought from a 2018 Ruthin Craft Centre exhibition of the artist's work. Everyday functional ceramics such as plates, cups, jugs, toast racks and ladles were Suttie's starting points for much more expressive sculptural forms. Originally working in earthenware he moved into stoneware for greater strength.[ii]

Suttie's work is postmodernist in the sense that it draws, often ironically and provocatively, upon eclectic historical influences such as south American ceramics and folk art, pre-Columbian architecture and surrealism. Visionary, witty, highly individualistic and emotionally charged, his ceramics are extravagant in form and painted in vivid colour.

Trained at Camberwell School of Art as a mature student, having originally studied drama, Suttie (1946-93) was born in Tealing, Angus, Scotland. He later taught at Morley College and Camberwell before becoming a full-time studio artist in Clerkenwell. Ceramics became a way in which he was able to explore his identity, sexuality and emotions. The works became more serious as he addressed the death from AIDS of his partner and, sadly, he would also die from similar complications.

A slightly earlier purchase by the Derek Williams Trust was Edmund de Waal's 2005 *Group of fourteen porcelain dishes from the Arcanum exhibition* (fig. 74). The exhibition referred to had been held at the museum that year. De Waal has moved away from making single pots to create installations of transparent celadon-glazed white porcelain ceramics in minimalist settings that are often responses to specific collections and places. The simple, yet elegant, forms of his ceramics, such as shallow dishes or cylindrical jars, may reveal tiny indentations and subtle changes in both

---

ii   Philip Hughes and Simon Olding eds., *Angus Suttie*, Ruthin Craft Centre, 2018

colour and texture. He has also written extensively about ceramics.[iii]

De Waal, born in 1964, has spent time studying in Japan and lives in London. He was invited to be a guest curator and creator of a place-specific installation as part of a project at the museum entitled 'Arcanum: Mapping 18th-century porcelain'. The title alluded to the perceived mystical process of making porcelain. De Waal chose items from the museum's comprehensive de Winton collection of continental porcelain, created in the nineteenth century, and considered issues relating to them such their origin, manufacture, trade, use, patronage, taste and collection.[iv]

Exploring ways of displaying the porcelain, de Waal made vessels as part of the process. 'I have tried to isolate some objects and mass others,' he wrote, 'to change the rhythms of display.'[v] Groups of his dishes were placed in dialogue with historic pieces to suggest domestic place settings. In another installation, he made a wall of a hundred and fifty of his small pots in a contemporary response to historic traditions of displaying porcelain. This *Porcelain Wall* was acquired by the museum with support from the trust and other funders.

---

iii   Edmund de Waal, *20th Century Ceramics*, Thames & Hudson, 2003; Edmund de Waal, *The White Road: A Journey into Obsession,* Chatto and Windus, 2015

iv   Michael Tooby ed., *Aracanum – Mapping Eighteenth-Century European Porcelain: Edmund de Waal*, National Museum and Gallery, Cardiff, 2005

v   De Waal in Tooby, *ibid.*, 8

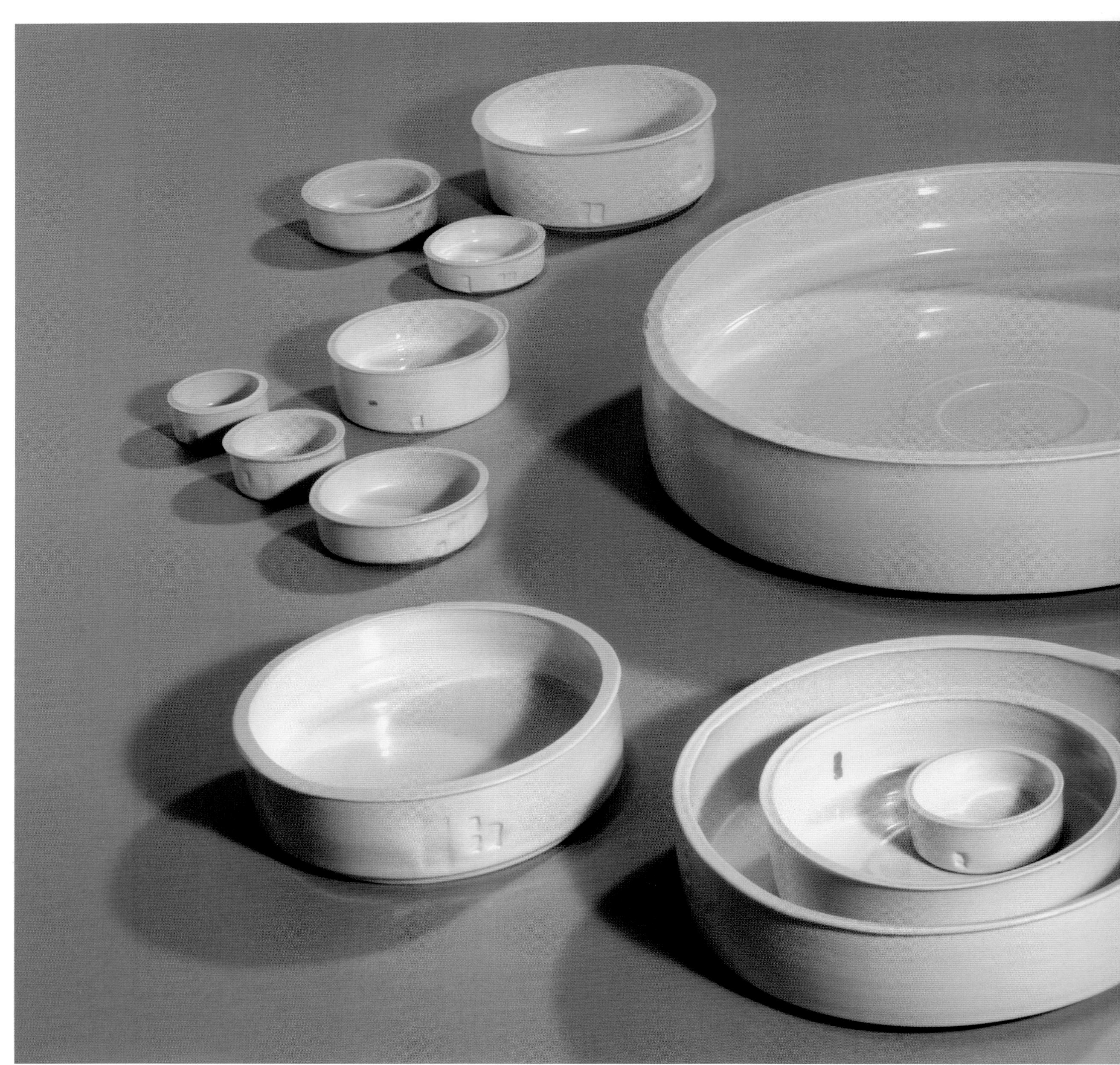

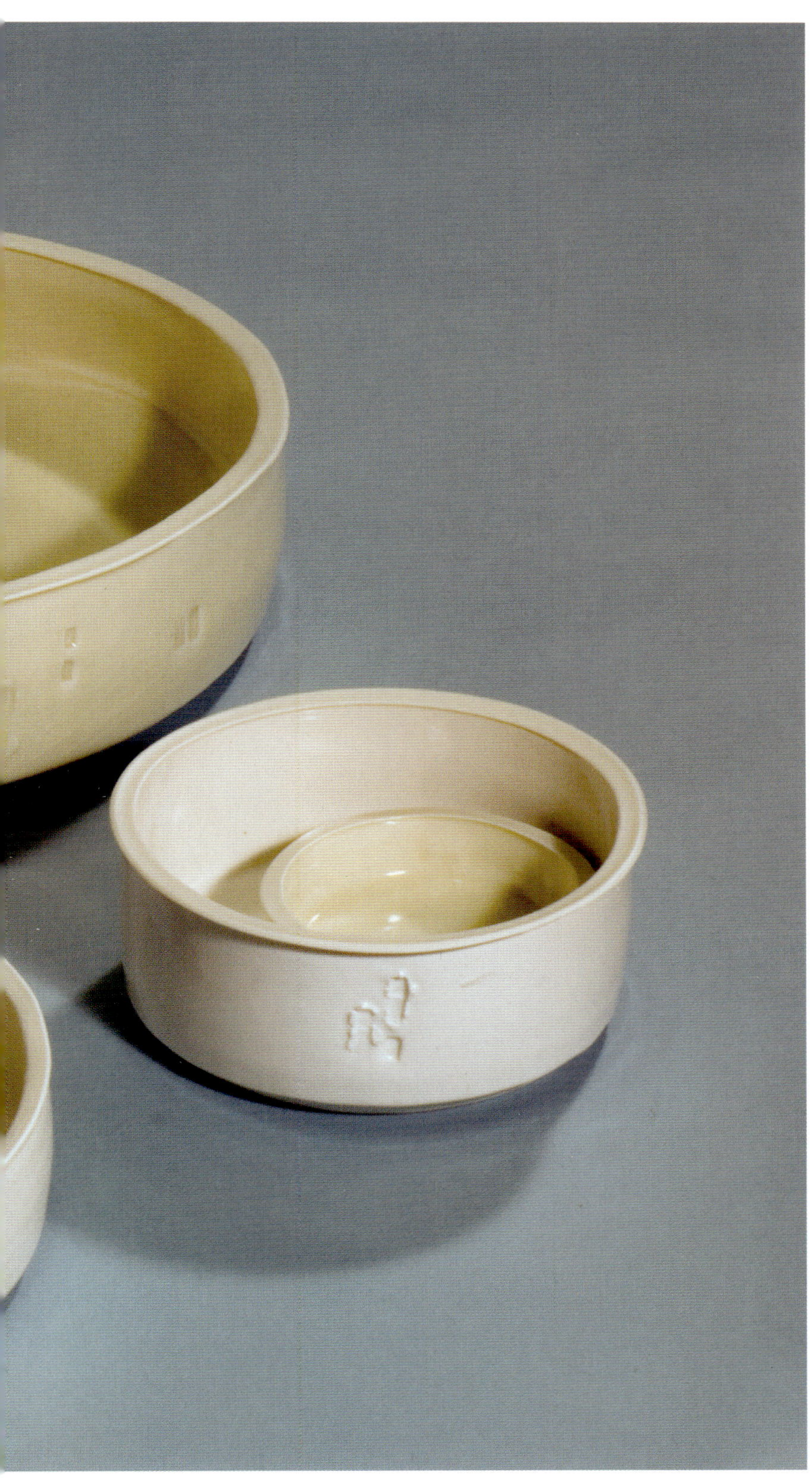

74. Edmund de Waal, *Group of fourteen dishes from the Arcanum exhibition*, porcelain, 2005, varied sizes up to 9 x 46 cm. Trust purchase, 2006.

Exploring ways of displaying the porcelain, de Waal made vessels as part of the process. 'I have tried to isolate some objects and mass others,' he wrote, 'to change the rhythms of display.'

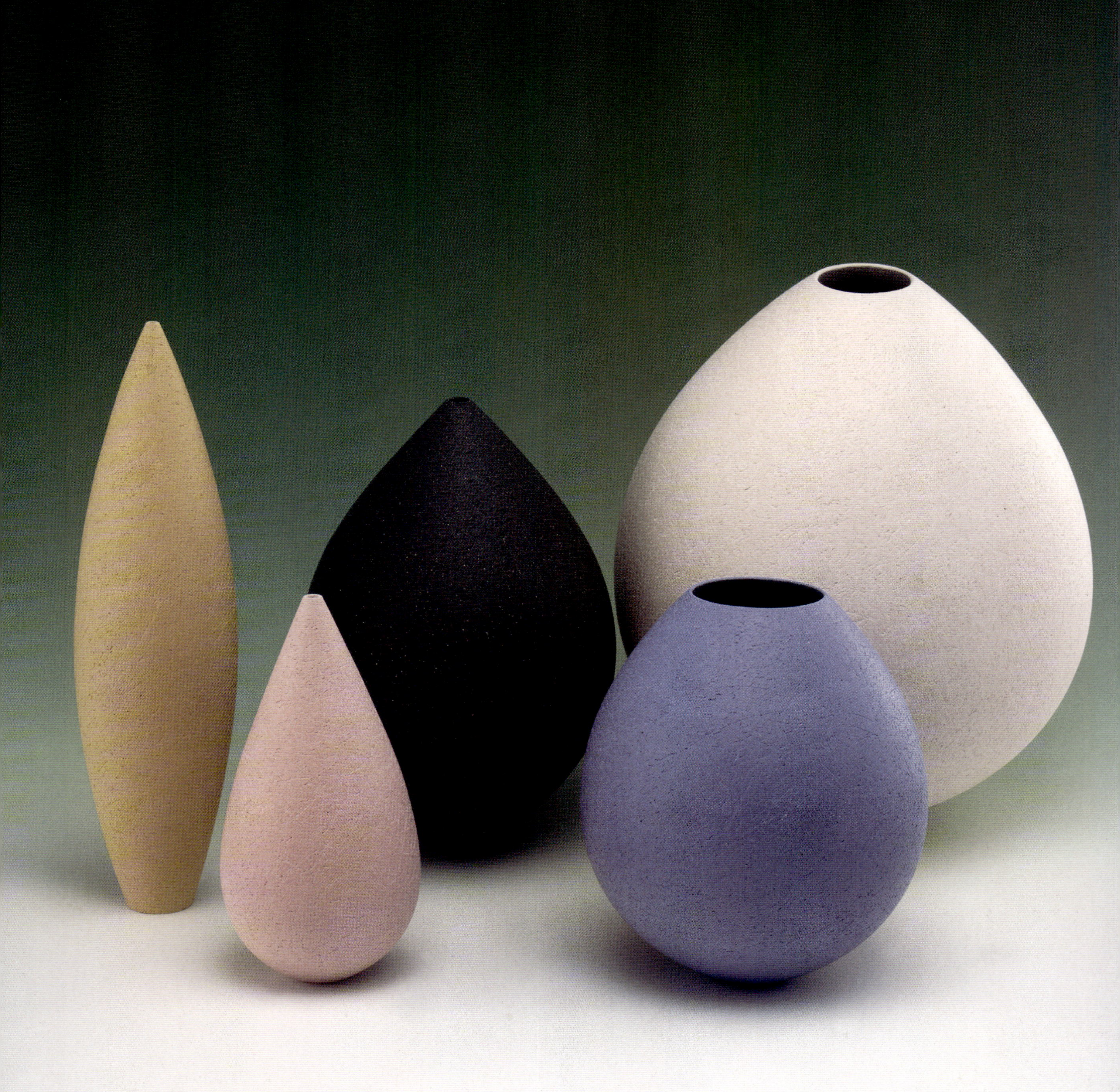

75. Christine Jones, *Vessels,* earthenware and stained earthenware, 2001, heights 21-34 cm, widths 11-29 cm. Trust purchase, 2001.

With the Derek Williams Trust's interest in studio ceramics, it is not surprising that it has been attracted to the work of remarkable ceramicists in Wales. This chapter considers some of these trust purchases and grant-aided works.

In 2001 the trust purchased a group of five earthenware and stained earthenware *Vessels* by Christine Jones (fig. 75). Born in 1955 and working from a Swansea studio, her ceramics are works for contemplation. They are influenced by the artist's receptivity to light over the sea and landscapes. Distinctive in both poised elegant form and gentle unglazed saturated colour, they exude a calm grounded tension. They absorb light and respond strongly to space, whether individually or in groups. Curiously, their pitted and scored surfaces reveal little about their making. With colour mixed in from the start, they have been coiled upwards and then pared down in a lengthy, repetitive process using grogged clay. The ground-up fired-clay particles have been dragged repeatedly across the surface. A craft and design gold-medal winner at the National Eisteddfod of Wales, Llanelli, in 2000, her more recent work sometimes includes patterns which are unified with the colour and form.[i]

Distinctive in both poised elegant form and gentle unglazed saturated colour, they exude a calm grounded tension. They absorb light and respond strongly to space, whether individually or in groups.

Ceramics as well as mixed-media landscape drawings by James Campbell (1942-2019) were acquired by the trust in 2006. His earthenware *Landscape with Road* (fig. 76) and *Man Bird* feature stylised, rhythmic and romantic landscapes. His work was often derived from childhood memories of the Campbell estates at Cawdor Castle, Scotland, and Stackpole in Pembrokeshire. The west Wales coast, where he lived at Manorbier, was a particularly strong influence. He strove to balance the forms of his hand-built slabbed and coiled pots, made from Staffordshire red clay overlain by white slip, with his landscape imagery.

---

i   Philip Hughes ed., *Christine Jones*, Ruthin Craft Centre, 2003

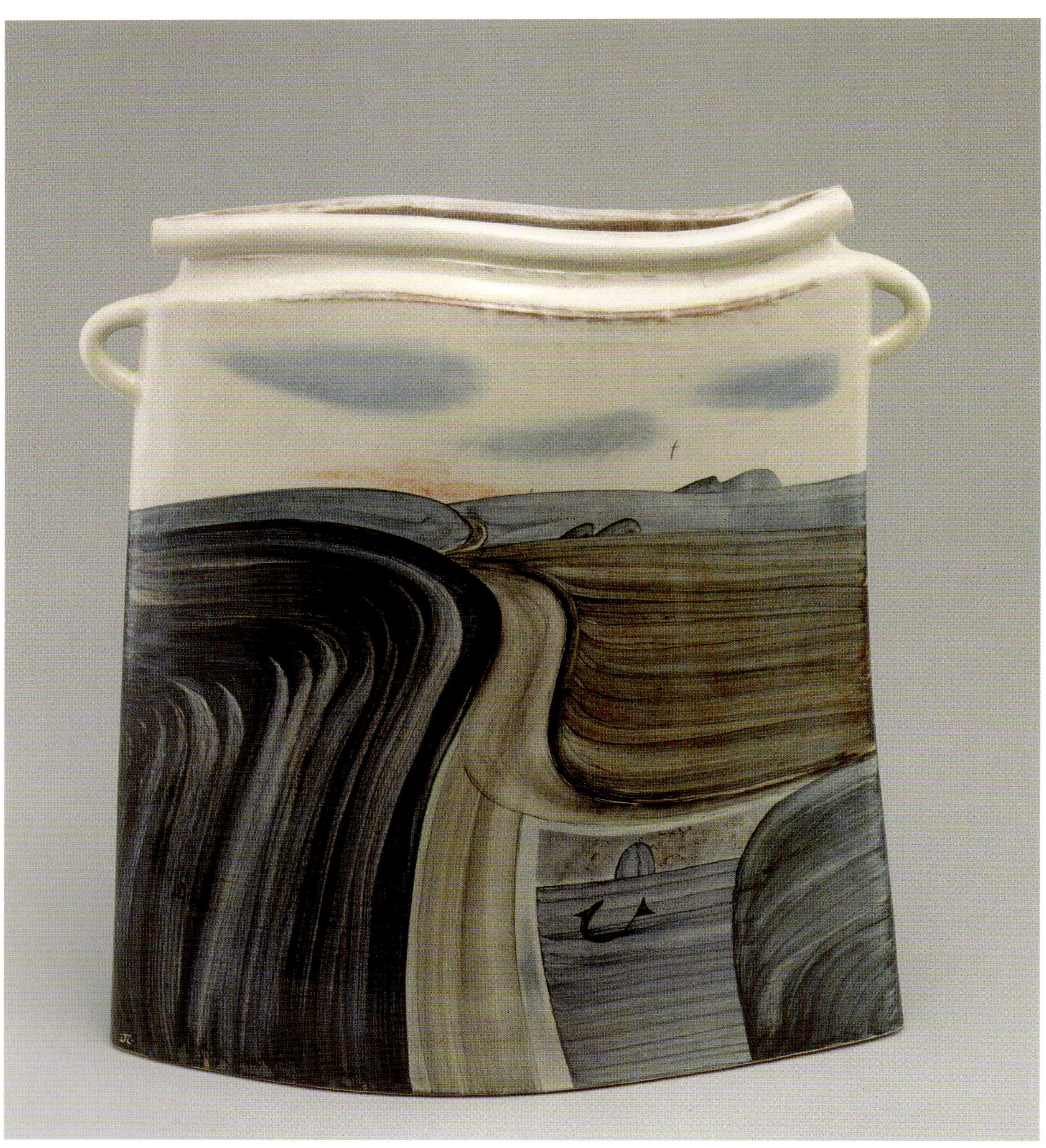

Amgueddfa Cymru – National Museum Wales purchased, with the support of the Derek Williams Trust, Cardiff ceramicist Claire Curneen's 2007 matt terracotta *In the Tradition of Smiling Angels* in 2009 (fig. 77). While Claire's earlier figures were female, these angels, as traditionally depicted, are male. Individuality emerges through the gestures of hands. Smiles convey both inner and outer blessedness and happiness and a spiky tree connects the figures to a landscape.[ii]

Claire's spiritual figures are influenced by Christian iconography and derive from the visual culture of Catholic Ireland, where she was born in 1968, as well as imagery from early Italian and Flemish painting. While saints and martyrs are often depicted, her work is deeply concerned with the human condition and the transience of life. She often uses porcelain, attracted by its pure whiteness, modelling upwards by hand and retaining a sense of the material used. Splashes of gold, suggesting blood, are a metaphor for interior value. They also reference a domestic ceramic decorative tradition.

In 2014 the trust acquired an intriguing group of related ceramic objects by Anne Gibbs entitled *Shift* (fig. 78). Born in 1966 and living in south Wales, she makes intricate, playful, yet often sinister, works in pastel-coloured bone china. These, as here, may be small-scale installations exploring spatial harmony and contrasts with a close attention to visual detail. Initially these works may induce a sense of peace and wellbeing but closer familiarity – awareness, perhaps, of a hard edge or sharp form – can reveal tension, disharmony, even a ritualistic or fetishistic quality. The objects in *Shift* are made from bone china, silk thread, wire and pins.

A former landscape architect, Anne is particularly affected by the texture and colour of landscape. Drawing, sometimes with liquid clay, and collecting found, and otherwise

ii   Philip Hughes ed., *Claire Curneen: Succour*, Ruthin Craft Centre, 2003; Amanda Roderick and Philip Hughes eds., *Claire Curneen: To this I put my name*, Ruthin Craft Centre / Mission Gallery, 2014

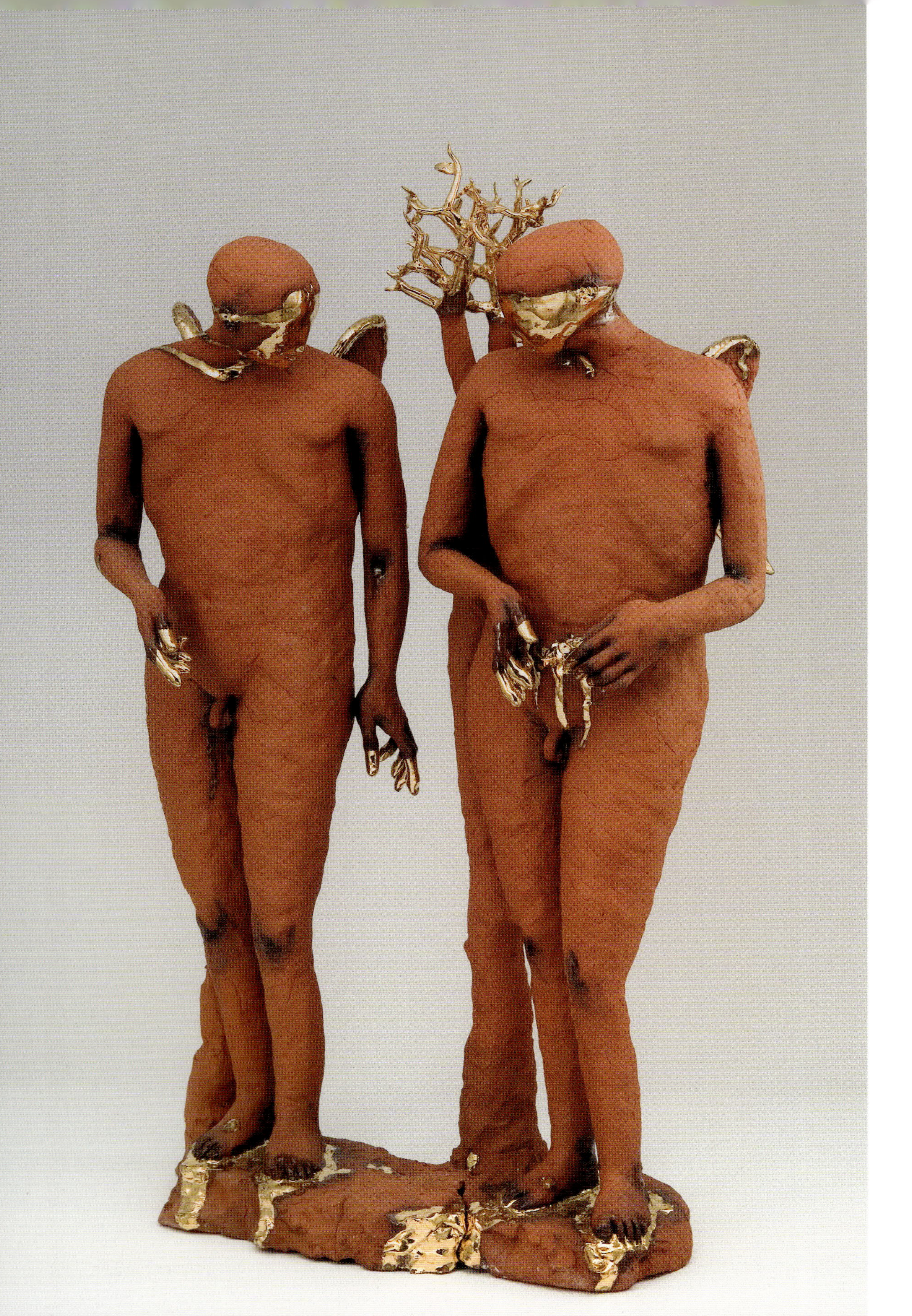

acquired, objects is important to her. Through casting she likes to change their shape and is interested in the relationships which may form between objects. She was a craft and design gold-medal winner at the 2012 National Eisteddfod of Wales.[iii]

The Trust has supported the purchase by the museum of work by other ceramicists in Wales including Philip Eglin's 2010 earthenware *Assholes Tipped Ripely* and two of David Cushway's 2008 *Fragments* videos. Commissioned ceramics supported by the trust in 2014-15 include a creamware commission, *Flailed,* by Walter Keeler, a stoneware *Massive Intertidal Jar* by Adam Buick and back-lit lithophanes, *Casglu,* by Lowri Davies. Works by Elizabeth Fritsch, born on the Welsh borders into a Welsh family, have also been supported by the trust.

Alongside other studio ceramic acquisitions by the museum, a stimulating selection may be found around the entrance-hall balcony at Amgueddfa Genedlaethol Caerdydd – National Museum Cardiff.

Claire's spiritual figures are influenced by Christian iconography and derive from the visual culture of Catholic Ireland, where she was born in 1968, as well as imagery from early Italian and Flemish painting.

iii   Ceri Jones ed., *Anne Gibbs: The Language of Clay*, Mission Gallery / Ruthin Craft Centre, 2016

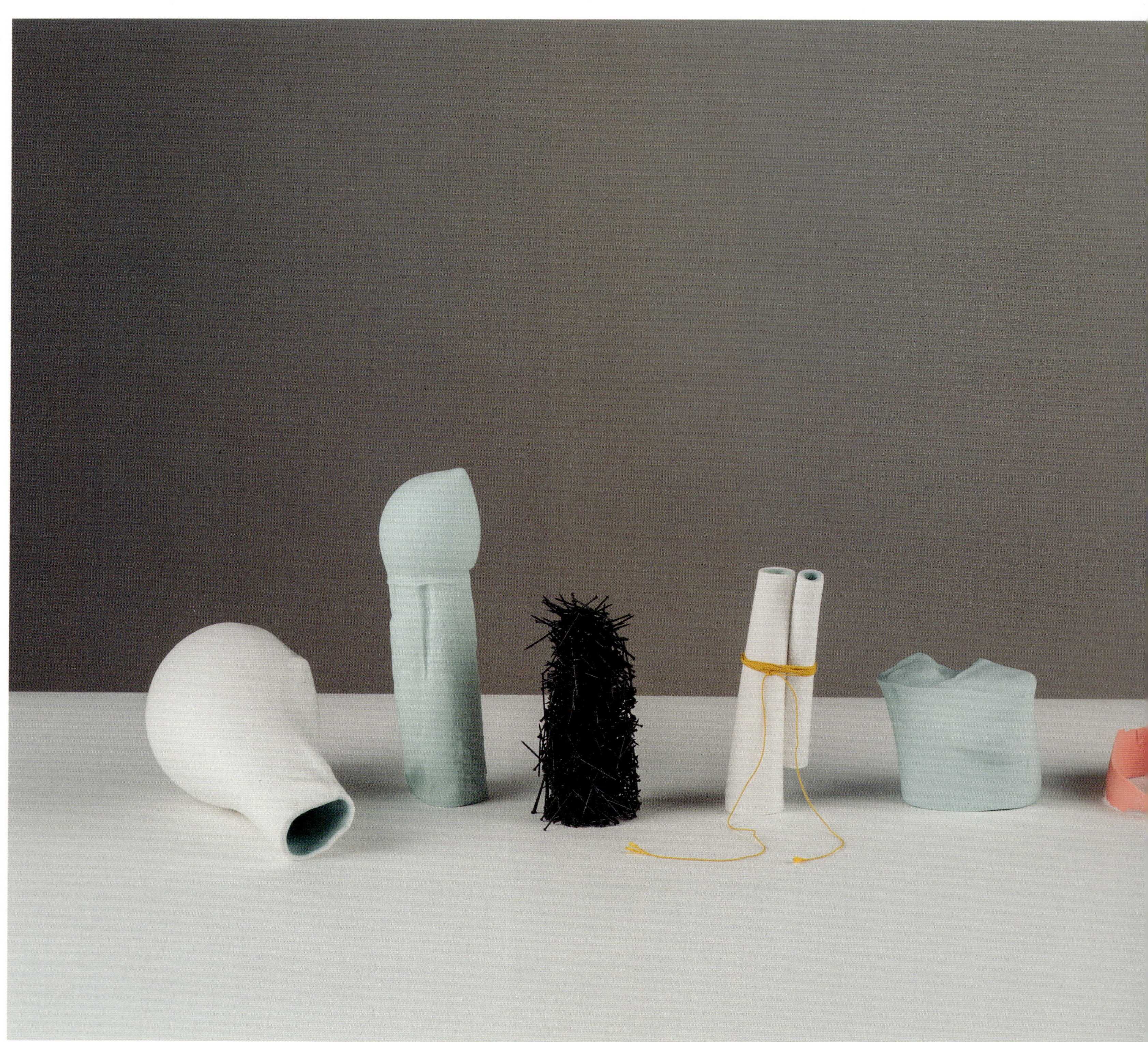

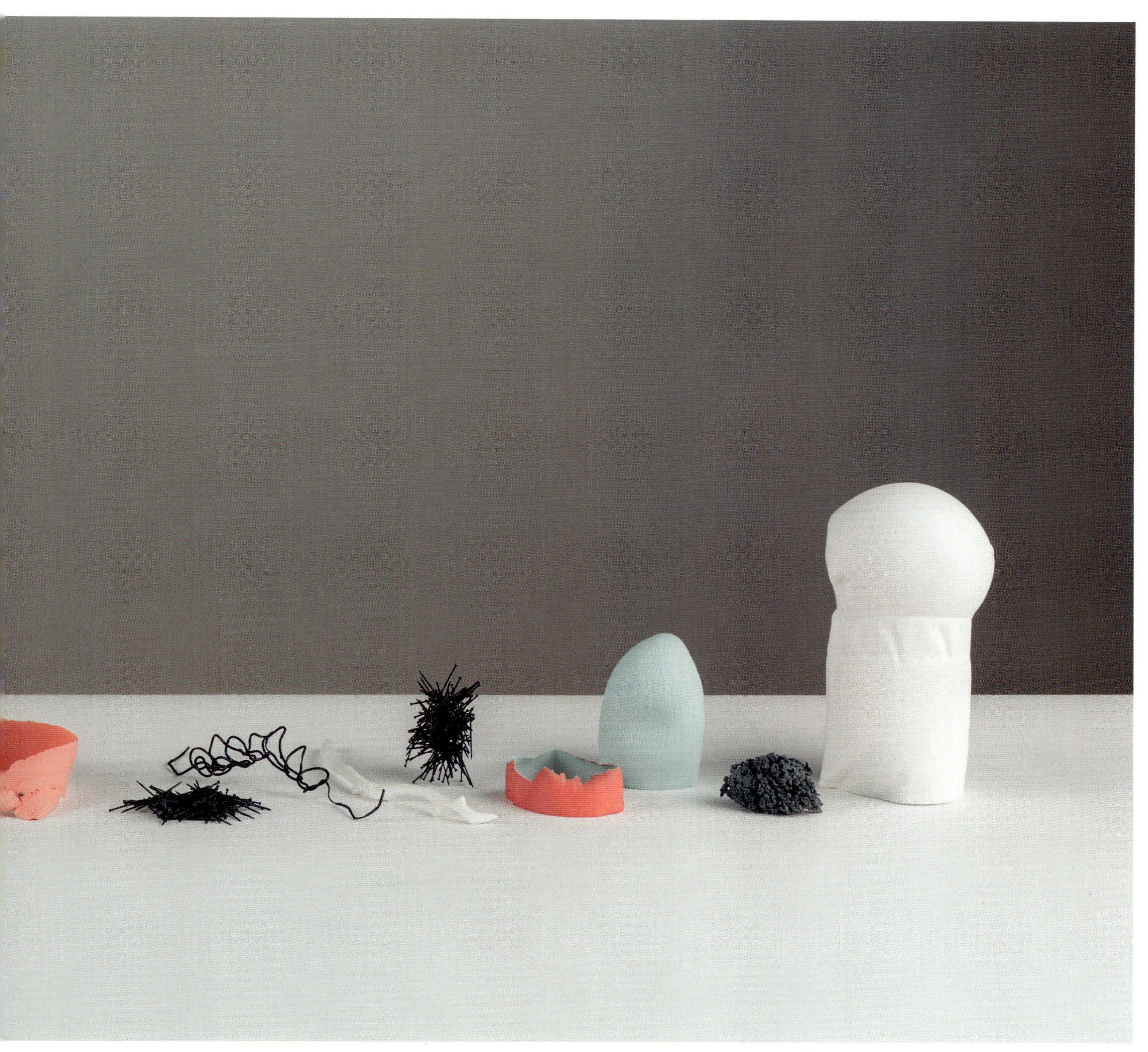

APPENDIX I: ARTWORKS BEQUEATHED TO A TRUST BY DEREK WILLIAMS IN 1984

Source of artworks purchased:
[HR] – Howard Roberts Gallery, 1956-69.
[Marlborough] – Directly from Marlborough Fine Art, London, 1968-78.
[Fosse] – Fosse Gallery, Stow-on-the-Wold, 1983-84.

Compiled from: Mark L. Evans, *The Derek Williams Collection at the National Museum of Wales*, Amgueddfa Genedlaethol Cymru – National Museum Wales. 1989.

Lucian Freud (1922-2011):
Falling Skeleton, ink on paper, c.1939-40 [Fosse]
Man and Bird with Worm, chalk and ink on paper, c.1939-40 [Fosse]

Simon Hardimé (1672-1737):
A Vase of Flowers, oil on canvas, early 18th century [Ronald Cook, London, 1972]

Norman Hepple (1908-1994):
Coming Home after Work, Valencia, oil on canvas, c.1981 [Fosse]

Josef Herman (1911-2000):
The Gardener, oil on canvas, 1963 [HR]
Two Figures with Bucket, pencil, ink and wash on paper, 1965 [HR]
Two Men near Trees and a Hut, pencil, ink and wash on paper, 1965 [HR]
Mexican Peasants with Baskets, pencil, watercolour and ink on paper, 1966 [HR]
Three Welsh Miners, oil on canvas, c.1966 [HR]
Figures with Tractor, pencil, ink and wash on paper, c.1967-68 [HR]

Ivon Hitchens (1893-1979):
Arched Trees No.12, oil on canvas, 1954 [Fosse]

Augustus John (1878-1961):
Study for the Valley of Time, ink and wash, 1904-6 [HR]

David Jones (1895-1974):
Standing female nude, viewed from behind, pencil, ink and chalk, 1920s [HR]
Landscape in France, pencil and watercolour, c.1928 [HR]
View from the Verandah Door, pencil and watercolour, 1927-31 [HR]
Still Life with Lamp on Table, pencil and watercolour, late 1920s/early 1930s
Half-length Woman, pencil, charcoal and coloured chalk, 1948 [HR]
Child with Garland, pencil and coloured chalk, 1948 [Lord Clwyd]

Richard Lin (1933-2011):
Hers, oil on canvas, 1971 [Marlborough]

L.S. Lowry (1887-1976):
Study of a Head, black chalk on paper, 1919 [Sotheby's, 1971]
Old Salford Street Scene, oil on panel, 1922 [Fosse]
The Doctor's Visit, oil on board, 1930s [HR]
Men Fishing, oil on board, 1966 [Fosse]

Henry Moore, (1898-1986):
Maquette for Reclining Interior Oval, bronze, 1965 [Marlborough]

Ben Nicholson, (1894-1982):
Painting, pencil and watercolour on board, 1944-45 [Marlborough]

Spring Landscape, etching with watercolour and ink, 1968 [Marlborough]

Victor Pasmore, (1908-1998):
Landscape with Cattle, oil on panel, 1925 [Fosse]
Pink Roses, oil on canvas laid down on card, 1944 [HR]

John Piper, (1903-1992):
Hope Inn, collage, gouache and ink on paper, 1930 [HR]
Still Life with Window and Ship, pencil, watercolour and gouache, 1932 [HR]
Still Life with Window, Paddle Steamer and Pier, pencil, watercolour and gouache, 1932 [HR]
A Ruined House, Hampton Gay, Oxfordshire, oil and ink on canvas over board, 1941 [HR]
Grongar Hill with Paxton's Tower in the distance, ink, gouache and watercolour on card, 1942 [HR]
Wolverton Church, ink, gouache and watercolour, 1944 [Marlborough]
Sidmouth, pencil, ink and wash over collage on paper, 1946 [HR]
Entrance to the Harbour, Aberaeron, chalk, gouache and ink, mid 1940s [HR]
Capel Curig, ink, gouache, watercolour and chalk, c.1950 [HR]
Foliate Head, crayon, watercolour, ink, gouache and collage, 1953 [HR]
Foliate Head, crayon, watercolour, ink, gouache and collage, 1953 [HR]
Portland on a Wet Day, pencil, wash, ink and gouache, 1954 [HR]

Two Studies of a Lake near Aberaeron, chalk, wash and ink on paper laid down on board, late 1950s [HR]
The Beach, Llantwit Major, chalk, watercolour, gouache and ink, 1957 [HR]
The Church and Scuola di San Rocco, Venice, pencil, ink and body colour, 1959 [HR]
Oppède-le-Vieux, watercolour, gouache and chalk, late 1950s [HR]
Lleyn Peninsula, pencil, watercolour, ink and gouache, early 1960s [HR]
Rudbaxton near Haverfordwest, pencil, watercolour, ink and gouache, 1963 [HR]
Chateau de Chambord II, pencil, wash and ink, 1964 [HR]
Study for Chichester Tapestry – Element Earth, oil on linen, 1965 [Marlborough]
Llanfair Orllwyn, watercolour, chalk, gouache and ink, c.1964-66 [HR]
Garden Follies at Stowe, chalk, ink, gouache and watercolour, date unknown [Sotheby's]

Ceri Richards (1903-1971):
The Force that through the green fuse drives the flower, pencil, ink and gouache, 1945 [HR]
The Force that through the green fuse drives the flower, ink, watercolour and gouache, 1945 [HR]
The Pianist, oil on canvas, 1948 [HR]
The Pianist, pencil, ink and watercolour, 1949 [HR]
The Dragon Pot, ink and watercolour, 1950 [HR]
Homage to Dylan Thomas, pencil, watercolour and ink, 1954-55 [HR]

Trafalgar Square, ink and gouache, 1957 [HR]
La Cathédrale Engloutie, pencil, ink and watercolour, 1958 [Marlborough]
Ce qu'a vu le vent d'Ouest, charcoal and crayon, 1958 [HR]
Rose Windows, pencil, ballpoint, crayon and wash, 1959 [HR]
La Cathédrale Engloutie, oil on canvas, 1960 [Marlborough]
Lion Hunt, oil on canvas, 1963 [HR]
Homage to Dylan Thomas, charcoal and gouache, 1965 [?HR]

Frances Richards (1901-1985):
Mystic, tempera on hardboard prepared with gesso, 1960s-early 1970s [HR]

William Roberts (1895-1980):
Before the Race, pencil, squared off, c.1928-30 [Fosse]
The Shooting Party, oil on canvas, 1976 [Fosse]

Spear Ruskin (1911-1990):
China Clay Pits, St. Austell, oil on cardboard, 1939 [Fosse]

Stanley Spencer (1891-1959):
Study for the Resurrection, Cookham, pencil and wash on six sheets of paper laid on card, 1922 [HR]

Graham Sutherland (1903-1980):
Landscape with Pointed Rocks, pencil, watercolour and crayon, 1944 [HR]
Crucifix Figure, silver on marble base, 1965 [HR]

Keith Vaughan (1912-1977):
Lovers, ink, pencil and wash, 1943 [HR]

Kyffin Williams (1918-2006):
Snow on Siabod, oil on canvas, c.1968 [HR]

Jack B. Yeats (1871-1957):
Sea Wind, oil on hardboard, 1954 [Victor Waddington Galleries, London and Dublin, 1974]

APPENDIX II: ARTWORKS ACQUIRED BY THE DEREK WILLIAMS TRUST SINCE 1992

Eileen Agar, *An Exceptional Occurrence*, oil on canvas, 1950

Craigie Aitchison, *Yellow Painting*, oil on canvas, 1974

Craigie Aitchison, *Georgeous Macaulay in a Sou'wester*, oil on canvas, 1976

Michael Andrews, *Lovers*, oil on board, 1956

Michael Andrews, *The Cathedral, The Southern Faces / Uluru (Ayers Rock)*, acrylic on canvas, 1987

Gillian Ayres, *Untitled*, oil and collage on paper, 1963

Gillian Ayres, *Calypso*, oil on canvas, 1985

Gillian Ayres, *Juno and the Paycock,* hand-painted colour etching, 1992

Gillian Ayres, *Myrrh of Marib*, carborundum etching with acrylic hand painting, 1998

Gillian Ayres, *Thuban*, woodcut on Japanese paper, 2017

Iwan Bala, *Raise High Your Ruins*, mixed media, 1992 (following Gold Medal in Fine Art at National Eisteddod of Wales, 1997)

Iwan Bala, *El Mundo Profundo*, mixed media on paper, 2005

Iwan Bala, *Carta Fragmentada*, mixed media on paper, 2005

Iwan Bala, *Captive (Enslaved) World*, mixed media on paper, 2005

Iwan Bala, *Eicon (Icon)*, mixed media on paper, 2005

John Banting, *Mutual Congratulations*, oil on canvas, c.1937

Theodor Bogler, *Combination Teapot*, tin-glazed earthenware, 1923

Brendan Stuart Burns, *Swish-Back-West*, oil on canvas, 1997 (after the National Eisteddfod of Wales)

Brendan Stuart Burns, *As Well As Being*, oil and wax on canvas, 2002

Edward Burra, *The Red Cloaked Figure*, watercolour, 1936

James Campbell, *Headland (Manorbier)*, pastel, charcoal, ink and pencil, 2005

James Campbell, *The Dream Boat*, charcoal and pastel, 2005

James Campbell, *Moon Bird*, earthenware, 2006

James Campbell, *Landscape with Road*, earthenware, 2006

Anthony Caro, *Serenade*, painted steel, 1970

Anthony Caro, *Can Co Slide*, stoneware, 1975

Claudi Casanovas, *Portic Mari 1 and 2*, stoneware, 2001

Patrick Caulfield, *Black Light with Letter*, oil on canvas, 1990

Roger Cecil, *Weeping Woman*, oil on canvas, 1990

Prunella Clough, *Broken Bottle*, oil on canvas, 1945

Prunella Clough, *Yard with Scrap Metal II*, oil on canvas, 1954

Maurice Cockrill, *Well You Needn't*, mixed media on canvas, 2008

Thomas Joshua Cooper, *A Premonitional Work (Message to Friedrich and Frith), Blaenau Ffestiniog, Gwynedd*, photograph, 1992

Hans Coper, *Dish*, stoneware, c.1952

Keith Coventry, *Avonley Road Estate*, oil on canvas, 1994

Michael Craig-Martin, *Cello*, aluminium, steel and wood, c.1985

Michael Craig-Martin, *Untitled*, emulsion on canvas, 1989

Ivor Davies, *Prefiguration – Eryr*, mixed media on hessian, 1956

Ivor Davies, *Caethni*, oil on canvas, 1996

Ogwyn Davies, *Mae Hen Wlad fy Nhadau*, mixed media on board, 1975 (following National Eisteddfod of Wales, 1996)

Edmund de Waal, *Tall lidded jars*, porcelain, 2004

Edmund de Waal, *Group of fourteen dishes from the Arcanum exhibition*, porcelain, 2005

Natalia Dias, *Transfiguration – As Above So Below*, porcelain, 2012

Ruth Duckworth, *Wall Mural*, porcelain on wooden framework, 2009

Ruth Duckworth, *Untitled*, porcelain, 2009

Terry Duffy, *Is there anything to show?* oil on board, 1995 (following National Eisteddfod of Wales, 1996)

Geraint Evans, *Loner*, oil on canvas, 2014

Roger Fry, *Coffee Pot*, blue tin-glazed earthenware, c.1916-18

Arthur Giardelli, *The Sea's Edge*, mixed media on board, 1990

Anne Gibbs, *Shift*, bone china, silk thread, wire and pins, 2013-14

Simon Hantaï, *Blancs*, acrylic on canvas, 1973

Adrian Heath, *Interlocking Forms*, oil on board, 1950

Josef Herman, *Mother and Child,* oil on canvas, c.1968

Amber Hiscott, *Designs for glazed screens at the former Centre for Visual Arts*, Cardiff, 1998

Howard Hodgkin, *Bedtime*, oil on wood, 1999-2001

Howard Hodgkin, *You Again*, hand-painted lift-ground etching with aquatint, 2001

Harry Holland, *Labyrinth*, oil on canvas, 2003

Steve Howlett, *Bowl*, sycamore, c.1996 (following Gold Medal for Craft and Design, National Eisteddfod of Wales, 1996*)

Steve Howlett, *Vessel*, holly, c.1996*

Steve Howlett, *Vase*, holly, c.1996*

James Hugonin, *Untitled (XIV)*, oil and wax on board, 2004

Andrzej Jackowski, *Standing Train II*, oil on canvas, 1997

Merlin James, *Unabstract*, acrylic on canvas, 2009

Merlin James, *A Pier at Night*, acrylic on canvas, 2005

Merlin James, *Figure (Framed)*, mixed media, 2009

Merlin James, *Horse with Jockey Up*, acrylic on canvas, 2008

Christine Jones, *Five Vessels*, earthenware, c.2000 (following Gold Medal for Craft and Design, National Eisteddfod of Wales, 2000)

Mary Lloyd Jones, *Swyn I*, mixed media on paper, 2008

Peter Kinley, *Swing,* oil on canvas, 1974

John Knapp-Fisher, *Porthgain*, oil on card, 2005

Yasuhisa Kohyama, *Kaze*, stoneware, 2012

Peter Lanyon, *Vase*, glazed earthenware, 1951

Stuart Lee, *Water Level Series, No. 6-9*, C-print photographs, 2004 (following Gold Medal in Fine Art, National Eisteddfod of Wales, 2004)

Jacqueline Lerat, *Petit Corps*, stoneware, 1995

Richard Long, *A Line of Ground 226 Miles Long*, Wales, text work, 1980

Richard Long, *Snowdonia Stones (along a five day walk in North Wales)*, inkjet print, 2006

Fausto Melotti, *Cavaliere*, terracotta, c.1945

Fausto Melotti, *Coppa*, ceramic, c.1955

Shozo Michikawa, *Natural Ash Vase*, stoneware, 2005

Shozo Michikawa, *Tanka Square Vase*, stoneware, 2005

John Minton, *Welsh Landscape*, pen, ink and watercolour on paper, 1943

Henry Moore, *Sleeping Shelterer*, pencil, wax crayon, watercolour wash, pen and ink, 1941

Henry Moore, *Two Reclining Figures*, pencil, watercolour, pen, ink and wax cayon on paper, 1946

Sally Moore, *Remains*, oil on panel, 2000

Georgio Morandi, *Natura morta con il panneggio a sinistra*, etching on zinc, 1927

Sigrid Müller, *Black Tulips*, mixed media, 2001

David Nash, *Wooden Boulder Portfolio no. 170*, (including bronze maquette, DVD, photographs and lithographs), 1978-2003

David Nash, *Ash Dome*, two black and white photographs, 1999-2000

David Nash, *Ash Dome*, charcoal on paper, 2000

David Nash, *Ash Dome*, twelve black and white photographs, 2000

David Nash, *Ash Dome*, charcoal, crayon and chalk on paper, 2000

David Nash, *Multi-Cut Column*, beech, 2000

Philip Nicol, *Paw*, oil on canvas, 2001 (following Gold Medal in Fine Art, National Eisteddfod of Wales, 2001)

Victor Pasmore, *Line and Space*, oil and charcoal on board, 1957

Gustavo Pérez, *Sculpture*, stoneware, 2010

Gustavo Pérez, *Vase*, stoneware, 2012

John Piper, *Landscape Triptych*, ink and wash over pencil and paper, 1940s

John Piper, *Nant Ffrancon Farm*, watercolour and ink on paper, 1950

Peter Prendergast, *King's Cross II*, oil on board, 1967

Peter Prendergast, *Orange Sunset*, acrylic on rag paper, 2000

Peter Prendergast, *Two Sketchbooks*, 2002-03

Peter Prendergast, *Close to Tŵr Elin*, Anglesey, oil on canvas, 2004

Peter Prendergast, *Preliminary drawing for Tŵr Elin*, gouache, chalk, charcoal and pencil on paper, 2004

Nicholas Pryke, *Display Cabinet for Works on Paper*, walnut, sycamore and stainless steel, 1998-2000 (commission)

Shani Rhys James, *Black Cot and Latex Glove*, oil on linen, 2003

Ceri Richards, *Rollerman (South Wales Sulphate Worker)*, ink and chalk on paper, 1942

Ceri Richards, *Yellow Interior*, oil on canvas, 1950

Lucie Rie, *Vase*, glazed earthenware, c.1928

Lucie Rie, *Bowl*, stoneware, 1989

Will Roberts, *Third Class Carriage (The Reading Room)*, oil on board, undated

John Selway, *'As I Rode to Sleep', Fern Hill series*, oil on canvas, 2002

Terry Setch, *Axminster II*, oil on canvas, c.1972

Sean Scully, *Sketchbook*, pen and ink on paper, 2000

Sean Scully, *Day Leaving*, oil on canvas, 2004

Terry Setch, *Yeah*, oil, pigment and wax on canvas board, 2003

George Shaw, *The End of Care*, humbrol enamel on board, 2013

Luke Shepherd, *Derek Williams*, bronze, 2004 (commission)

Jeffrey Steele, *Four sets of 4 chromatic oppositions in a system of rotation*, oil on canvas, 1973

Robert Thomas, *Independence*, bronze, 1965-66 [on loan to University of South Wales]

Robert Thomas, *Girl*, bronze, 1968-69 [on loan to University of South Wales]

Joe Tilson, *Ziggurat II*, acrylic on wood relief, 1964

Gertrud Vasegaard, *Bowl*, stoneware, 1976

Gertrud Vasegaard, *Kumme*, stoneware, 2001

William Wilkins, *Santa Maria Gloriosa dei Frari*, oil on canvas, 1994

Lois Williams, *A Reconstructed Thing*, wool and yarn, 1994 (following Gold Medal in Fine Art, National Eisteddfod of Wales, 1999)

Clare Woods, *Handsome Devil*, oil on aluminium, 2015

Bryan Wynter, *Tidal Surge*, oil on canvas, 1964

Ernest Zobole, *Painter and Subject Matter*, oil on canvas, 1996-97

APPENDIX III: ARTWORKS GRANT SUPPORTED BY THE DEREK WILLIAMS TRUST SINCE 1992

Unless specified these are in the collection of Amgueddfa Cymru – National Museum Wales. Items acquired with the trust's dedicated fund for the museum's centenary are labelled 'Centenary Fund'.

Lida Abdul, *Tree*, 16mm film transfer to DVD, 2005 [from Artes Mundi 3]

Heather Ackroyd and Dan Harvey, *Bull's Head*, grass on hessian on board, 2004

Alexander Adams, *Boy* (C), oil on canvas, 1998-99

Eija-Liisa Ahtila, *The Hour of Prayer*, DVD installation for four projections, 2005 [from Artes Mundi 2]

John Akomfrah, *Vertigo Sea*, video installation, 2015 [with Art Fund, Contemporary Art Society and Towner Collection Development Fund]

Keith Arnatt, *The Visitors*, 46 silver gelatin prints, 1974-76

Shimon Attie, *The Attraction of Onlookers: Aberfan – An Anatomy of a Welsh Village*, five-screen video projection, 2008

Frank Auerbach, *Park Village East – Winter*, oil on canvas, 1998-99 [with Art Fund]

Frank Auerbach, *Park Village East – Winter*, felt tip pen, pencil, ink and crayon on paper, 1998-99 [with Art Fund]

Frank Auerbach, *Park Village East – Winter*, felt tip pen, pencil, ink and crayon on paper, 1998-99 [with Art Fund]

Felicity Aylieff, *Vase: Still Life with Three Chinese*, porcelain, 2001 [with Art Fund]

Fiona Banner, *Superhuman Nude*, inkjet, screenprint, glaze, 2011 (London Olympic and Paralympic Portfolio)

Alice Mary Barton, *Portrait of Margaret Haig Thomas, 'Viscountess Rhondda'*, oil on canvas, c.1930 [with Friends of Museum]

Richard Billingham, *River (Three Cliffs)*, photograph on aluminium, 2001

Peter Blake, *Kamikaze*, cryla and collage on board, 1965 [with Art Fund]

John Bonner, *The St. Winefride Necklace*, silver, enamel and opals, c.1905

Frank Bowling, *Caesar's Plume*, acrylic on canvas, 1975

Alison Britton, *Influx*, earthenware, poured slips and glazes, 2012

Abigail Brown, *Square Fruit Bowl*, silver, 2006-07 [with P&O Makower Trust]

Tania Bruguera, *Destierro*, performance, recording, costume, 1998-99 (Derek Williams Trust Artes Mundi 5 Purchase Prize)

Adam Buick, *Massive Intertidal Jar*, stoneware with Waun Lodi clay, 2015 (commission)

Brendan Stuart Burns, *Etch*, oil and wax on board, 2009

Brendan Stuart Burns, *Pulse*, oil and wax on board, 2009

Brendan Stuart Burns, *Throb*, oil and wax on board, 2009

Brendan Stuart Burns, *Ooze*, oil and wax on board, 2009

Brendan Stuart Burns, *Shimmer*, oil and wax on board, 2009

Andrea Büttner, *Little Works*, five films, 2007 [with Contemporary Art Society]

Andrea Büttner, *Dancing Nuns*, two-panel woodcut on paper, 2007 [with Contemporary Art Society]

Andrea Büttner, *Vogelpredigt (Sermon to the birds)*, 2 panel woodcut on paper, 2010

Andrea Büttner, *Grille*, screenprint, 2010

Michael Cardew, *Winchcombe Pottery Dish*, earthenware, c.1930-35

Claudi Casanovas, *Deep Form*, stoneware, 2009

Claudi Casanovas, *Camp d'urnes Series*, Urn no. 17, stoneware, 2009

Patrick Caulfield and Jean-Paul Llandreau, *Flowers, Lily Pad, Picture and Labels*, ceramic mosaic, 1994 (commission)

Olga Chernysheva, *The Train*, video, 2003 (Derek Williams Trust Artes Mundi 4 Purchase Prize)

Hans Coper, *Vessels*, stoneware, 1948-76

Keith Coventry, *White Abstract (Royal Family at Windsor)*, oil on canvas, 1994

Michael Craig-Martin, *GO*, sreenprint, 2011 (London Olympic and Paralympic Portfolio)

Martin Creed, *Work No. 1273*, lithograph, 2011 (London Olympic and Paralympic Portfolio)

Claire Curneen, *In the Tradition of Smiling Angels*, terracotta with gold lustre, 2007

Claire Curneen, *Touched*, black stoneware, glaze and cotton, 2015 (commission)

David Cushway, *Teacup 1 (Bounce) and Teacup 2 (Break) from Fragments series*, DVD, 2008 (following 2008 National Eisteddfod of Wales)

Steffan Dam, *Fossil Panel*, hand-blown and cut glass, 2010

Alan Davie, *Crazy Gondolier*, oil on canvas, 1960 [with Art Fund]

Lowri Davies, *Casgliad Nantgarw*, slip-cast bone china with screen-printed and digital transfers, 2012

Lowri Davies, *Casglu*, seven bone-china lithophanes and oak-framed light box, c.2015 (commission)

Tim Davies, *Postcard Series III – Figures in Landscape*, ink, lithograph, figure shapes cut out of postcards, 2003 (Gold Medal for Fine Art, National Eisteddfod of Wales, 2003)

Tim Davies, *Drift*, video, 2011

Richard Deacon, *Tall Tree in the Ear*, mixed media sculpture, 1983-84 [with private donor]

Richard Deacon, *Empirical Jungle*, stoneware, 2003 [with Art Fund]

Edmund de Waal, *Porcelain Wall*, porcelain, 2005 [with Art Fund and Colwinston Charitable Trust and, in 2007, additional gifts from the artist]

Mauricio Dias and Walter Riedweg, *Throw*, video, 2004 (from Artes Mundi 2)

Peter Doig, *Riding in Water (Blue)*, oil on canvas, 2012

Philip Eglin, *Assholes Tipped Ripely*, earthenware, 2010

Tracey Emin, *Birds 2012*, lithograph, 2011 (London Olympic and Paralympic Portfolio)

Peter Finnemore, *Base Camp*, DVD projection, 35 short films, 2005 (Gold Medal for Fine Art, National Eisdeddfod for Wales, 2005)

Barry Flanagan, *Carving No. 5*, marble, 1982

Laura Ford, *Glory Glory (Hat and Horns)*, mixed media sculpture, 2005

Michael Freeman, *The Minotaur's Funeral*, oil on board, 1969

Michael Freeman, *Boats*, oil on board, 1971

Michael Freeman, *Forgotten Emperor IV*, 1993

Michael Freeman, *Fierce Red King*, oil on board, 2008

Lucian Freud, *Cedric Morris*, oil on canvas, 1940 [also accepted in lieu of inheritance tax by HM Government]

Elizabeth Fritsch, *Optical Bowl with Fractured Rim*, hand-built stoneware, coloured matt glazes and slips, 1974

Elizabeth Fritsch, *Counterpoint Vase in Twelve Tones*, stoneware and slip, 1975 [with Art Fund]

Elizabeth Fritsch, *Blown-away Vase, Over the Edge, Firework XII*, hand-built stoneware with coloured slips, 2008 [with Art Fund]

Elizabeth Fritsch, *Vase: Water of Greenness*, hand-built stoneware painted with coloured slips, 2008 [with Art Fund]

Ryan Gander and Bedwyr Williams, *Both before and after I had to write your obituary*, screenprint, 2008

David Garner, *Last Punch of the Clock*, mixed media installation, 2009

Rajesh Gogna, *Hanging Ice Coffee Pot*, sterling silver, 2009

Miriam Hamid, *Coriolis Centrepiece*, silver, 2010 [with P&O Makower Trust]

Anthea Hamilton, *Divers*, screenprint, 2011 (London Olympic and Paralympic Portfolio)

Josef Herman, *Miner with dog*, oil on canvas, 1968 [with V&A Purchase Grant Fund] (for Brecknock Museum and Art Gallery)

Rauni Higson, *Glacier II*, Britannia silver (commission) [Funded by Rita Plowman through the trust]

David Hockney, *The Actor*, acrylic on canvas, 1964 [with Art Fund and the Honourable James Butler Charitable Trust]

Howard Hodgkin, *Venice*, Evening, hand-painted lift-ground etching and aquatint with carborundum, 1995

Howard Hodgkin, *Swimming*, screenprint, 2011 (London Olympic and Paralympic Portfolio)

Carole Hodgson, *For Morandi*, bronze, 1993

Catrin Howell, *Head with Thorns*, stoneware, 2011

Gary Hume, *Capital*, 2011 (London Olympic and Paralympic Portfolio)

Bethan Huws, *Boats*, glass and maple vitrine with ten rush boat models, 1983-2000

James Dickson Innes, *Chepstow Castle*, oil on canvas, 1907

Dilys Jackson, *Flow through Circle*, bronze sculpture, 2006

Gwen John, *A Corner of the Artist's Room in Paris*, oil on canvas on board, 1907-09 [with the estate of Mrs J. Green]

Gwen John, *The Japanese Doll*, oil on canvas, 1920s [with Art Fund]

David Jones, *Elephant*, oil on canvas, 1928

Mo Jupp, *Standing Figure*, terracotta, 1995

Mo Jupp, *Sitting Figure*, terracotta, 2003

Marion Kalmus, *Thirty-Three Thousand, Seven Hundred and Ninety-Eight*, sculpture, 2001 (for National Botanic Garden of Wales)

Wassily Kandinsky, *Acid Green Crescent*, watercolour, ink, bodycolour on paper, 1927 (Centenary Fund)

Walter Keeler, *Flailed*, creamware and glaze, 2014 (commission)

Ragnar Kjartansson, *The Sky in a Room*, installation, performance, recording, 2018 (Derek Williams Trust Artes Mundi 6 Purchase Prize) [with Art Fund]

Archibold Knox, *Clock*, silver and enamels, 1902 [funded in memory of Jack and Dolci Josephson by their daughter Rita Plowman through the trust]

Leon Kossoff, *From Willesdon Green*, Autumn, oil on board, 1991

Radovan Kraguly, *Reflections*, mixed media installation, 1989

Peter Lanyon, *Beach Girl*, oil on canvas, 1961 [with Art Fund]

Jacqueline Lerat, *Untitled*, stoneware sculpture, 1990s

Simon Ling, *Untitled*, oil on two-panel canvas, 2018 [Contemporary Art Society and Knapping Fund]

Richard Long, *Blaenau Ffestiniog Circle*, slate, 2011 (Commissioned through Centenary Fund for opening of new modern and contemporary art galleries, 2011-12) [with Art Fund]

Kate Malone, *Ribbed Fennel Vase*, crystalline-glazed stoneware, c.2012

Shozo Michikawa, *Twisted Pot*, stoneware wood-fired with ash, 2009

Cedric Morris, *Jeanette Horowicz*, oil on canvas, 1921

Cedric Morris, *Golden Auntie*, oil on canvas, 1923

Cedric Morris, *Heritage of the Desert*, oil on canvas, 1925

Cedric Morris, *Paul Odo Cross*, oil on canvas, 1925

Cedric Morris, *Brocas Harris*, oil on canvas, 1928

Cedric Morris, *Two Sisters,* oil on canvas, 1935

Cedric Morris, *Gladys Hynes*, oil on canvas, 1936

Cedric Morris, *Lougher from Penclawdd*, oil on canvas, 1936

John Meirion Morris, *Cofeb Tryweryn*, bronze, 1997-98

Mali Morris, *Angel and People*, acrylic on canvas, 1978

Sarah Morris, *Big Ben 2012*, sreenprint, 2011 (London Olympic and Paralympic Portfolio)

Peter Nicholas, *Ivor Novello*, bronze, 2009 (for Cardiff Bay)

Chris Ofili, *For the unknown runner*, lithograph, 2011 (London Olympic and Paralympic Portfolio)

Martin Parr, *Snowdonia, Wales*, colour photograph, 1989

Martin Parr, *Newport, Wales*, colour photograph, 1988

Martin Parr, *Tenby, Wales*, colour photograph, 2018

Martin Parr, *Tower Colliery*, Wales, colour photograph, 1993

Martin Parr, *Blaengwynfi*, Wales, colour photograph, 2008

Martin Parr, *Abergavenny*, Wales, colour photograph, 2008

Tom Phillips, *Alive we thought beyond our lives...*, etching on marble panel with inset crushed bone, 2012 (for Cardiff University)

Pablo Picasso, *Nature Morte au Peron*, oil on canvas, 1948 (Centenary Fund) [with Art Fund]

Pablo Picasso, *Gothic pitcher with three women*, tin-glazed earthenware, 1948 (Centenary Fund)

Pablo Picasso, *Zoomorphic vase*, 'La Tarasque', tin-glazed earthenware, painted in slips and incised, 1954 (Centenary Fund)

Pablo Picasso, *Jug depicting the artist and his models*, tin-glazed earthenware, 1954 (Centenary Fund)

Pablo Picasso, *Vase depicting head and figure*, tin-glazed earthenware, 1955-60 (Centenary Fund)

John Piper collection of twenty works [with Heritage Lottery Fund and Art Fund**]:

John Piper, *Llanthony Abbey*, oil on canvas on panel, 1941**

John Piper, *The Rise of the Dovey*, oil on canvas on board, 1943-4**

John Piper, *Rocky Valley, North Wales*, oil and gesso on canvas on board, 1948**

John Piper, *Trawsallt, Cardiganshire*, monotype, 1939**

John Piper, *The Vale of Clwyd*, watercolour, 1940**

John Piper, *Pistyll Rhaeadr*, monotype, 1940**

John Piper, *Welsh Landscape*, ink, chalk and watercolour, c.1946**

John Piper, *Cwm Glas with Grib Goch*, pen and ink, 1947**

John Piper, *The Snowdon Range*, ink and watercolour, c.1947**

John Piper, *Head of the Nant Ffrancon Pass, Tryfan, Snowdonia*, ink, chalk and watercolour, 1949**

John Piper, *Rocks on Tryfan*, ink, chalk and watercolour, c.1948-50**

John Piper, *Fynnon Lloer*, ink and watercolour, c.1949-50**

John Piper, *Jagged Rocks under Tryfan*, ink, watercolour and gouache, 1949-50**

John Piper, *Rocks at Capel Curig*, ink, watercolour and gouache, c.1950**

John Piper, *Rock Formations*, ink, watercolour and gouache, c.1950**

John Piper, *Near and Far Rocks, Tryfan*, ink, watercolour and crayon, 1950**

John Piper, *Rocks, Capel Curig, Snowdonia*, ink, chalk and watercolour, 1950**

John Piper, *Escarpment, Snowdonia*, ink and gouache, 1950**

John Piper, *Tryfan Mountain*, ink, watercolour, wax resist and crayon, 1950**

John Piper, *Llansanffraid, Llanon*, ink, chalk and watercolour, 1954**

John Piper, *Curly Dish*, earthenware, c.1982

William Pye, *Scaladaqua Tonda (Curving Water Steps)*, sculpture, 2000 (for National Botanic Garden of Wales)

Pamela Rawnsley, *Shadow Vessel*, oxidised silver, 2005*

Pamela Rawnsley, *Shadow Vessel*, silver, 2004*

Pamela Rawnsley, *Pair of Cwm Cwareli Vessels*, silver, 18ct gold handles, 2006* [*funded in memory of Jack and Dolci Josephson by their daughter Rita Plowman through the trust] (Rawnsley won the Gold Medal for Craft and Design, National Eisteddfod of Wales, in 2005)

Pamela Rawnsley, *Mad March*, two vessels in silver with gilding and black gilding, 2008 [with Contemporary Art Society for Wales]

Dan Rees, *Untitled (Triptych)*, plasticine on board, 2012

Dan Rees, *Artex Painting*, oil on canvas, 2014

Dan Rees, *Gravel Master*, oil and pebbles on canvas, 2014

Paula Rego, *Female Genital Mutilation Series: Lullaby, Night Bride, Circumcision, Stitched and Bound, Mother Loves You, Escape*, etching and aquatint on paper, 2009

James Reilly, *Pet*, oil on canvas, 2000

Ceri Richards, *'And freely he goes lost'*, Dylan Thomas, watercolour, c.1954

Bridget Riley, *4 Colours*, gouache on paper, 1983

Bridget Riley, *Kashan*, oil on linen, 1984

Bridget Riley, *Rose Rose*, screeprint, 2011 (London Olympic and Paralympic Portfolio)

Helen Sear, *Blocked Field (Raglan)*, sixteen-panel inkjet print on aluminium, 2012

Helen Sear, *Company of Trees*, DVD projection, 2015

Berni Searle, *Snow White*, DVD, c.2004 (from Artes Mundi 1)

Paul Seawright, *Between II and Between IX*, aluminium, fuji crystal archive photographic prints, 2003

Anthony Shapland, *A Setting*, DVD, 2007

Robert Sheriff, *Ivor Novello in 'Glamorous Night'*, pen and ink, 1935

Walter Sickert, *The Rialto Bridge and the Palazzo dei Camerlenghi*, oil on canvas, c.1902-04

Bob and Roberta Smith, *Love*, screenprint, 2011 (London Olympic and Paralympic Portfolio)

Stanley Spencer, *Souvenir of Switzerland*, oil on three canvases, 1934 [with Art Fund and Heritage Lottery Fund]

Julian Stair, *Crouch Jar II*, Etruria marl, oiled finish, 2008 [with Arts Council England]

Julian Stair, *Three Floating Cinerary Jars*, Etruria marl, porcelain, Venetian plaster, 2011 [with Arts Council England]

Angus Suttie, *Cup*, hand-built earthenware, 1985

Angus Suttie, *Theatre Container*, hand-built stoneware, 1986

Angus Suttie, *Extended Teapot*, hand-built stoneware, 1991

Hiroshi Suzuki, *Miyabi-Fire II*, Britannia silver, hammer-raised, 2005 [funded in memory of Jack and Dolci Josephson by their daughter Rita Plowman through the trust]

James Tower, *Pod-Form Vase*, tin-glazed earthenware, 1985

Annie Turner, *Sinker*, hand-built stoneware with brushed lithium glaze, 2006 [with Art Fund]

James Turrell, *Raethro Pink*, light projection, 1968 [with Art Fund and Bilstone Foundation]

Rachel Whiteread, *Untitled (History)*, plaster cast, 2002 [with Art Fund]

Rachel Whiteread, *LOndOn 2012*, screenprint, 2011 (London Olympic and Paralympic Portfolio)

Bedwyr Williams, *Bard Attitude*, photograph, 2005

Bedwyr Williams, *Writ Stink*, fourteen drawings, 2015 (Derek Williams Trust Artes Mundi 7 Purchase Prize)

Bedwyr Williams, *Writ Stink*, film, 2015 (Derek Williams Trust Artes Mundi 7 Purchase Prize)

Bedwyr Williams, *Tyrrau Mawr*, digital projection, 2016 (Derek Williams Trust Artes Mundi 7 Purchase Prize)

Evelyn Williams, *I went into the garden of love*, No.1, oil on canvas, 2003

Christopher Wood, *The Rug Seller, Tréboul*, oil on card, 1930 [with Art Fund, Brecknock Art Trust, Wolfson Foundation and a donation]

Betty Woodman, *Puccini*, soft-paste porcelain, enamelled and gilded, 1989

Betty Woodman, *Diptych: The Balcony*, glazed earthenware, epoxy resin, laquer and paint, 2007 [with Art Fund]

Bill Woodrow, *The Red Hat*, mixed media installation, 1981 [with Contemporary Art Society]

Sophie Woodrow, *Carningli*, soft-paste porcelain, 2013

Sophie Woodrow, *Owl*, soft-paste porcelain, 2013

Sophie Woodrow, *Amroth*, soft-paste porcelain, 2013

Sophie Woodrow, *Fox*, soft-paste porcelain, 2013

Sophie Woodrow, *Antelope*, soft-paste porcelain, 2013

Clare Woods, *Hill of Hurdles*, oil and enamel on aluminium, 2010 [with Contemporary Art Society]

Catherine Yarrow, *Bowl with Fabulous Beast*, terracotta, c.1945

APPENDIX IV: CERAMICS BEQUEATHED BY ANITA BESSON TO THE DEREK WILLIAMS TRUST IN 2015

Compiled from: William Wilkins et al., *Anita Besson: The Derek Williams Bequest*, Erskine, Hall & Coe / The Derek Willams Trust / Amgueddfa Cymru – National Museum Wales, 2016.

Michael Cardew (1901-1983):
Group of six jars, earthenware, c.1928.

Claudi Casanovas (b.1956):
Rectangular wall plate, stoneware and porcelain, 1989; *Large amphora*, stoneware, 1991.

Hans Coper (1920-1981):
[stoneware] *Cup with disc*, 1970s; *Bottle with disc top*, 1960s; *Early round pot*, 1950s; *Pot with tapered waist*, c.1968; *Large Thistle*, c.1965.

Bernard Dejonghe (b.1942):
Petite Meule Vive, optical glass, 2002.

Ian Godfrey (1942-1992):
[stoneware] *Large dish with pierced rim*, 1960s; *Landscape*, 1970s; *Vessel with animals*, 1970s; *Cup*, 1970s; *Barrel with animal*, 1970s; *Barrel with animal and funnel*, 1970s; *Flask with beast*, 1970s; *Peep bowl*, 1970s;
[earthenware] *Footed bowl*, 1960s.

Ewen Henderson (1934-2000):
Dark Torso, mixed laminated clay, 1986.

Ryoji Koie (b.1938):
Tea bowl, stoneware, c.1990; *Pot*, porcelain, 1990; *Open bowl*, 1990s, porcelain; *Pot*, porcelain, 1990.

Jacqueline Lerat (1920-2009):
Untitled No. 13, stoneware, 2006.

Lucie Rie (1902-1995):
[stoneware] *White-glazed vase*, 1969; *Knitted bowl*, 1980s; *Bowl*, 1969; *Bowl with bronze rim*, 1980s; *Footed bowl*, c.1981; *Jug*, 1950s; *Small jug*, 1950s; *Turquoise bowl with bronze rim*, 1980s; *Bowl*, 1989; *Bottle*, 1970s; *Salad bowl*, 1950s; *Spiral vase*, 1980s; *Knitted bowl*, c1980; *Pot*, c.1972; *Vase*, 1980s; *Small vase*, 1980s; *Pink bowl*, c.1980; *Small vase*, c.1970; *Bottle*, 1970s; *White-glazed vase*, c.1970; *Bowl*, 1969; *Casserole*, 1950s; *Bowl*, early 1980s; *Yellow-glazed dish*, c.1960;

[porcelain] *Small yellow bowl*, c.1965; *Bottle*, c.1968; *Small vase*, c.1960; *Vase with sgraffito*, c.1953; *Lidded bowl*, 1966; *Green bowl*, 1980s; *Bowl*, c.1980; *Two yellow cups and saucers*, 1950s; *Black bowl*, c.1980; *Vase with cylindrical drum foot*, c.1965; *Bowl*, 1970s; *Bowl*, 1972; *Open bowl*, c.1980; *Four cups and saucers*, 1958; *Cruet*, c.1960;

[earthenware] *Bowl*, c.1947;

[various] *Thirty-five buttons*, 1940s; *Two button moulds*, 1940s.

Tatsuzo Shimaoka (1919-2007):
Large vase, stoneware, 2000.

William Staite Murray (1881-1962):
Untitled, stoneware, 1930s.

Vladimir Tsivin (b.1949):
[chamotte] *The Family Pair*, on wooden base, 1994; *Egyptian Portrait*, 1998; *Torso*, 1983.

Shiro Tsujimura (b.1947):
[stoneware] *Vase*, c.1990s; *Tea bowl*, 1990s; *Tea bowl*, 1990s.

DEREK WILLIAMS TRUST BIBLIOGRAPHY

Anon., *Derek Williams Trust Website:* derekwilliamstrust.org

Mark L. Evans, *The Derek Williams Collection at the National Museum of Wales*, Amgueddfa Genedlaethol Cymru / National Museum of Wales, 1989

Oliver Fairclough ed., *A Companion Guide to the Welsh National Museum of Art*, Amgueddfa Cymru – National Museum Wales, 2011

David Fraser Jenkins and Melissa Munro, *John Piper: The Mountains of Wales – Paintings and Drawings from a Private Collection*, Amgueddfa Cymru – National Museum Wales, 2012

David Moore, A series of sixteen articles marking the twenty-fifth anniverary of the Derek Williams Trust in *Western Mail Weekend*: 'How the work of world-renowned artists was given to the nation', 21 October 2017; 'Art really is for everyone', 18 November 2017; 'Taking art to another level', 23 December 2017; 'The world renowned sculptors of Wales', 13 January 2018; 'Visual art and the human condition', 10 February 2018; 'A genuine appreciation of ceramics', 10 March 2018; 'The man behind our finest art legacy', 7 April 2018; 'A champion of Welsh art', 12 May 2018; 'Collection that won't have you glazing over', 2 June 2018; 'The challenges and joys of abstract art', 30 June 2018; 'Welsh artists exploring their identity', 28 July 2018; 'Landscape into art', 25 August 2018; 'Figuratively speaking...', 24 November 2018; 'Echoes of the unconscious', 23 February 2019; 'Ceramic artworks of the modern era', 25 May 2019;

'Paintings for Wales – Derek Williams' legacy', 24 August 2019

Tania Pirsig-Marshall, *A Catalogue of the Derek Williams Trust Collection*, 1993-2006, The Derek Williams Trust, 2007

Andrew Renton, 'Contemporary Silver in the Welsh National Collection', in Philip Hughes, ed., *Silverstruck*, Ruthin Craft Centre, 2011, 44-63

William Wilkins et al., *Anita Besson: The Derek Williams Trust Bequest*, Erskine, Hall & Coe for the Derek Williams Trust in association with Amgueddfa Cymru – National Museum Wales, 2016.

THE AUTHOR

David Moore, who lives in Brecon, has worked extensively, both directly and independently, for museums and galleries in Wales and has developed an interest in modern Welsh art and Welsh public art collections. Originally from Brentwood, Essex, where he was born in 1958, he attended Brentwood School and worked briefly as a rent collector in a local housing department before reading geography at Keble College, Oxford.

Originally moving to Aberystwyth in 1981 to study upland historic landscapes, he then worked for Pembrokeshire Museum Service where he developed an interest in material culture, social history and Welsh art and worked closely with the museum friends. As curator of Brecknock Museum and Art Gallery between 1992 and 2004 he continued to pursue these interests and established an extensive and well supported programme of exhibitions focusing upon Welsh artists. He also built a significant regionally-focused art collection and, in 2000, founded, with William Gibbs, an art trust to support this work. It is an outstanding Welsh regional public art collection.

David has written books and catalogues on Welsh art under the Crooked Window imprint, which he runs with artist Sue Hiley Harris (www.crookedwindow.co.uk). These include catalogues for the Contemporary Art Society for Wales which demonstrate the substantial impact of the society's gifts upon regional public art collections. His books include *A Taste of the Avant-Garde: 56 Group Wales, 56 Years*, which was published in 2012, and *Y Grŵp Cymreig yn 70 / The Welsh Group at 70*, which was commissioned by the group and published in 2018.

Concerned about mental health issues, he endeavours to raise their profile in his local community and has chaired Brecon and District Mind.

PLATE INDEX

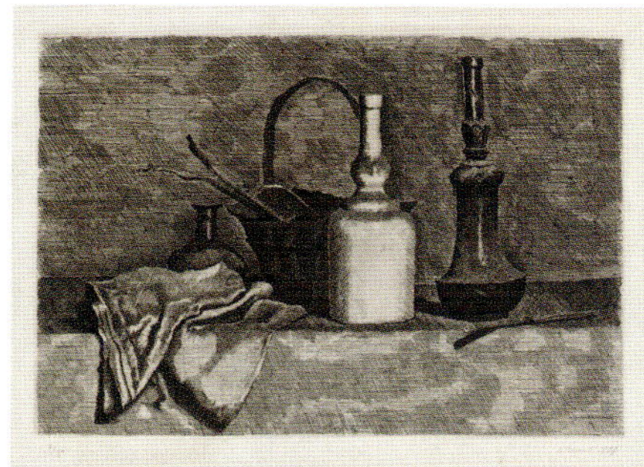

1. Georgio Morandi, *Natura morta con il panneggio a sinistra*, etching on zinc, 1927, sheet size 35 x 50 cm. Trust purchase, 2017. © DACS 2020. Photograph courtesy of Amgueddfa Cymru – National Museum Wales.

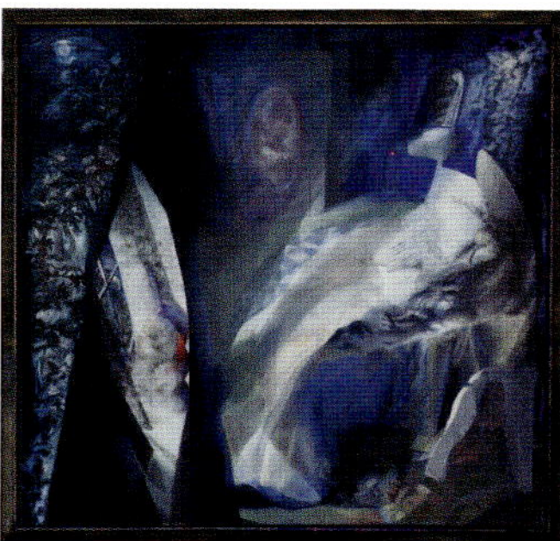

2. John Selway, *'As I rode to sleep'*, **Fern Hill series,** oil on canvas, 2002, 183 x 183 cm. Trust purchase, 2011. © Estate of John Selway. Photograph courtesy of Amgueddfa Cymru – National Museum Wales.

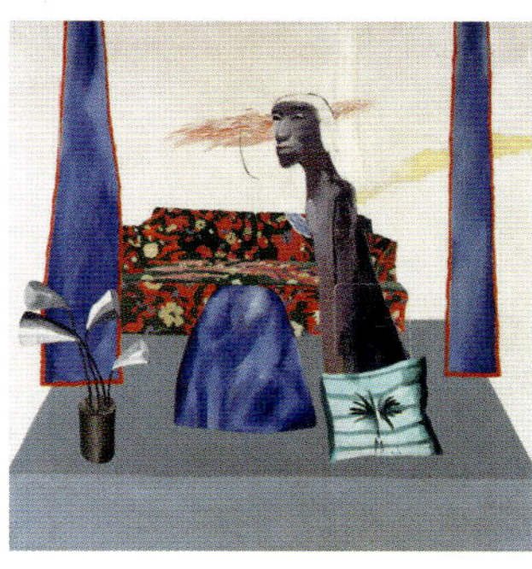

3. David Hockney, *The Actor*, acrylic on canvas, 1964, 167 x 167 cm. Acquired by Amgueddfa Cymru - National Museum Wales with support from the Derek Williams Trust, 1999. © David Hockney. Photograph courtesy of Amgueddfa Cymru – National Museum Wales.

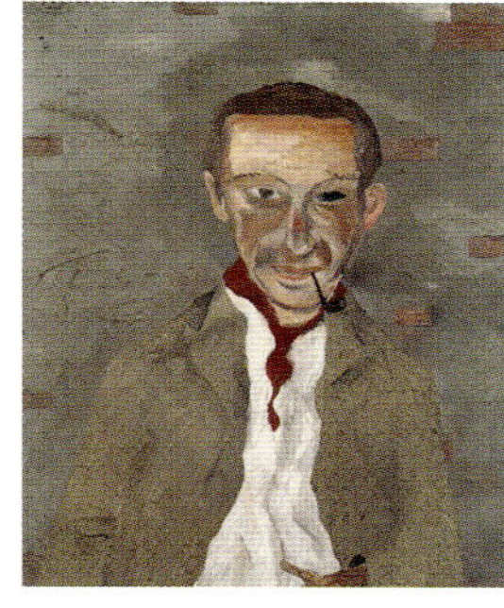

4. Lucian Freud, *Cedric Morris*, oil on canvas, 1940, 31 x 36 cm. Accepted in lieu of inheritance tax by HM Government and purchased by Amgueddfa Cymru – National Museum Wales with support from the Derek Williams Trust, 1998. © Estate of Lucian Freud. All rights reserved / Bridgeman Images. Photograph courtesy of Amgueddfa Cymru – National Museum Wales.

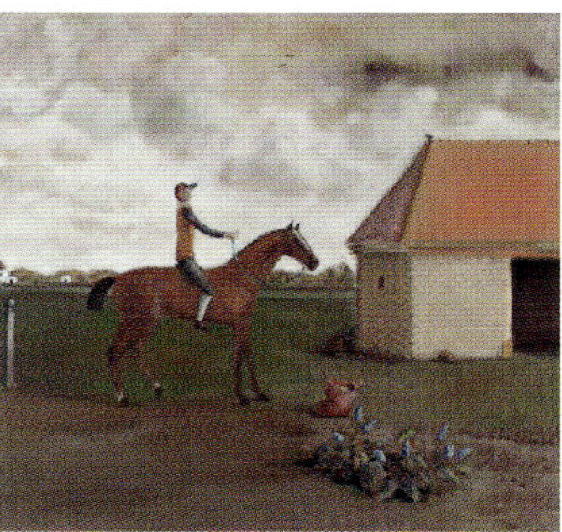

5. Merlin James, *Horse with Jockey Up*, acrylic on canvas, 2008, 109 x 118 cm. Trust purchase, 2009. © Merlin James. Photograph courtesy of Amgueddfa Cymru – National Museum Wales.

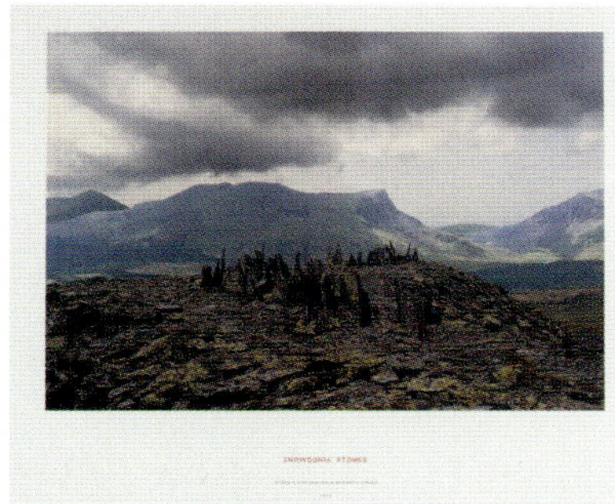

6. Sir Richard Long, *Snowdonia Stones (along a five day walk in North Wales)*, inkjet print, 2006, 100 x 113 cm. Trust purchase, 2010. © Richard Long. All rights reserved, DACS 2020. Photograph courtesy of Amgueddfa Cymru – National Museum Wales.

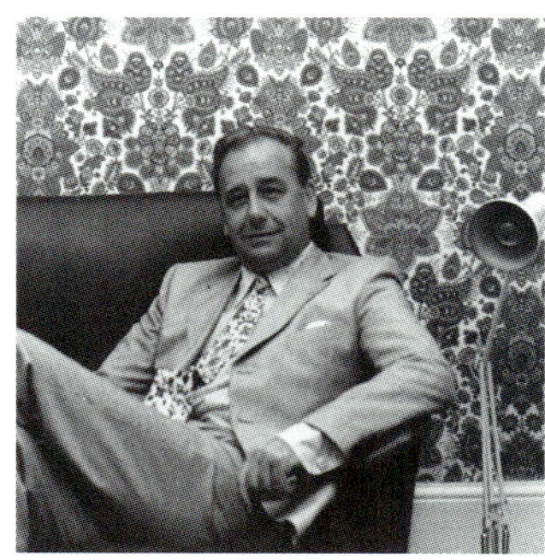

7. Derek Williams in the 1970s. Photographer unknown. Image courtesy of Amgueddfa Cymru – National Museum Wales.

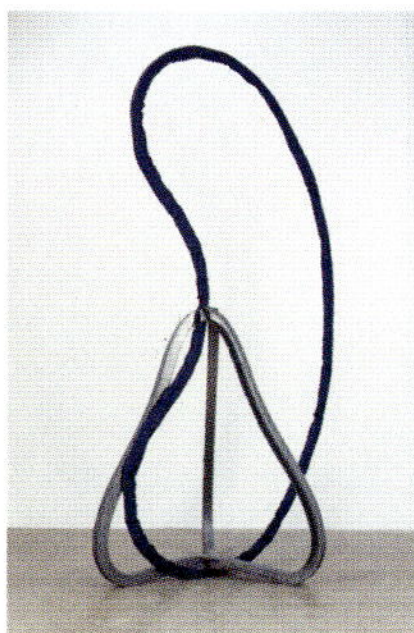

8. Richard Deacon, *Tall Tree In The Ear*, 1984, galvanised steel, laminated wood, canvas, 308 x 105 x 205 cm. Acquired by Amgueddfa Cymru – National Museum Wales with the support of the Derek Williams Trust and a private donor, 2015. © Richard Deacon. Photograph by John Riddy courtesy of Lisson Gallery.

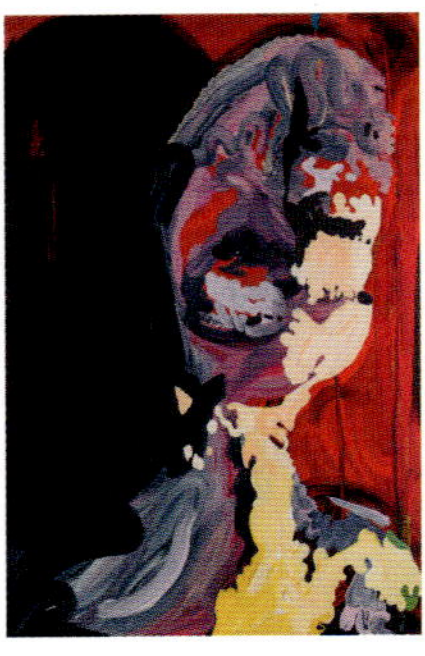

9. Clare Woods, *Handsome Devil*, oil on aluminium, 2015, 150 x 100 cm. Trust purchase, 2016. © Clare Woods. Photograph courtesy of Amgueddfa Cymu – National Museum Wales.

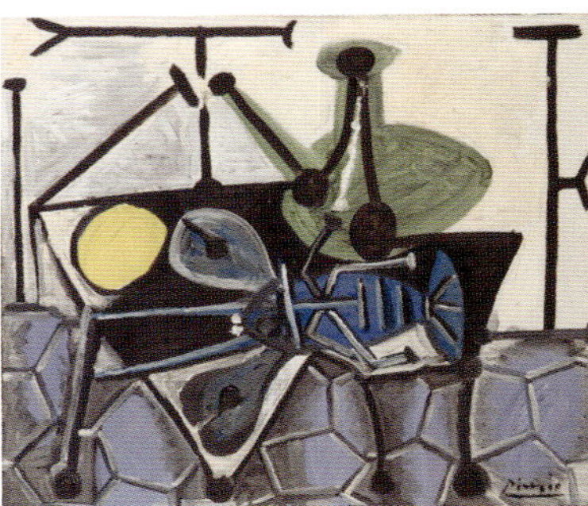

10. Pablo Picasso, *Nature Morte au Poron*, oil on canvas, 1948, 50 x 61 cm. Acquired by Amgueddfa Cymru – National Museum Wales with the support of the Derek Williams Trust (Centenary Fund) and the Art Fund, 2009. © Succession Picasso / DACS, London 2020. Photograph courtesy of Amgueddfa Cymu – National Museum Wales.

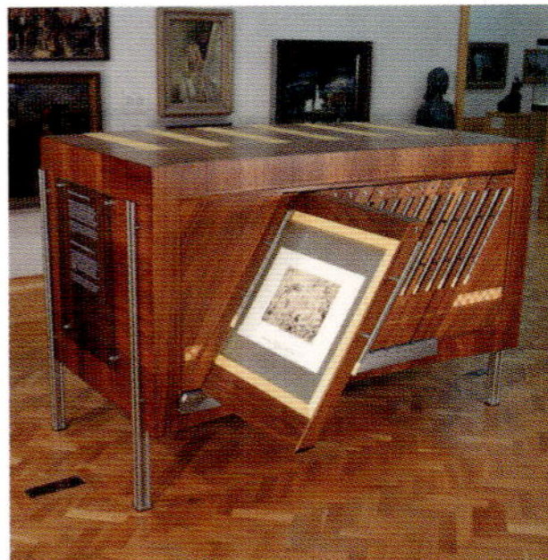

11. Nicholas Pryke, *Display Cabinet for Works on Paper*, walnut and sycamore veneer and stainless steel, 1998-2000,140 x 217 x 125 cm. Trust commission, 1998. © Nicholas Pryke. Photograph courtesy of Amgueddfa Cymru – National Museum Wales.

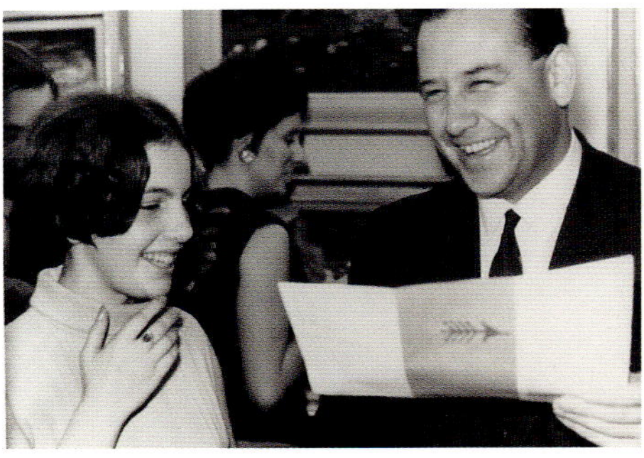

12. Derek Williams at an exhibition launch. Photographer unknown. Image courtesy of Amgueddfa Cymru – National Museum Wales.

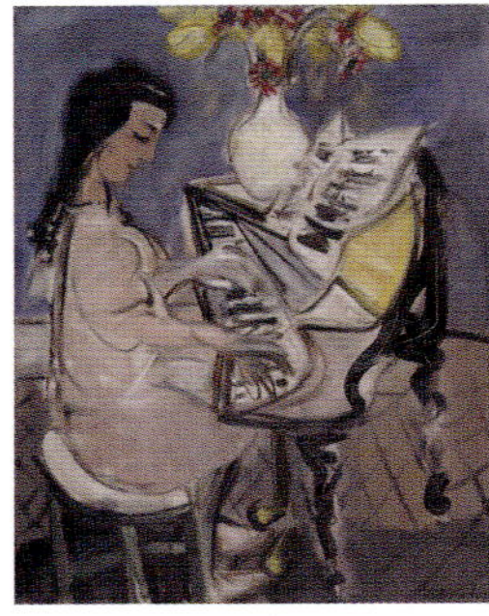

13. Ceri Richards, *The Pianist*, oil on canvas, 1948, 53 x 43 cm. Bought by Derek Williams from Howard Roberts Gallery, Cardiff. © Estate of Ceri Richards. All rights reserved, DACS 2020. Photograph courtesy of Amgueddfa Cymru – National Museum Wales.

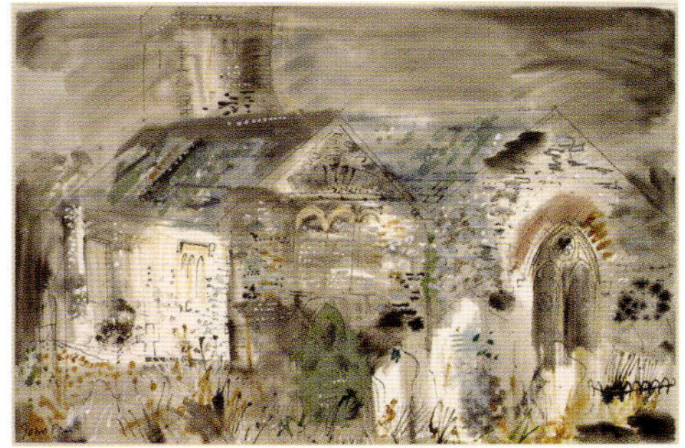

14. John Piper, *Rudbaxton near Haverfordwest*, pencil, watercolour, indian ink and gouache, 1963, 40 x 57 cm. Bought by Derek Williams from Howard Roberts Gallery, Cardiff, c.1964. © The Piper Estate / DACS 2020. Photograph courtesy of Amgueddfa Cymru – National Museum Wales.

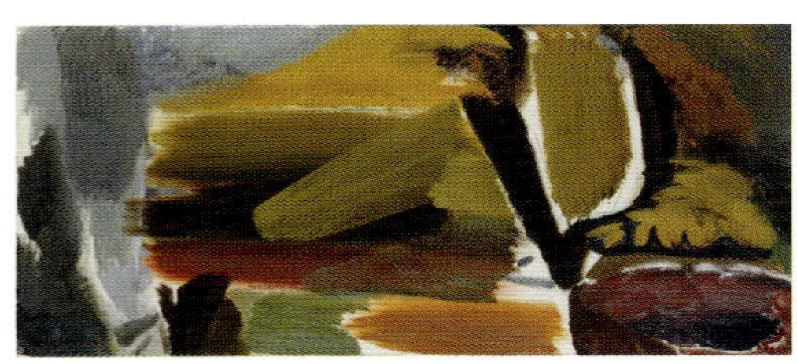

15. Ivon Hitchens, *Arched Trees No.12*, oil on canvas, 1954, 46 x 110 cm. Bought by Derek Williams from Fosse Gallery, Stow-on-the-Wold, 1984. © The Estate of Ivon Hitchens. All rights reserved, DACS 2020. Photograph coutesy of Amgueddfa Cymru – National Museum Wales.

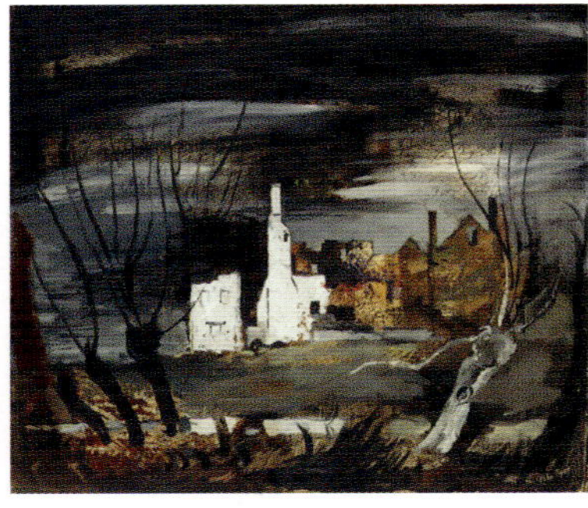

16. John Piper, *A Ruined House, Hampton Gay, Oxfordshire*, oil and ink on canvas, 1941, 64 x 77 cm. Purchased by Derek Williams from Howard Roberts Gallery, Cardiff. © The Piper Estate / DACS 2020. Photograph courtesy of Amgueddfa Cymru – National Museum Wales.

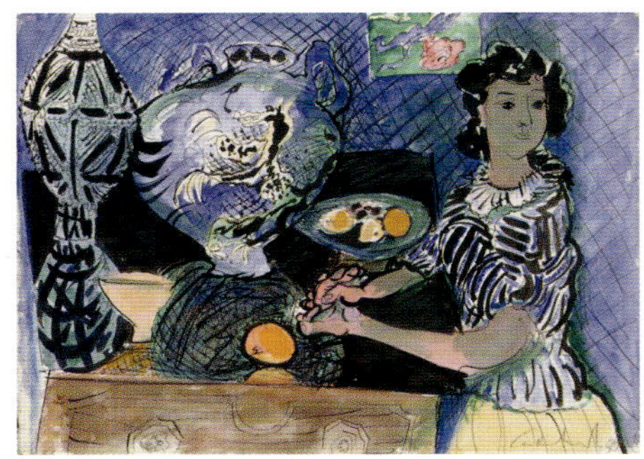

17. Ceri Richards, *The Dragon Pot*, ink and watercolour, 1950, 39 x 56 cm. Bought by Derek Williams from Howard Roberts Gallery, Cardiff. © Estate of Ceri Richards. All rights reserved, DACS 2020. Photograph courtesy of Amgueddfa Cymru – National Museum Wales.

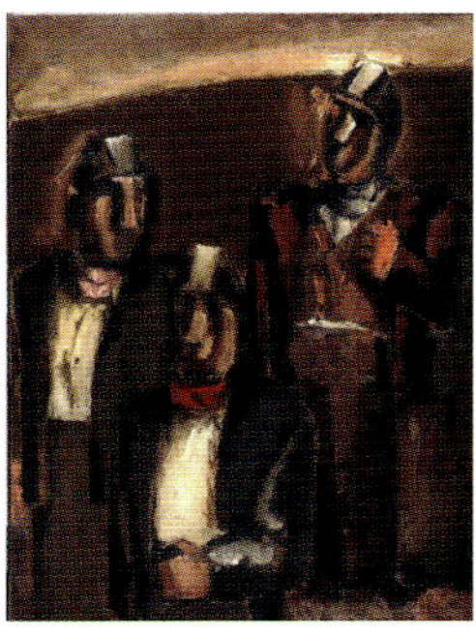

18. Josef Herman, *Three Welsh Miners,* oil on canvas, c.1966, 66 x 51 cm. Purchased by Derek Williams from Howard Roberts Gallery, Cardiff. © Estate of Josef Herman. All rights reserved, DACS 2020. Photograph courtesy of Amgueddfa Cymru – National Museum Wales.

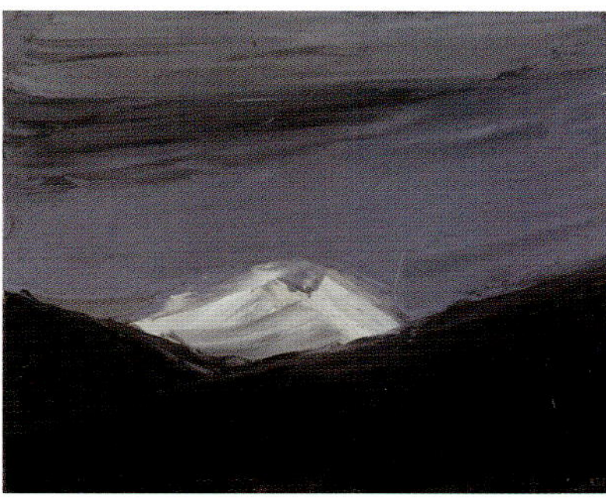

19. Kyffin Williams, *Snow on Siabod,* oil on canvas, c.1968, 41 x 51 cm. Purchased by Derek Williams from Howard Roberts Gallery, Cardiff. © Llyfrgell Genedlaethol Cymru / The National Library of Wales. Photograph courtesy of Amgueddfa Cymru – National Museum Wales.

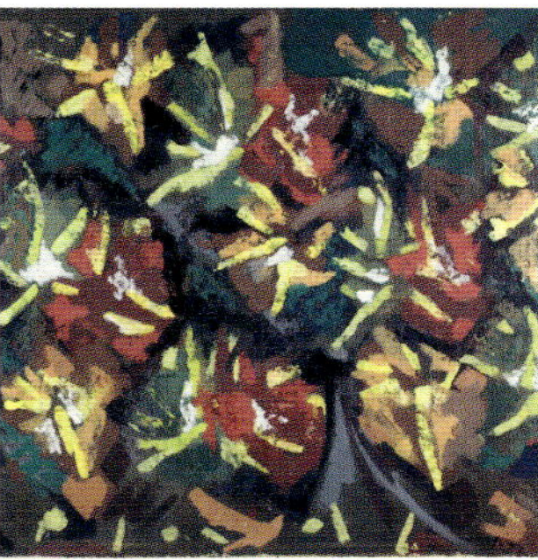

20. Terry Setch, *Axminster II,* oil on canvas, 1972, 152 x 151 cm. Trust purchase, 2008. © Terry Setch. Photograph courtesy of Amgueddfa Cymru – National Museum Wales.

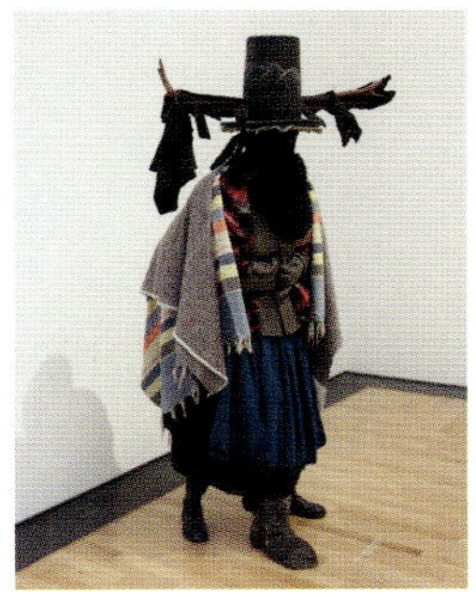

21. Laura Ford, *Glory Glory (Hat and Horns),* mixed-media sculpture, 2005, 261 x 125 x 190 cm. Acquired by Amgueddfa Cymru – National Museum Wales with support from the Derek Williams Trust, 2011. © Laura Ford. Photograph courtesy of Amgueddfa Cymru – National Museum Wales.

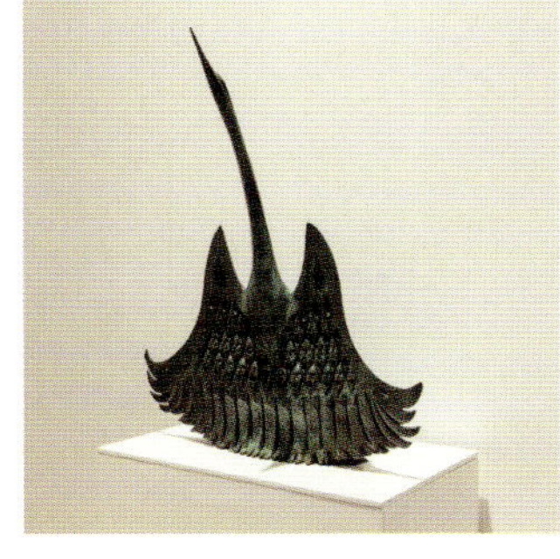

22. John Meirion Morris, *Cofeb Tryweryn,* bronze, 1996, 72 x 60 x 39 cm. Acquired by Amgueddfa Cymru – National Museum Wales with support from the Derek Williams Trust, 2008. © John Meirion Morris. Photograph courtesy of Amgueddfa Cymru – National Museum Wales.

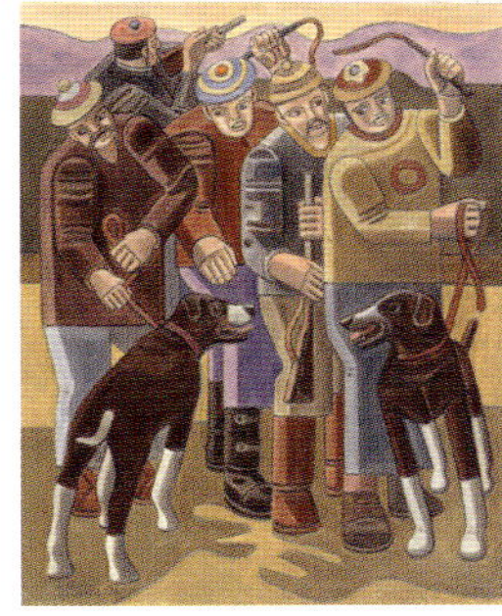

23. William Roberts, *The Shooting Party,* oil on canvas, 1976, 51 x 41 cm. Purchased by Derek Williams from Fosse Gallery, Stow-on-the-Wold, 1984. © Estate of William Roberts. Photograph courtesy of Amgueddfa Cymru – National Museum Wales.

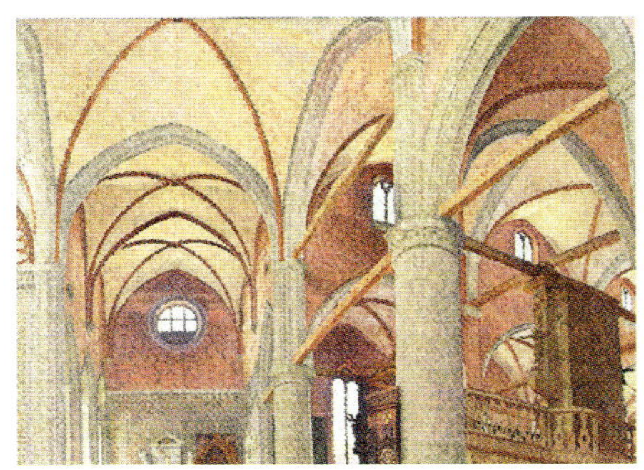

24. William Wilkins, *Santa Maria Gloriosa dei Frari,* oil on canvas, 1994, 47 x 67 cm. Trust purchase, 1994. © William Wilkins. Photograph courtesy of Amgueddfa Cymru – National Museum Wales.

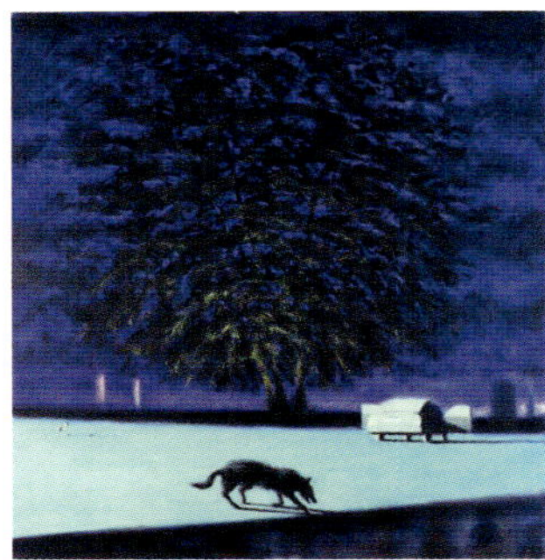

25. Philip Nicol, *Paw,* oil on canvas, 2001, 144 x 144 x 3 cm. Trust purchase, 2002. © Philip Nicol. Photograph courtesy of Amgueddfa Cymru – National Museum Wales.

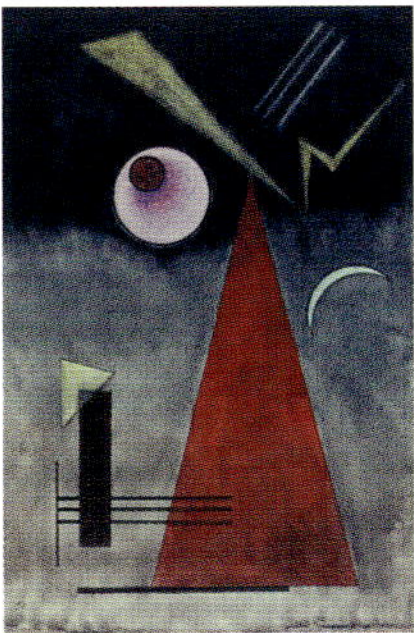

26. Wassily Kandinsky, *Acid Green Crescent,* watercolour, ink and bodycolour on paper, 1927, 48 x 32 cm. Acquired by Amgueddfa Cymru – National Museum Wales with support from the Derek Williams Trust (Centenary Fund), 2007. Photograph courtesy of Amgueddfa Cymru – National Museum Wales.

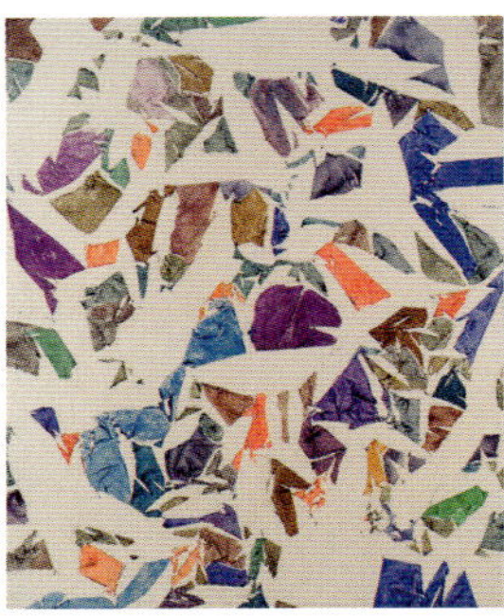

27. Simon Hantaï, *Blancs,* acrylic on canvas, 1973, 228 x 192 cm. Trust purchase, 2017. © Archives Simon Hantaï / ADAGP, Paris and DACS, London 2020. Photograph courtesy of Amgueddfa Cymru – National Museum Wales.

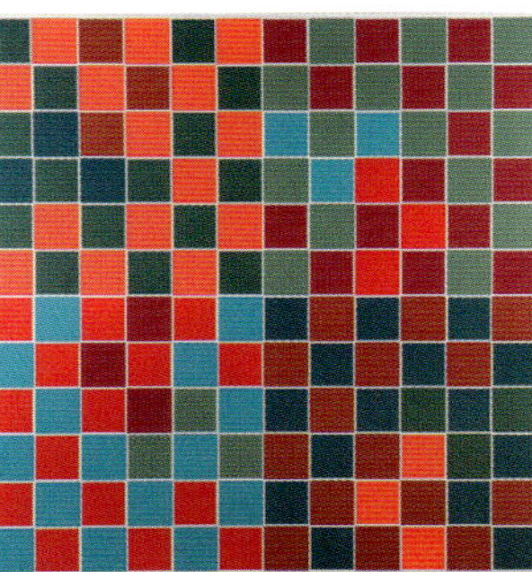

28. Jeffrey Steele, *Four sets of 4 chromatic oppositions in a system of rotation,* oil on canvas, 1973, 127 x 127 cm. Trust purchase, 2008. © Jeffrey Steele. Photograph courtesy of Amgueddfa Cymru – National Museum Wales.

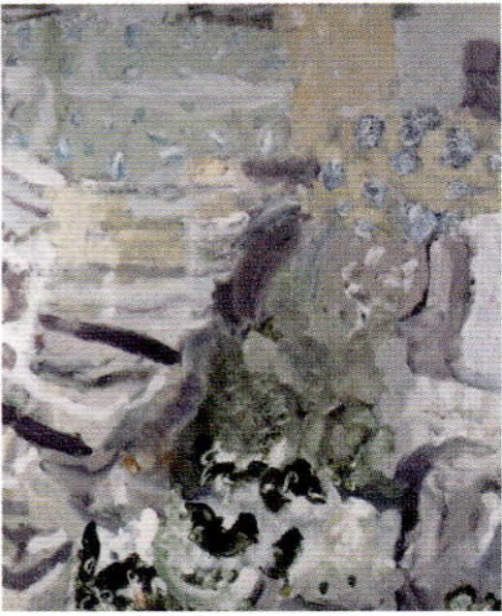

29. Brendan Stuart Burns, *Swish-Back-West,* oil on canvas, 1997, 241 x 201 cm.Trust purchase, 1997. © Brendan Stuart Burns. Photograph courtesy of Amgueddfa Cymru – National Museum Wales.

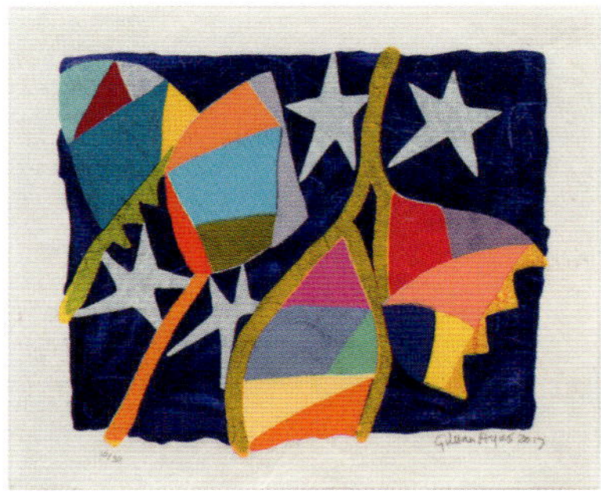

30. Gillian Ayres, *Thuban,* woodcut on Japanese paper, 2017, sheet size 48 x 58 cm. Trust purchase, 2018. © Gillian Ayres Estate and Cristea Roberts Gallery, London. Photograph courtesy of Amgueddfa Cymru – National Museum Wales.

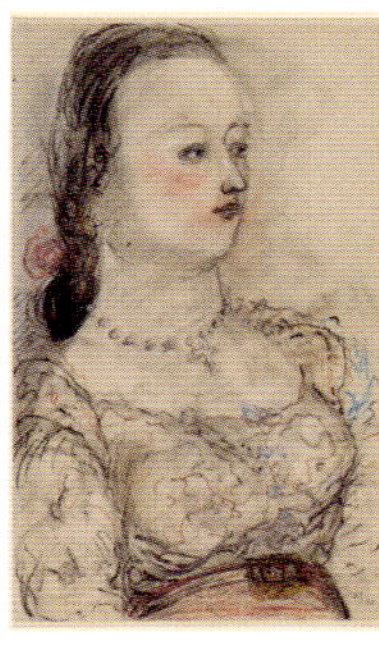

31. David Jones, *Half-Length Woman,* pencil, charcoal and coloured chalk, 1948, 33 x 20 cm. Purchased by Derek Williams from Howard Roberts Gallery, Cardiff. © Estate David Jones. All rights reserved / Bridgeman Images. Photograph courtesy of Amgueddfa Cymru – National Museum Wales.

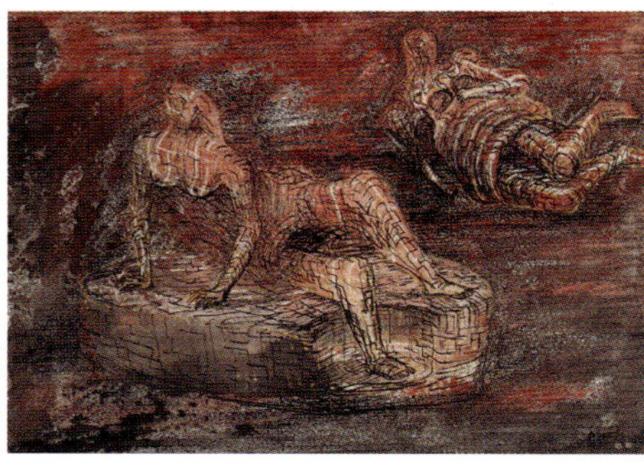

32. Henry Moore, *Two Reclining Figures,* pencil, watercolour, pen, ink and wax crayon, 1946, 25 x 35 cm. Trust purchase, 2006. © The Henry Moore Foundation. All rights reserved, DACS / www.henry-moore.org 2020. Photograph courtesy of Amgueddfa Cymru – National Museum Wales.

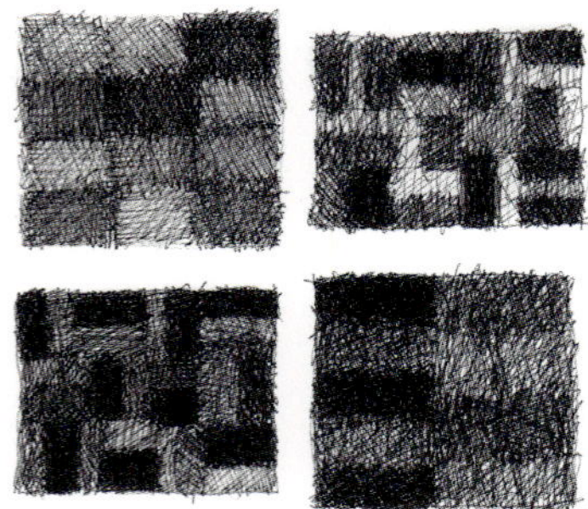

33. Sean Scully, Four drawings from a sketchbook, ink, 2000, sketchbook size 16.8 x 15.6 x 2.5 cm. Trust purchase, 2007. © Sean Scully Studio. Photograph courtesy of Amgueddfa Cymru – National Museum Wales.

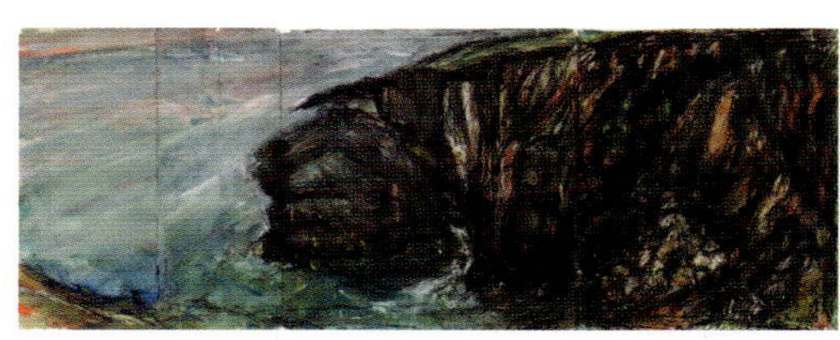

34. Peter Prendergast, *Preliminary Drawing for Tŵr Elin,* gouache, chalk, charcoal and pencil, 2004, 92 x 276 cm. Trust purchase, 2008. © Estate of Peter Prendergast. All rights reserved, DACS 2020. Photograph courtesy of Amgueddfa Cymru – National Museum Wales.

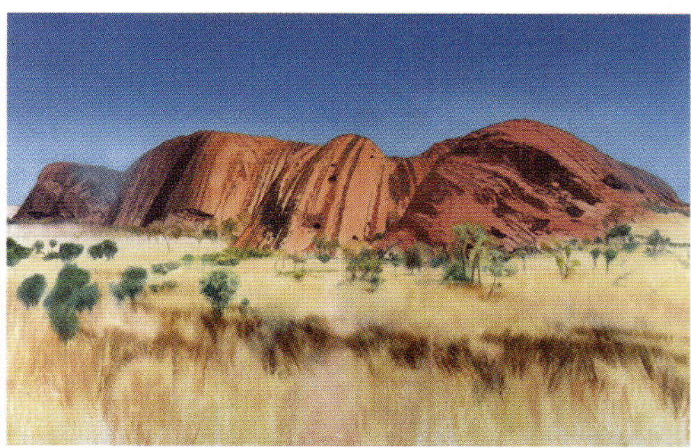

35. Michael Andrews, *The Cathedral, The Southern Faces / Uluru (Ayers Rock),* acrylic on canvas, 1987, 244 x 389 cm. Trust purchase, 1993. © Estate of Michael Andrews. Photograph courtesy of Amgueddfa Cymru – National Museum Wales.

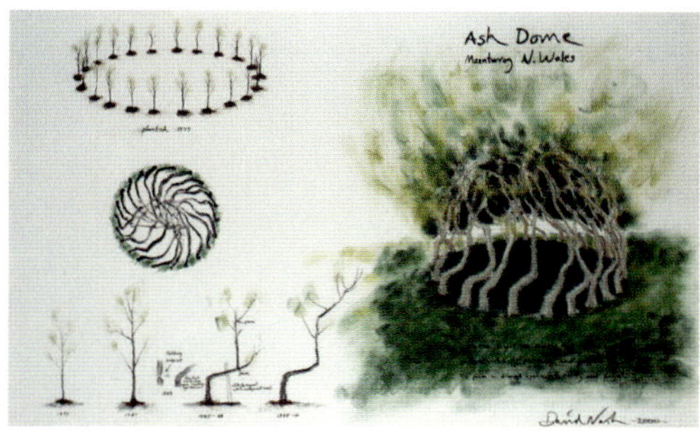

36. David Nash, *Ash Dome,* charcoal, crayon and chalk on paper, 2000, 117 x 188 cm. Trust purchase, 2000. © David Nash. All rights reserved, DACS 2020. Photograph courtesy of Amgueddfa Cymru – National Museum Wales.

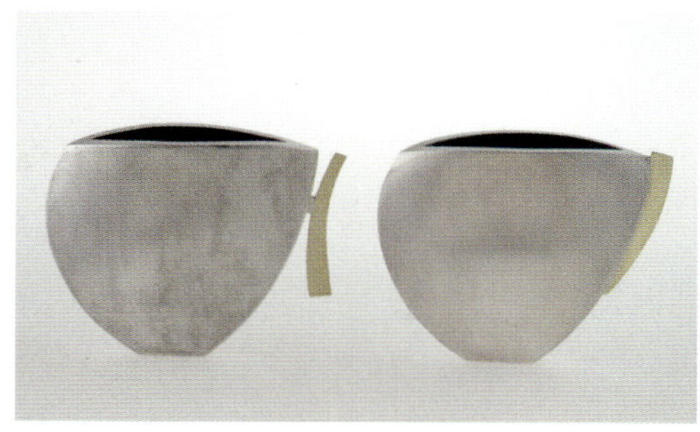

37. Pamela Rawnsley, *Cwm Cwareli Vessels,* silver with gold attachments, 2006, 9 x 9 cm and 12 x 11.5 cm. Gifted to Amgueddfa Cymru – National Museum Wales by the Derek Williams Trust with funding from Rita Plowman in memory of her parents Jack and Dolci Josephson, 2006. © Estate of Pamela Rawnsley. Photograph courtesy of Amgueddfa Cymru – National Museum Wales.

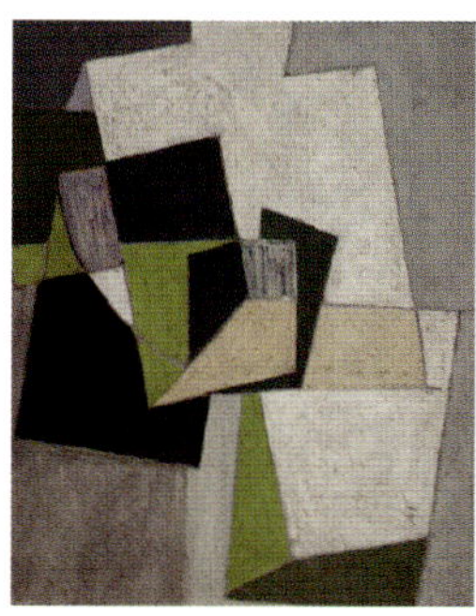

38. Adrian Heath, *Interlocking Forms,* oil on board, 1950, 46 x 36 cm. Trust purchase, 2010. © Estate of Adrian Heath. All rights reserved, DACS 2020. Photograph courtesy of Amgueddfa Cymru – National Museum Wales.

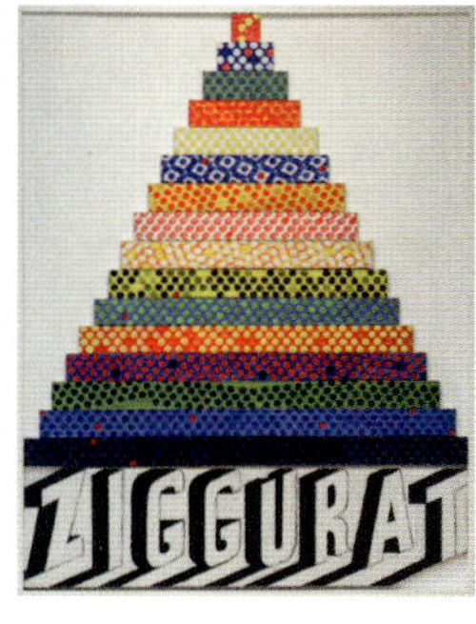

39. Joe Tilson, *Ziggurat II,* acrylic on wood relief, 1964, 203 x 157 cm. Trust purchase, 2013. © Joe Tilson. All rights reserved, DACS 2020. Photograph courtesy of Amgueddfa Cymru – National Museum Wales.

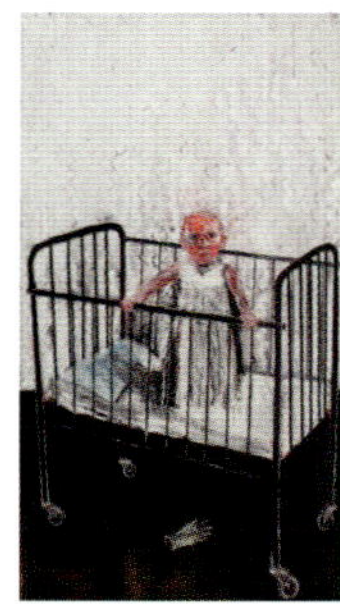

40. Shani Rhys James, *Black Cot and Latex Glove,* oil on linen, 2003, 360 x 180 cm. Trust purchase, 2008. © Shani Rhys James. All rights reserved, DACS 2020. Photograph courtesy of Amgueddfa Cymru – National Museum Wales

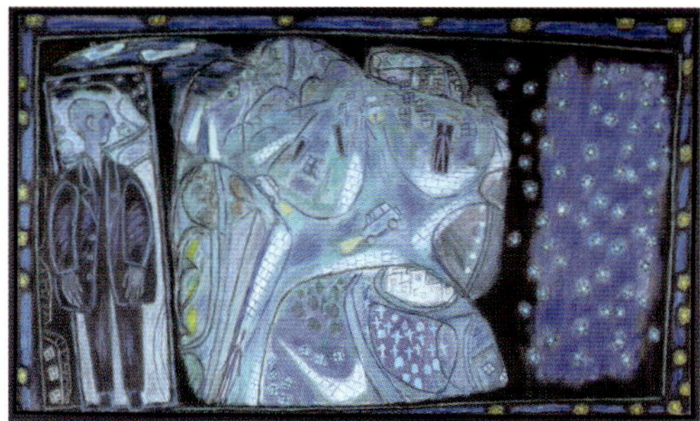

41. Ernest Zobole, *Painter and Subject Matter,* oil on canvas, 1996-97, 115 x 189 cm. Trust purchase, 1998. © Estate of Ernest Zobole. Photograph courtesy of Amgueddfa Cymru – National Museum Wales.

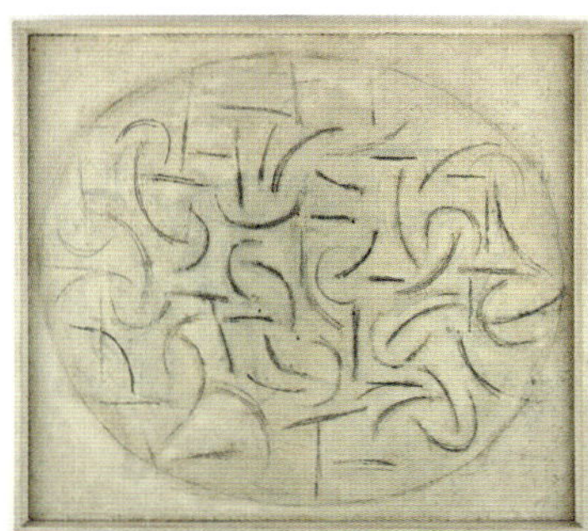

42. Victor Pasmore, *Line and Space,* oil and charcoal on board, 1957, 69 x 79 cm. Trust purchase, 2019. © Estate of Victor Pasmore. All rights reserved, DACS 2020. Photograph courtesy of Amgueddfa Cymru – National Museum Wales.

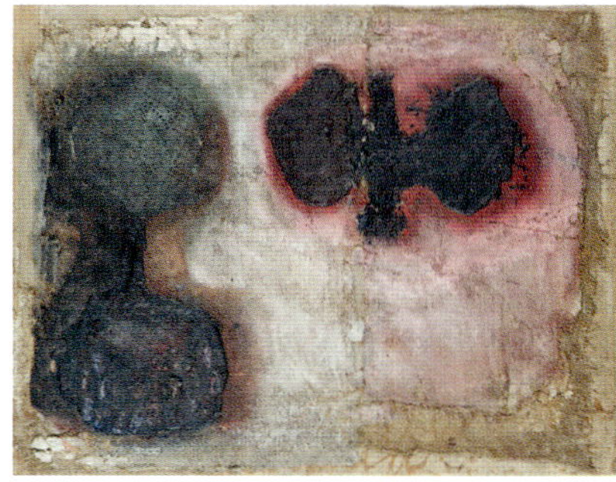

43. Ivor Davies, *Prefiguration – Eryr,* mixed media on hessian, 1956-61, 94 x 122 cm. Trust purchase, 2009. © Ivor Davies. Photograph courtesy of Amgueddfa Cymru – National Museum Wales.

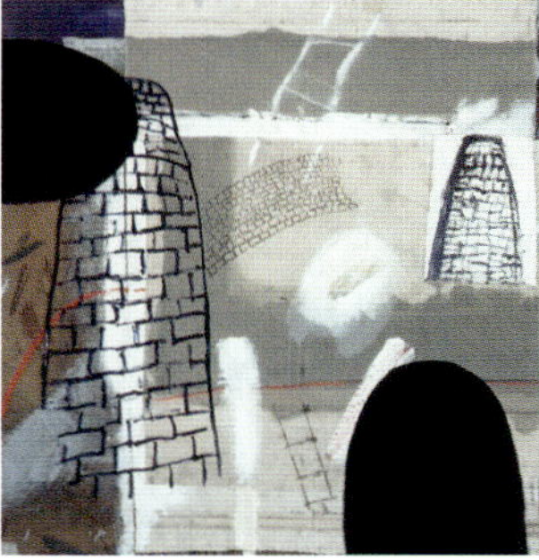

44. Iwan Bala, *Raise High Your Ruins,* mixed media on canvas, 1992, 133 x 133 cm. Trust purchase, 1998. © Iwan Bala. Photograph courtesy of Amgueddfa Cymru – National Museum Wales.

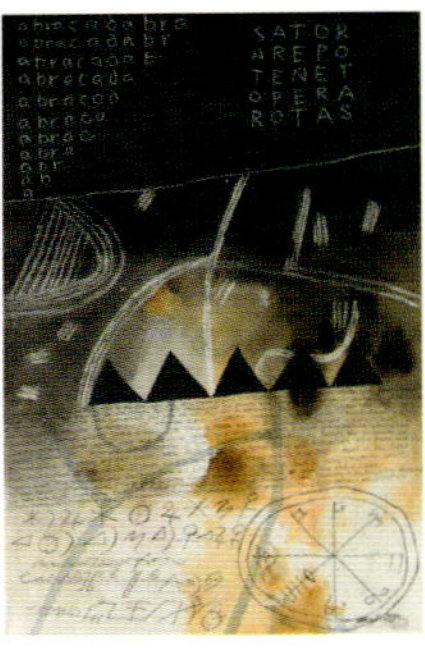

45. Mary Lloyd Jones, *Swyn I,* mixed media, 2007, 69 x 110 cm. Trust purchase, 2008. © Mary Lloyd Jones. Photograph courtesy of Amgueddfa Cymru – National Museum Wales.

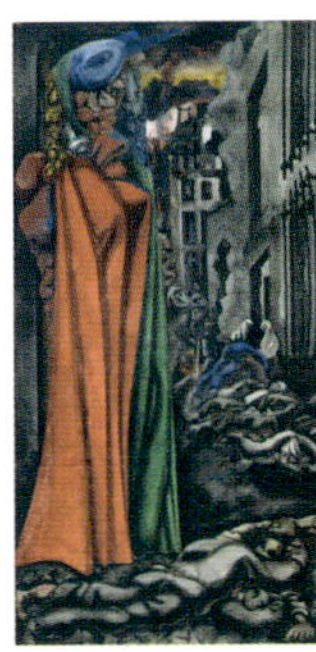

46. Edward Burra, *The Red Cloaked Figure,* watercolour on paper, 1936, 112 x 57 cm. Trust purchase, 1994. © Estate of the Artist, c/o Lefevre Fine Art Ltd, London. Photograph courtesy of Amgueddfa Cymru – National Museum Wales.

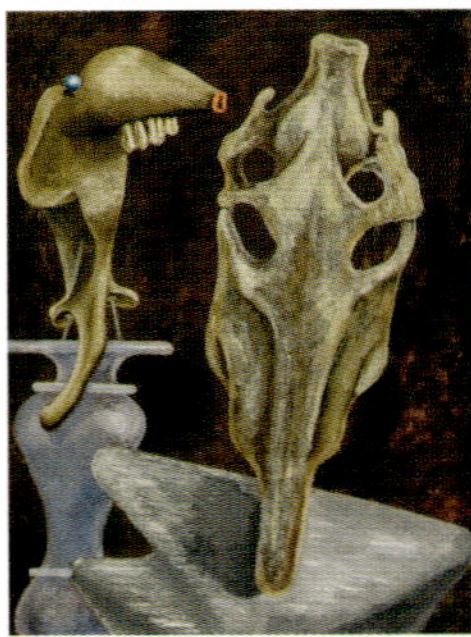

47. John Banting, *Mutual Congratulations,* oil on canvas, c.1937, 102 x 76 cm. Trust purchase, 2009. © Estate of John Banting. All rights reserved / Bridgeman Images. Photograph courtesy of Amgueddfa Cymru – National Museum Wales.

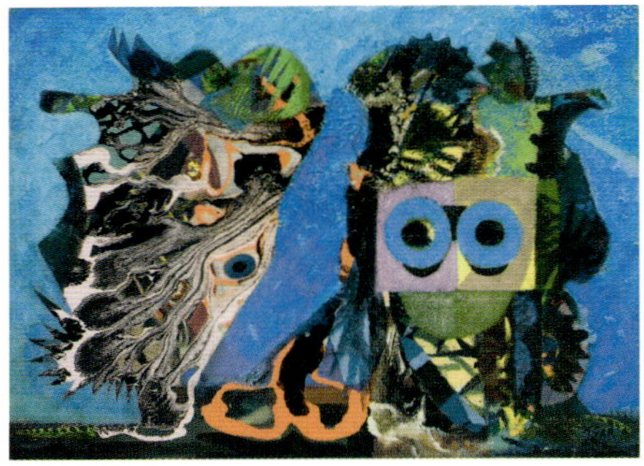

48. Eileen Agar, *An Exceptional Occurrence,* oil on canvas, 1950, 64 x 80 x 6 cm. Trust purchase, 2009. © Estate of Eileen Agar. All rights reserved / Bridgeman Images. Photograph courtesy of Amgueddfa Cymru – National Museum Wales.

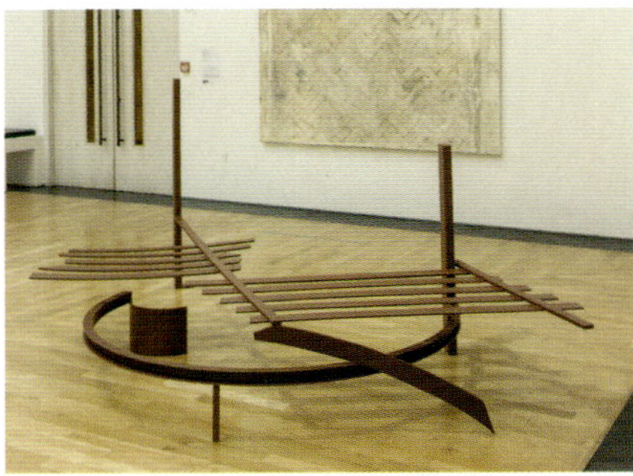

49. Sir Anthony Caro, *Serenade,* painted steel, 1970-71, 119 x 264 x 229 cm. Trust purchase, 2016. © Barford Sculptures Ltd. Photograph courtesy of Amgueddfa Cymru – National Museum Wales.

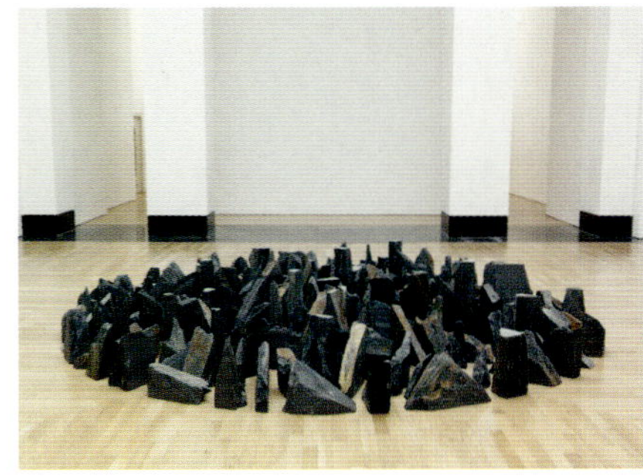

50. Sir Richard Long, *Blaenau Ffestiniog Circle,* slate, 2011, 59 x 400 cm. Acquired by Amgueddfa Cymru – National Museum Wales with support from the Art Fund and the Derek Williams Trust, 2012. © Richard Long. All rights reserved, DACS 2020. Photograph courtesy of Amgueddfa Cymru – National Museum Wales.

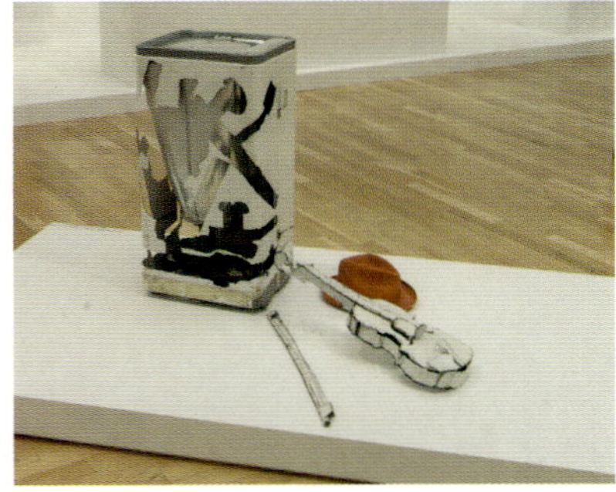

51. Bill Woodrow, *The Red Hat,* mixed-media installation, 1981, 78 x 88 cm. Acquired by Amgueddfa Cymru – National Museum Wales with support from the Derek Williams Trust and the Contemporary Art Society, 2012. © Bill Woodrow. Photograph courtesy of Amgueddfa Cymru – National Museum Wales.

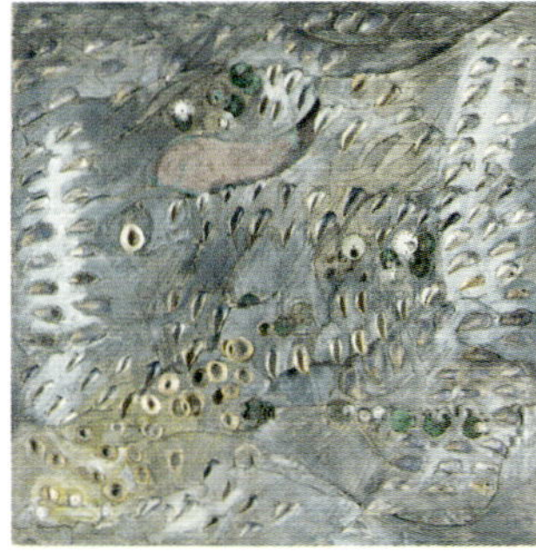

52. Arthur Giardelli, *The Sea's Edge,* mixed-media relief on board, 1990, 92 x 91 cm. Trust purchase, 2001. © Estate of Arthur Giardelli. Photograph courtesy of Amgueddfa Cymru – National Museum Wales.

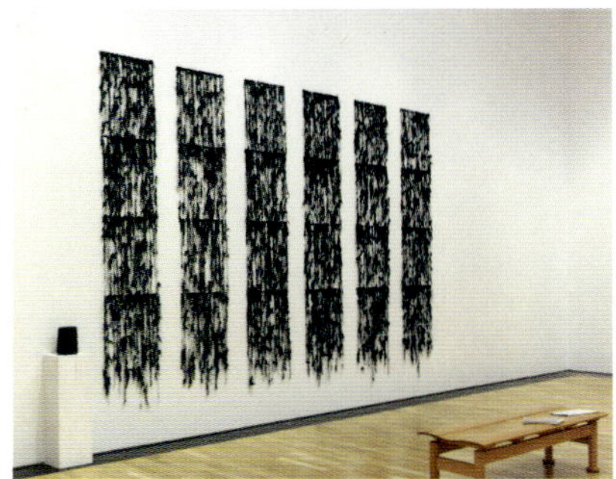

53. Lois Williams, *A Reconstructed Thing,* wool and woven yarn, 1994, 280 x 850 cm. Trust purchase, 2000. © Lois Williams. Photograph courtesy of Amgueddfa Cymru – National Museum Wales.

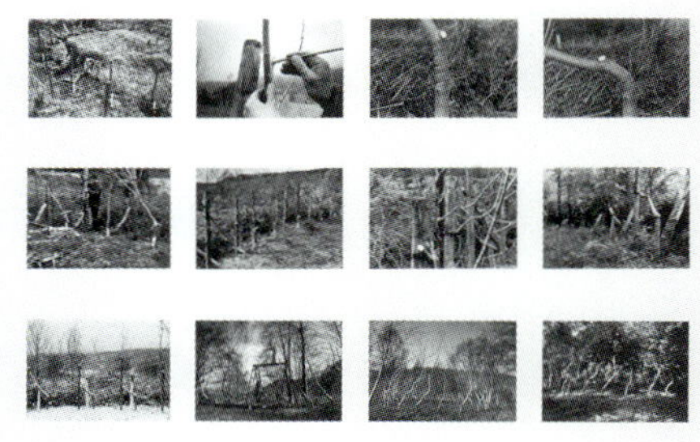

54. David Nash, *Ash Dome,* Twelve black and white board-mounted photographs, 2000, 117 x 162 cm. Trust purchase, 2000. © David Nash. All rights reserved, DACS 2020. Photograph courtesy of Amgueddfa Cymru – National Museum Wales.

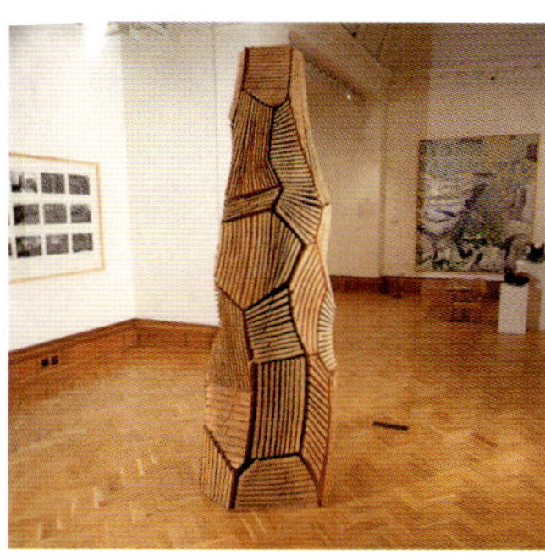

55. David Nash, *Multi-Cut Column,* beech, 2000, 241 x 76 x 77 cm. Trust purchase, 2000. © David Nash. All rights reserved, DACS 2020. Photograph courtesy of Amgueddfa Cymru – National Museum Wales.

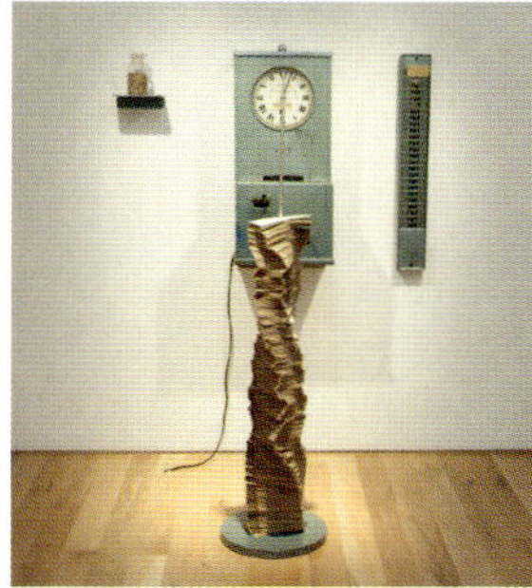

56. David Garner, *Last Punch of the Clock,* mixed-media installation, 2009. Acquired by Amgueddfa Cymru – National Museum Wales with support from the Derek Williams Trust, 2012. © David Garner. Photograph courtesy of Amgueddfa Cymru – National Museum Wales.

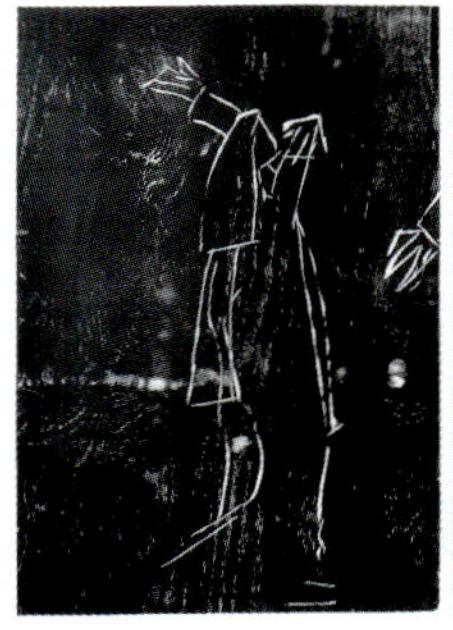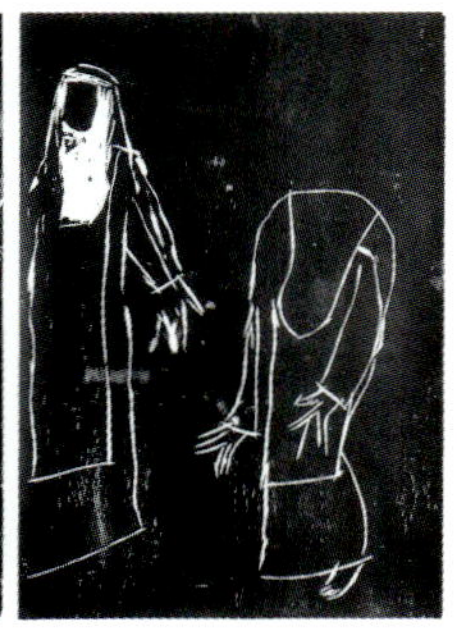

57. Andrea Büttner, *Dancing Nuns,* woodcut diptych on paper, 2007, each sheet 180 x 113 cm. Acquired by Amgueddfa Cymru – National Museum Wales with support from the Derek Williams Trust and the Contemporary Art Society. © Andrea Büttner / VG Bild-Kunst, Bonn 2019. Photograph courtesy of the artist and Hollybush Gardens, London.

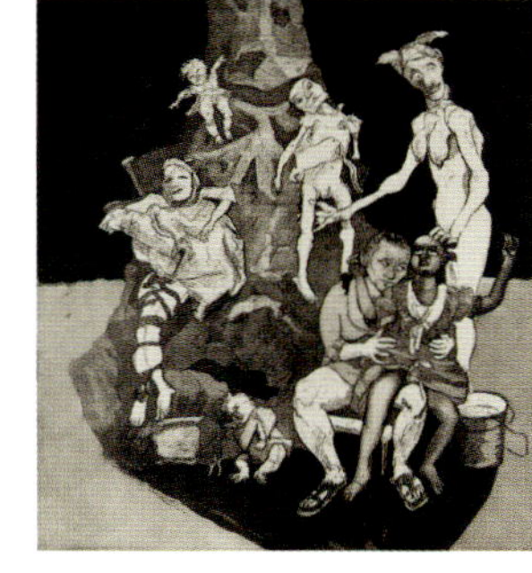

58. Dame Paula Rego, *Female Genital Mutilation Series: Stitched and Bound,* etching and aquatint on paper, 2009, sheet size 120 x 108 cm. Acquired by Amgueddfa Cymru – National Museum Wales with support from the Derek Williams Trust, 2012. © Paula Rego. Image courtesy of Amgueddfa Cymru – National Museum Wales.

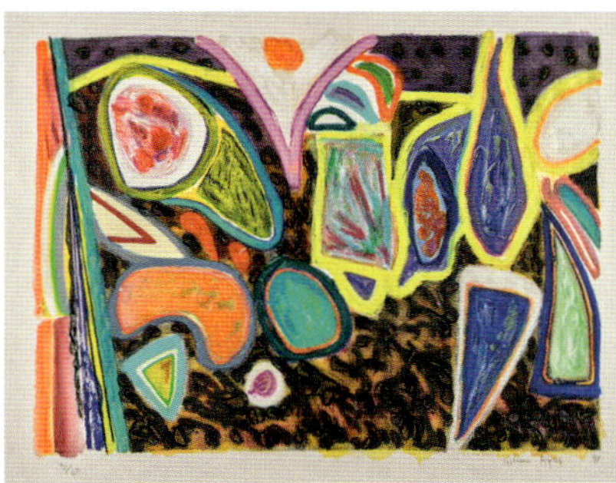

59. Gillian Ayres, *Myrrh of Marib,* carborundum etching with acrylic hand painting on paper, 1998, sheet size 80 x 102 cm. Trust purchase, 2018. © Gillian Ayres Estate and Cristea Roberts Gallery, London. Photograph courtesy of Amgueddfa Cymru – National Museum Wales.

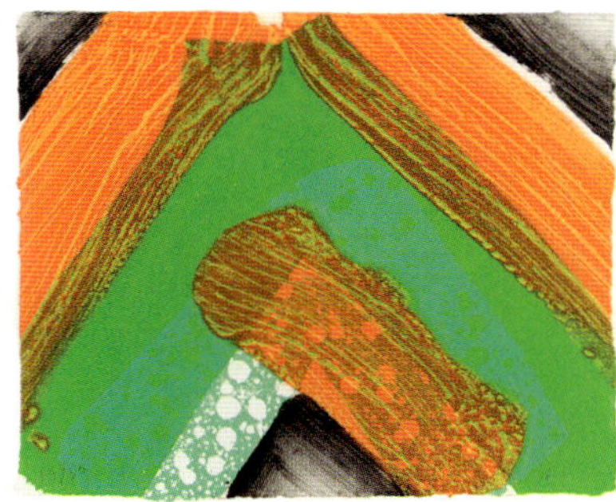

60. Sir Howard Hodgkin, *You Again,* hand-painted lift-ground etching with aquatint on paper, 2010-11, sheet size 38 x 48 cm. Trust purchase, 2011.© Estate of Howard Hodgkin. Photograph courtesy of Amgueddfa Cymru – National Museum Wales.

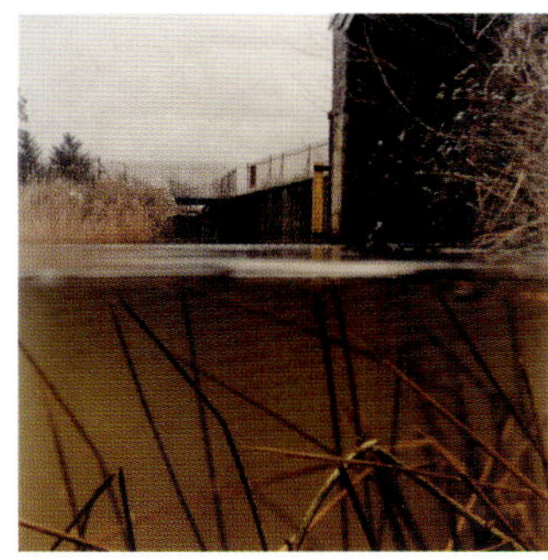

61. Stuart Lee, *Water Level Series, no 6,* photograph, 2004-05, 98 x 76 cm. Trust purchase after the National Eisteddfod of Wales, 2005. © Stuart Lee. Photograph courtesy of Amgueddfa Cymru – National Museum Wales.

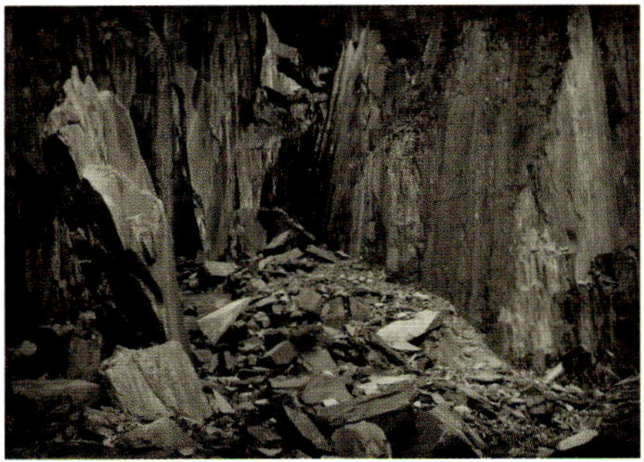

62. Thomas Joshua Cooper, *A Premonitional Work (Message to Friedrich and Frith), Blaenau Ffestiniog, Gwynedd, Wales,* photograph, 1992, 71 x 91 cm. Trust purchase, 2009. © Thomas Joshua Cooper. Photograph courtesy of Amgueddfa Cymru – National Museum Wales.

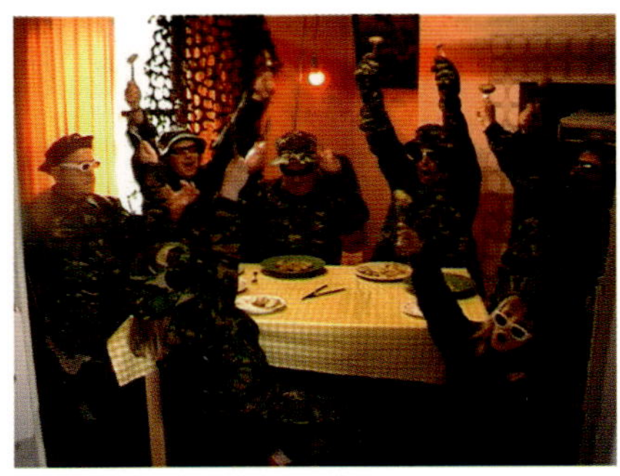

63. Peter Finnemore, *Base Camp*, still from DVD projection of thirty-five short films, 2005. Acquired by Amgueddfa Cymru – National Museum Wales with support from the Derek Williams Trust, 2006. © Peter Finnemore. Image courtesy of the artist.

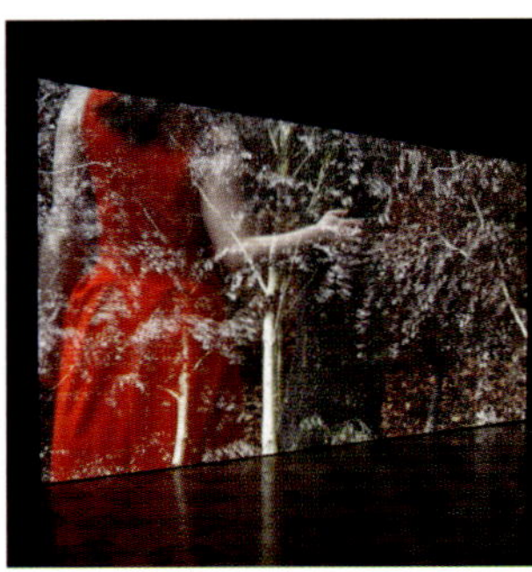

64. Helen Sear, *Company of Trees*, still from DVD projection at Santa Maria Ausiliatrice, Venice, 2015. Acquired by Amgueddfa Cymru – National Museum Wales with support from the Derek Williams Trust, 2017. © Helen Sear. Image courtesy of the artist.

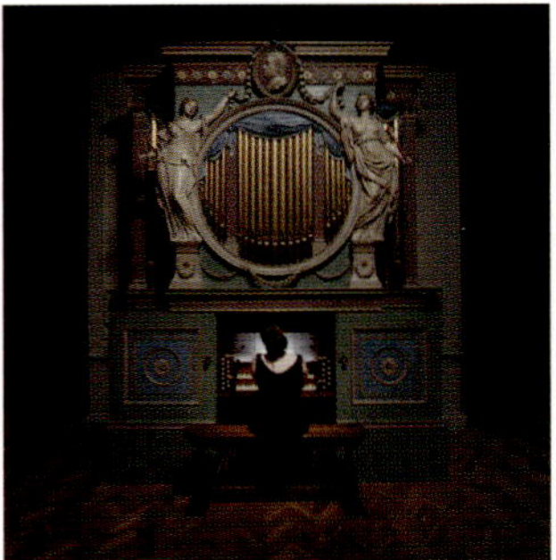

65. Ragnar Kjartansson, *The Sky in a Room*, installation and performance at the museum, 2018. Commissioned by Amgueddfa Cymru – National Museum Wales and *Artes Mundi* with Art Fund support after winning the Derek Williams Trust Purchase Prize, *Artes Mundi* 6, 2015. © Ragnar Kjartanssen courtesy of Luhring Augustine, New York, and i8 Gallery, Reykjavik. Photograph by Hugo Glendinning.

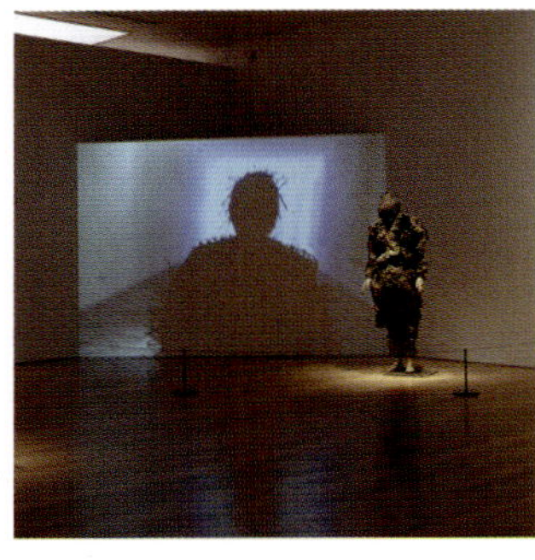

66. Tania Bruguera, *Destierro*, performance film recording with costume, 1998-99. Acquired by Amgueddfa Cymru – National Museum Wales after winning the Derek Williams Trust Purchase Prize, *Artes Mundi* 5, 2012. © ARS, NY and DACS, London 2020. Photograph courtesy of Amgueddfa Cymru – National Museum Wales.

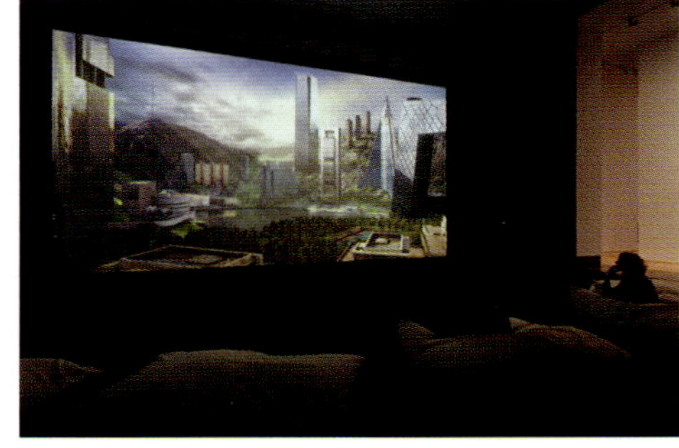

67. Bedwyr Williams, *Tyrrau Mawr*, still from twenty-minute video installation loop showing at the museum, 2016. Acquired by Amgueddfa Cymru – National Museum Wales after winning the Derek Williams Trust Purchase Prize, *Artes Mundi* 7, 2017. © Bedwyr Williams. Photograph by Jamie Williams courtesy of Artes Mundi.

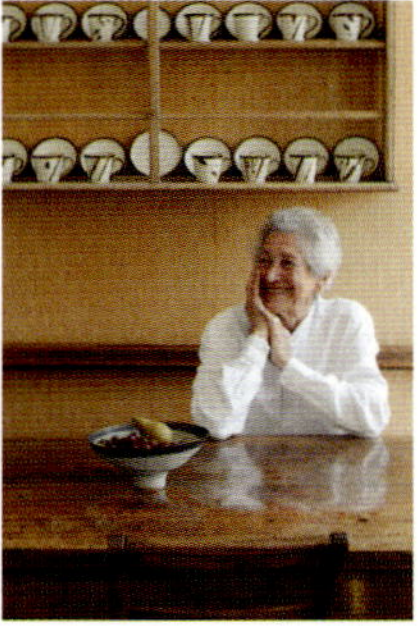

68. Anita Besson in her Hampstead home, 2015. Photograph by Miki Yamanouchi courtesy of Erskine, Hall & Coe.

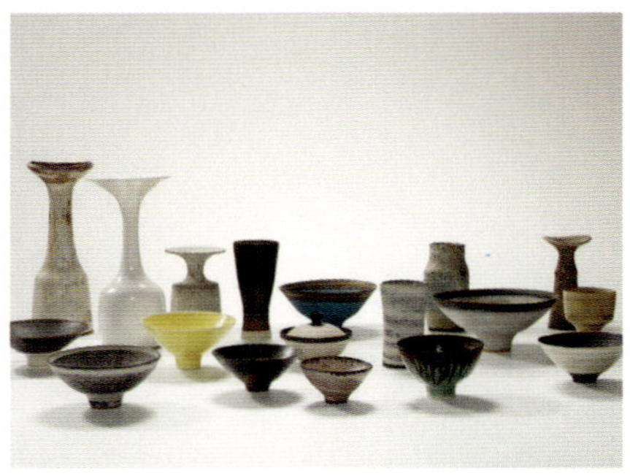

69. Lucie Rie, *Stoneware and porcelain bowls and vases*. Anita Besson bequest to the Derek Williams Trust, 2015. © Estate of the artist / DACS 2020. Photograph by Michael Harvey courtesy of Erskine, Hall & Coe.

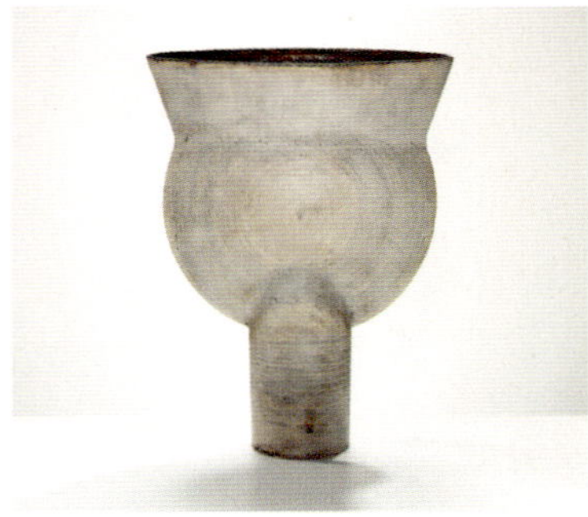

70. Hans Coper, *Large Thistle*, stoneware, c.1965, 32 x 24 cm. Anita Besson bequest to the Derek Williams Trust, 2015. © Estate of Hans Coper. Photograph by Michael Harvey courtesy of Erskine, Hall & Coe.

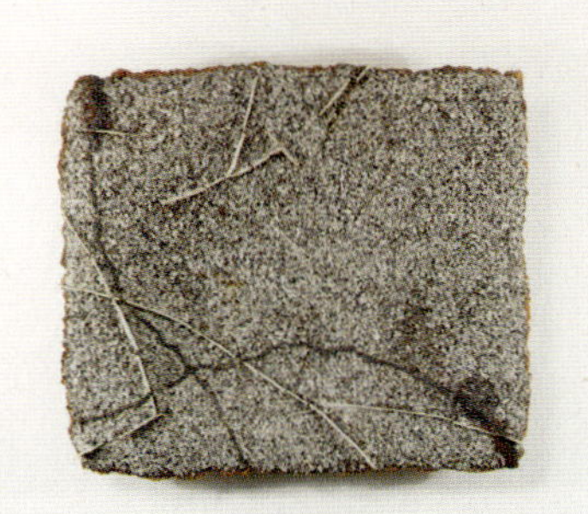

71. Claudi Casanovas, *Rectangular Wall Plate*, stoneware and porcelain, 1989, 100 x 87 cm. Anita Besson bequest to the Derek Williams Trust, 2015 © Claudi Casanovas. Photograph by Michael Harvey courtesy of Erskine, Hall & Coe.

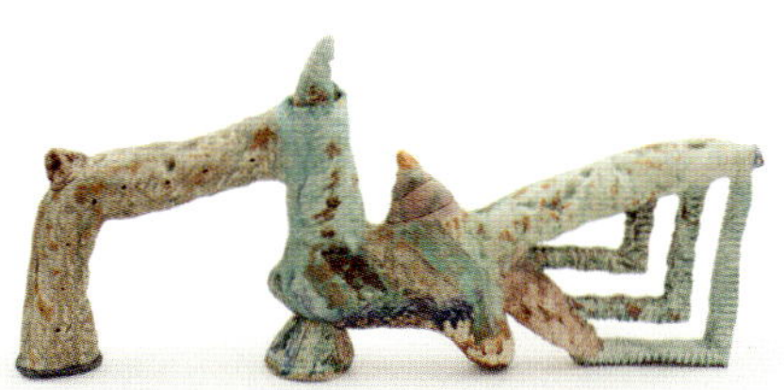
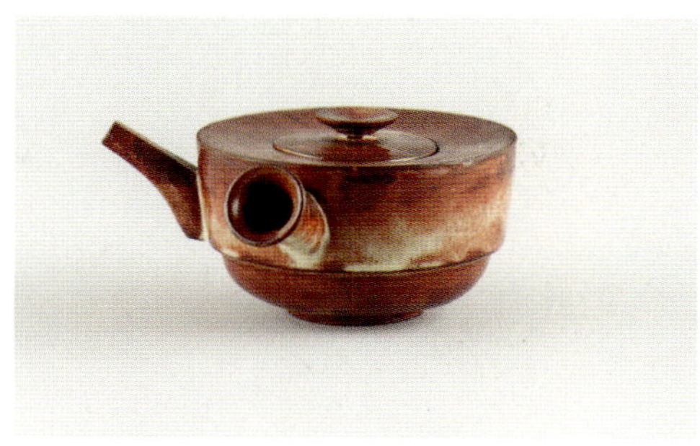
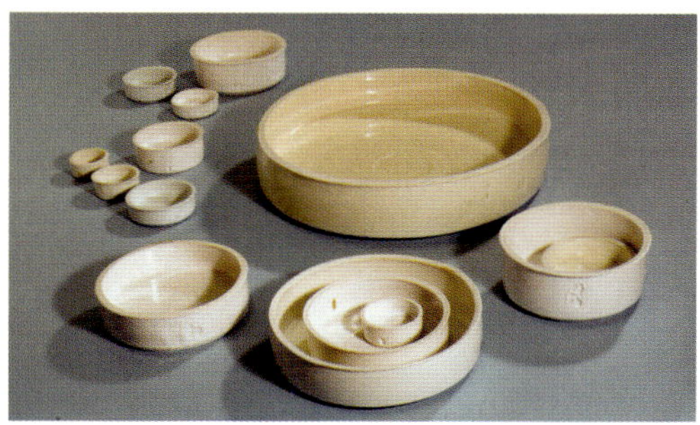

72. Angus Suttie, *Extended Teapot,* Stoneware, c.1991, 260 x 560 x 60 cm. Acquired by Amgueddfa Cymru – National Museum Wales with support from the Derek Williams Trust, 2018. © Estate of Angus Suttie. Photograph by Dewi Tannatt Lloyd courtesy of Ruthin Craft Centre.

73. Theodor Bogler, *Combination Teapot,* (Bauhaus Ceramic Workshop, Dornburg), stoneware with a tin glaze, cast and assembled, 1923, 16 x16 cm. Trust purchase, 2018. © Estate of Theodor Bogler. Photograph courtesy of Amgueddfa Cymru – National Museum Wales.

74. Edmund de Waal, *Group of fourteen dishes from the Arcanum exhibition,* porcelain, 2005, varied sizes up to 9 x 46 cm. Trust purchase, 2006. © Edmund de Waal. Photograph courtesy of Amgueddfa Cymru – National Museum Wales.

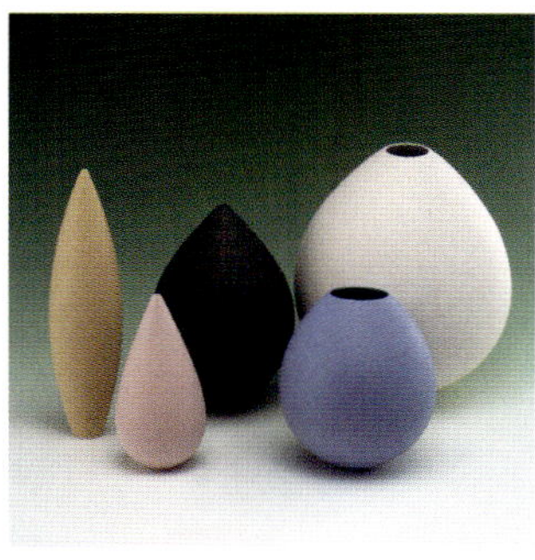
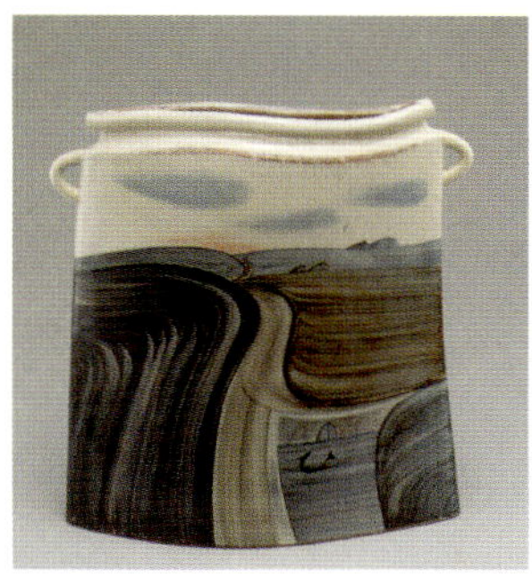
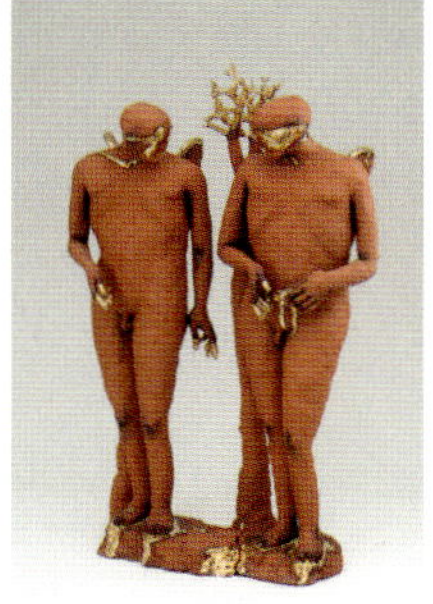

75. Christine Jones, *Vessels,* earthenware and stained earthenware, 2001, heights 21-34 cm, widths 11-29 cm. Trust purchase, 2001. © Christine Jones. Photograph courtesy of Amgueddfa Cymru – National Museum Wales.

76. James Campbell, *Landscape with Road,* earthenware, 2006, 41 x 38 x 10 cm. Trust purchase, 2000. © Estate of James Campbell. Photograph courtesy of Amgueddfa Cymru – National Museum Wales.

77. Claire Curneen, *In the Tradition of Smiling Angels,* terracotta, 2007, 78 x 50 cm. Acquired by Amgueddfa Cymru – National Museum Wales with support from the Derek Williams Trust, 2009. © Claire Curneen. Photograph courtesy of Amgueddfa Cymru – National Museum Wales.

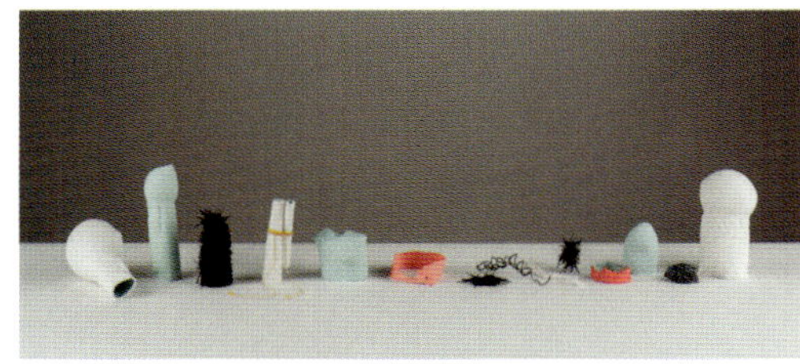
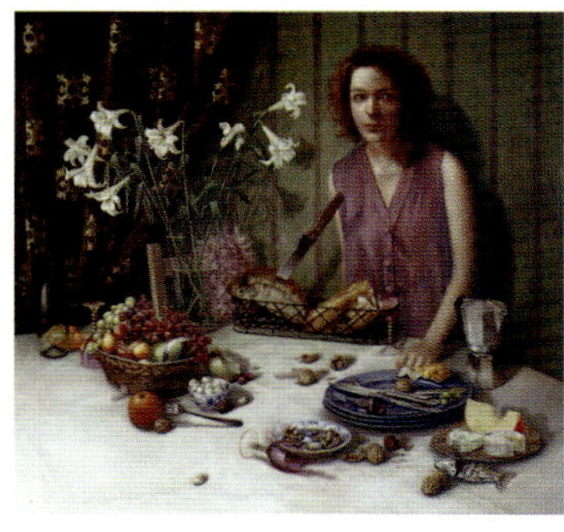

78. Anne Gibbs, *Shift,* bone china, silk thread, wire and pins, 2013, varied dimensions. Trust purchase, 2014. © Anne Gibbs. Photograph courtesy of Amgueddfa Cymru – National Museum Wales.

79. Sally Moore, *Remains,* 2000, oil on panel, 99 x 110 cm. Trust purchase, 2000. © Sally Moore. Photograph courtesy of Amgueddfa Cymru – National Museum Wales.

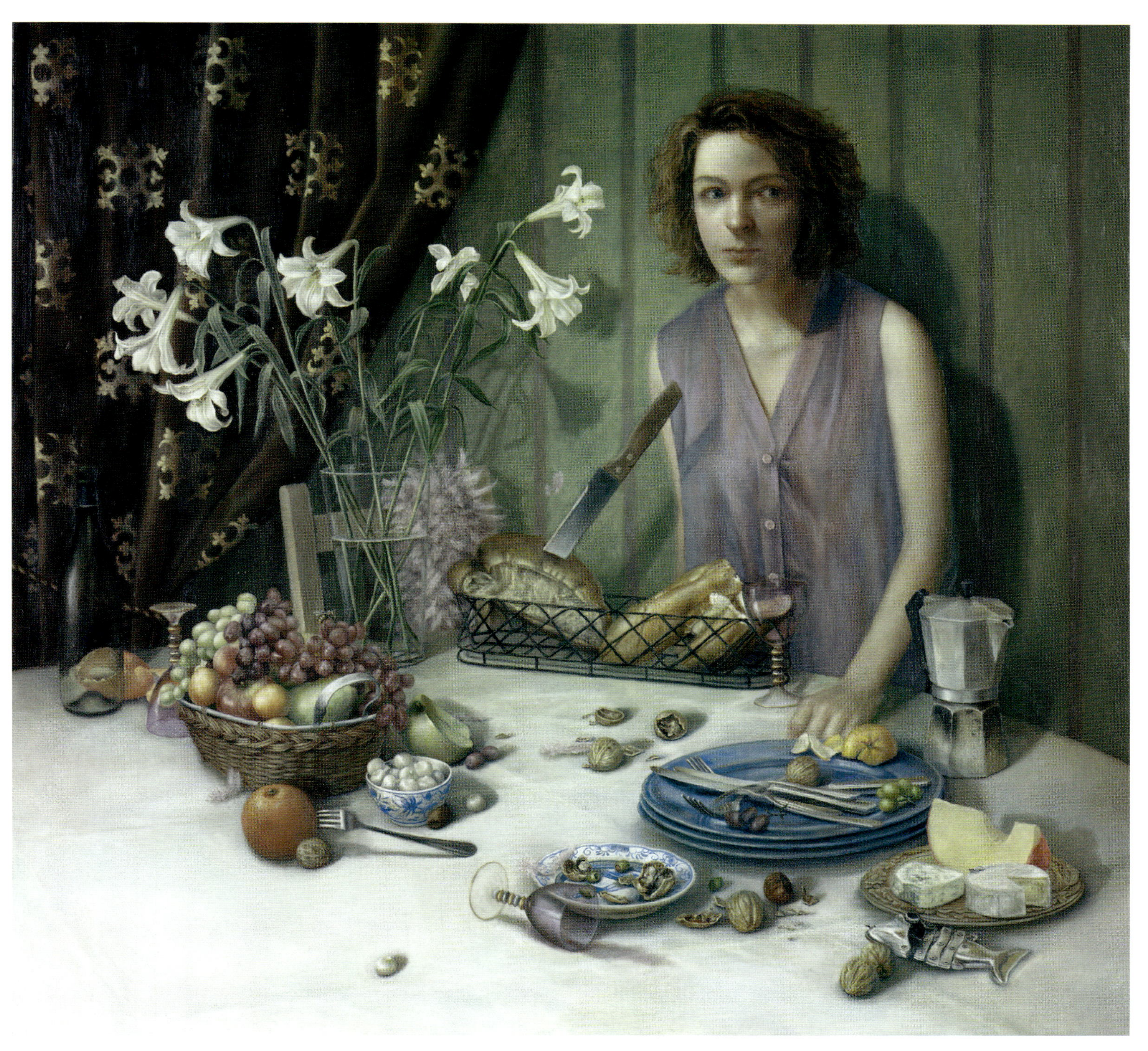

79. Sally Moore, *Remains,* 2000, oil on panel, 99 x 110 cm. Trust purchase, 2000.